Language Education in the School Curriculum

Also available from Bloomsbury

Content Knowledge in English Language Teacher Education,
edited by Darío Luis Banegas
Engaging with Linguistic Diversity, David Little and Deirdre Kirwan
Language Power and Hierarchy, Linda Tsung
Identity, Motivation and Multilingual Education in Asian Contexts,
Mark Feng Teng and Wang Lixun

Language Education in the School Curriculum

Issues of Access and Equity

Ken Cruickshank, Stephen Black, Honglin Chen,
Linda Tsung and Jan Wright

BLOOMSBURY ACADEMIC
LONDON • NEW YORK • OXFORD • NEW DELHI • SYDNEY

BLOOMSBURY ACADEMIC
Bloomsbury Publishing Plc
50 Bedford Square, London, WC1B 3DP, UK
1385 Broadway, New York, NY 10018, USA
29 Earlsfort Terrace, Dublin 2, Ireland

BLOOMSBURY, BLOOMSBURY ACADEMIC and the Diana logo are
trademarks of Bloomsbury Publishing Plc

First published in Great Britain 2020
This paperback edition published in 2021

Cover image: © pixelfusion3d/iStock
Cover design: Tjaša Krivec

A catalogue record for this book is available from the British Library.

ISBN: HB: 978-1-3500-6946-6
        PB: 978-1-3501-9258-4
        ePDF: 978-1-3500-6947-3
        eBook: 978-1-3500-6948-0

Typeset by Integra Software Services Pvt. Ltd.

To find out more about our authors and books visit www.bloomsbury.com
and sign up for our newsletters.

Contents

About the Authors

Stephen Black is currently an honorary research associate at the University of Technology Sydney. For many years he worked mainly in the field of adult literacy as a teacher, front-line manager and researcher. His research interests have focused on critical, sociocultural studies of the role of language and literacy in the lives of many groups of people, including prisoners, local council workers, adult literacy students, community groups, production workers and, more recently, children in school education.

Honglin Chen is Associate Professor in TESOL (Teaching English to Speakers of Other Languages) and language education at the University of Wollongong, Australia. Her research has focused on advancing understanding of how all students, native English speaking and second language, in school and tertiary contexts, can raise their literacy and language achievements. She has a keen interest in three interconnected areas in language and literacy education: literacy and languages studies, teacher knowledge and practice, and curriculum development and enactment.

Ken Cruickshank has been a teacher and teacher educator for many years at school and university. His principal work concerns languages and literacy in multilingual contexts. His first book *Teenagers, Literacy and School* (Routledge, 2006) drew on his doctoral study of literacy practices in Arabic-speaking families in Sydney and explored how young people's languages and literacies were extended or excluded in school contexts. He has published widely in the field of languages education.

Linda Tsung is Associate Professor and Associate Dean in the Faculty of Arts and Social Sciences, University of Sydney. Her research interests are multilingualism, multilingual education, language policy and cultural identity in Australia and Greater China. She has published widely on these topics. In particular, she has published two sole-authored books: *Language Power and Hierarchy: Multilingual Education in China* (Bloomsbury, 2014) and *Minority languages, Education and Communities in China* (Palgrave Macmillan, 2009). A/Professor Tsung has also co-authored a book *Bilingual Education and Minority Language Maintenance in China* (Springer, 2019) and co-edited books entitled *Contemporary Chinese Discourses and Social Practice in China* (Benjamins, 2015) and *Teaching and Learning Chinese in Global Contexts* (Continuum, 2010).

Jan Wright is Emeritus Professor of Education at the University of Wollongong. She has researched and taught in areas that examine curriculum from a critical/sociocultural perspective, particularly in the areas of curriculum health education and physical education. Her work has covered issues such as the relationship between language and ideology, media representations of sport and sporting 'bodies' and the health of young people.

Glossary

TERM	EXPLANATION
Language/s	We generally use the term "language/s" to refer to languages other than English. Where we compare types of languages or purposes for learning languages, we use terms such as 'Asian', 'modern'/'traditional', 'community/heritage'. We prefer the term 'community' to 'heritage' languages because the term implies something vibrant and in everyday use in the society. We avoid use of the terms 'foreign', 'immigrant', 'minority' languages because of their negative connotations.
Background and LBOTE	We often use the term 'background' for users of language/s – for example, English- /Chinese- /Macedonian language-speaking background. We try to avoid negative terms such as 'language background other than English (LBOTE)' because of negative connotations. LBOTE, however, is used in some government reporting. We are also aware that the terms 'background' and 'native' speakers are not useful terms when used to homogenize or 'other' learners. We use the term 'bilingual' in its broader sense of speakers who can operate successfully in bi/multilingual contexts.
SES	Our analysis relies on SEIFA (Socio-Economic Indices for Areas), an indicator of socio-economic status (SES). SEIFA is an Australian national census instrument derived from four summary measures: income, educational attainment, employment and housing expenditure (Australian Bureau of Statistics [ABS], 2014). This indicator consists of five quintiles from lowest to highest-SES and is mapped onto local government areas (LGAs).
ICSEA	School enrolments do not necessarily reflect local area SES. Hence, we also rely on the ICSEA measure (Index of Community Socio-Economic Advantage) which is

determined based on data from individual student enrolments. ICSEA variables include socio-economic characteristics of the small areas where students live, rural/regional/urban location and percentage of Aboriginal student enrolment (NSW Department of Education and Training, 2010). For the purposes of this study, ICSEA with a median value of 1081 and below was coded as low-SES and 1082 and over as high.

HSC   The Higher School Certificate is the award granted from external examinations that students in NSW sit at the end of Year 12.

ATAR   Australian Tertiary Admission Rank or ATAR, as it is more commonly known, is the ranking used for tertiary entry by universities across Australia. It is a number between 0.00 and 99.95 that indicates a student's position relative to all the students in their age group. Set by universities, it is calculated from student Year 12 marks.

NAPLAN   The National Assessment Program Literacy and Numeracy is an external test in literacy, numeracy and language administered to all students in Year 3, 5, 7 and 9 across Australia.

NALSAS   The National Asian Languages and Studies in Australia Schools strategy was one of two key programs implemented by the Australian government to increase the uptake of Asian languages in schools.

Issues in the Provision and Uptake of Languages

What's the problem?

The relationship between social inequality and access to the study of languages is becoming a key issue in Anglophone countries (Baggett, 2016; Lanvers, 2017; Nikolov and Mihaljević Djigunović, 2011; Pufahl and Rhodes, 2011; Tinsley and Board, 2017). In the UK, evidence is growing of a social divide in access and attitudes to languages study. Students from poorer backgrounds are less likely to choose languages, more likely to be withdrawn from mandatory languages study (e.g. for remedial Maths and English support) and less likely to study languages to the GCSE (Board and Tinsley, 2014, 2015a, 2017; Tinsley and Dolezal, 2018). In the United States, lower-socioeconomic status (SES) elementary and middle schools are less likely to offer languages and these schools find it hardest to get qualified languages teachers (Pufahl and Rhodes, 2011). There is also underrepresentation of lower-SES, African-American and Latino students in modern languages classes (O'Rourke, Zhou and Rottman, 2017). The answers to why this happens are unclear. Some studies point to funding differences (Pufahl and Rhodes, 2011). Some suggest a social divide in attitudes, with lower-SES parents and students having less positive attitudes to languages study (Gayton, 2010). Others point to how teachers and the school leadership see languages as less relevant to lower-SES students: the argument being that students from lower-SES backgrounds don't need languages because they will have fewer opportunities to travel and to use languages skills (Lanvers, 2017). To what extent does the social divide reflect a reality of low motivation and purpose for languages study or is this a construction *ex post facto*? Assumptions about low-SES students' lower motivation and need for languages have been taken for granted. It is only in the last few years that the divide in access to and uptake of languages has been examined through a more sociological lens, looking at broader social contextual factors as well as their implications for policy decision-making at national and state levels and in schools.

This broader lens provides the means to see how access to languages has changed over time and how languages were not always the preserve of the more affluent. For example, the introduction of comprehensive schooling in the 1960s and 1970s in North America, the UK and Australia prompted a shift from languages study as the preserve of elite schools with prestige languages as a mark of distinction to much wider access to languages in government primary and secondary schools. In Australia, this goal of 'languages for all' led to a 500 per cent increase in students taking languages between 1970 and 2000 (Lo Bianco, 2009). This promise of universal access to languages seems to have evaporated (Hagger-Vaughan, 2016). Neoliberal policy education reforms have resulted in specialization and selection within the 'comprehensive' system and dezoning has provided parents with greater 'choice' of government schools in order to maximize academic opportunities for their children (Campbell, Proctor and Sherington, 2009). These reforms have produced a highly differentiated market, where those who can afford it take measures to ensure their children are in the 'best' schools. This has had a flow-on effect on languages provision, where few comprehensive (non-selective) government schools now offer languages beyond a mandatory 100 hours in the first years of high school. Thus, the goal of 'languages for all' appears in the current context to be a lost hope.

The added factor in this has been the wider social and cultural change impacting on the range of language resources in communities, the result of global flows of populations through immigration and more recently refugee populations (Lo Bianco, 2009). The 1960s and 1970s in Australia were also the time when government policy responded to the major post-war migration schemes, with initiatives acknowledging the multicultural and multilingual makeup of the society. The study of community/heritage languages capitalized on these resources and provided pathways to education for many students whose parents had not had such access. These languages, taught mainly to students in lower-SES comprehensive schools, provided access to tertiary education for many students whose parents had not themselves completed secondary school (Teese, 2013). Their legacy is the now over thirty-four languages and over sixty-three courses counted for tertiary entry, the majority of which are community languages (NSW Education Standards Authority, 2019). Enrolments, however, are small and shrinking and the largest community language, Chinese, has a 94 per cent enrolment attrition rate by final year of schooling (Orton, 2008).

Again, the 1970s policy promise of multiculturalism and multilingualism has not been realized in practice. In this context, what is the narrative of community/ heritage languages and the interrelationship between class and ethnicity in access to languages?

The context: Four schools

In this chapter we illustrate the current state of languages in New South Wales (NSW) schools and the intersections of culture, language and social class as realized by language provision and access. We set up the problematic addressed in this book through case studies of languages study in four schools.[1] Forster High School is typical of government selective schools in our study: high-SES student enrolment, most speaking languages in addition to English in the home. Campbell High School, a regional secondary comprehensive, is typical of low-SES regional and rural comprehensives: majority English-speaking-background families and a single languages teacher. St Francis Primary School, a Catholic primary school in the eastern suburbs of Sydney, typifies the high-SES primary schools: majority English-speaking-background families with all students having access to languages but only thirty minutes a week. Cheswell Primary School, a low-SES government primary school in the inner west of Sydney, with 97 per cent of students speaking languages in addition to English at home, is an outlier. It is in a low-SES area but has a bilingual stream and strong languages program. Languages are central to the school curriculum. The school is a lighthouse school and attracts many students from out of area because of the programs. These four schools in their different ways point to the issues confronting students in their opportunities to access languages study.

Forster Selective High School

Forster is one of the forty-two government selective schools in NSW, most of them in Sydney (18 per cent of all government secondary schools). Forster is high-SES with 70 per cent of parents in the top quartile. Most of its 900 students

---

[1] Pseudonyms are used in the book for all schools, teachers, parents and students referred to in reference to the study.

come from a language background other than English, 40 per cent speaking Chinese at home. The post-school destination of all students is tertiary entry.

Forster has a strong languages program with a head teacher and nine languages teachers. The teachers are all experienced teachers and two are background speakers of the language. In Year 7 all students take 100 hours in French, Japanese, German or Chinese and then more classes in Year 8. In Year 9 there are strong elective classes in French. The languages program offers many extra-curricular activities with exchanges to Japan, France, Germany and China, and the school regularly hosts assistant teachers from Germany, France and China.

Wesley (pseudonym), aged fifteen, is a student in Year 10 at Forster HS. His mother is of Chinese background and his father Israeli. He grew up with Hebrew as his first language and learnt English when he came to Australia at the age of seven. He is studying Chinese and plans to keep studying it to Year 12 for his final Higher School Certificate (HSC) examination for tertiary entry.

> My Mum speaks Cantonese and some Mandarin and so Chinese has always been a point for me. I go to China relatively frequently. My Chinese is fluent but it will be nicer to expand on it with my relatives. My parents are happy with this.

His road to Chinese, however, has been rocky. He learnt Italian in primary school: 'It was negligible … I only remember numbers and colours.' He studied French for the compulsory 100 hours languages study in junior secondary school, and it wasn't until Year 8 that he could study Chinese.

> It's hard to develop languages in high school because it's not compulsory in primary, not like most countries in the world. Then it's compulsory in Year 7 and 8. If you have kids who aren't that keen, you cannot move ahead. You need that continuity in a subject.

He said he is one of the few studying Chinese who actually wanted to do it. In his class of thirty, he said that most are studying because their parents make them. He reported liking Chinese not only because of the teacher but also because of the relevance to his extended family. Sarah, one of Wesley's friends, with both parents of Chinese background, is studying French in Year 10. She chose French in Year 8 because her parents wanted her to do it.

> My parents have a kind of romanticised view of French. It's this international language. I could join the United Nations or something (laughs).

She kept going with French because of the cultural aspects, because 'I really like learning languages' and also the school has three-week language learning overseas tours every second year. She also practises her French with her piano teacher whose husband is French. Both Wesley and Sarah are at the point of deciding whether to take languages for their final exam in Year 12. The issue of marks and the difficulties with studying a language was a common theme in all our interviews with senior students. As Sarah says:

> The others in the class are better than me but I will keep on with French even though I know I won't get the marks I want. To be honest, the focus on the HSC marks, it kills my desire to study languages, they are difficult because they're something that's so unfamiliar.

Wesley is also going to choose Chinese despite the problem with marks.

> I know there'll only be four or five of us [studying Chinese] next year. It was easy in Year 8 and 9 but now we're … like … testing this HSC type of structure where the class is more intense and you can begin to see the difficulty in the jump between the Year 10 syllabus and the Year 11 syllabus. There's the other reason too. Most kids in Year 11, they choose subjects they can get a 95 in rather than a 90 in the HSC. They'll take that any day. The parents don't think Chinese is important in Year 11. They think okay now it's Physics, Chemistry. Chinese isn't important. It's not going to rank very well. So the Chinese classes go from being full classes in Year 10 to about four in Year 11.

Jack is a student in Year 7 doing the 100 hours compulsory language in Japanese, last school period on a hot Friday afternoon. The teacher has the thirty students practising interviews with each other about personal details. They revise key vocabulary and then move into pair work. She then gets them to switch pairs, do a second interview and jot down notes. The lesson is interactive and engaging. Jack intends to do Japanese in Year 9.

> I like it. I'm good at it and why not? I like the teacher, especially when she tells us about her growing up in Japan. Mum and Dad, we're going there next year for holidays.

Forster is typical of the government selective schools with its strong languages program and the opportunity for continuity of languages study from Year 7 to Year 10, and for many students in Year 12.

Campbell High School

Campbell is a regional comprehensive high school with 320 students; it is lower-SES with two-thirds of parents in the lowest quartile. Just under 20 per cent of its students are Indigenous and another 20 per cent have a language background in addition to English. It is what is called a 'residual' comprehensive school, with many local students attending selective and other schools out of area. Campbell has one full-time languages teacher, John, a German teacher who retrained in Chinese. He teaches the mandatory 100 hours to all students in Year 7 and Margo, a generalist, also teaches two small elective French classes in Years 9 and 10. Campbell has taken up the discourse of Chinese as a language of trade and opportunity, and the principal and languages teacher are working to make the school languages a marker of distinction in competing for student enrolments in the context of school-based management. According to John, languages 'struggle' at the school.

> There's no continuity from teaching Chinese in Year 7 to elective languages in Year 9 [no languages were offered in Year 8]. There's competition from other elective subjects, you know, photography, music, graphic design.

For Alan, the school principal, the switch from French to Chinese as the mandatory 100 hours language is a deliberate decision to enhance the profile of the school, with the hope that it might be the first step in establishing the school as a designated specialist languages school. Chinese is the language of choice because of 'the future-proofing needs of our students out in the employment force'. Chinese will 'set them up for employability over other people and that's important'. As John comments:

> I think he's looking for a distinction; it's looking for something to sell. I think when you're looking at different products the different schools are selling, some schools are looking down the line of sports high schools, there are IT schools, performing arts schools. So I think it's looking for a niche.

The school is typical of lower-SES secondary schools we visited: a single languages teacher focusing on the mandatory Year 7 or 8 classes. It is different because of the commitment of John, the languages teacher, and Alan, the principal, to the discourse of Asian languages and the engagement with the neoliberal language of the market, rarely apparent in working-class schools. Interview data from parents and students were mixed, with positive and negative comments in relation to the value of languages study. This is interesting because we found that staff in many schools believed that languages have no value or relevance for lower-SES parents and students. Our interviews at Campbell also suggest a greater diversity of languages in immediate or extended families, which was not evident in the school's demographics or in the talk about languages by the staff and principal. Students mention, for example, backgrounds in and/

or some family members speaking Danish, Serbian, Vietnamese, Indonesian, Malaysian, French and Hungarian.

Samantha is fifteen. She studied French in Year 7 for the compulsory 100 hours and has chosen it as an elective in Year 9: 'I just like the culture and friends and stuff and I just thought learn a different language ... just something new to learn.' She says that French might be good for travelling one day and is 'something to back you up as a job career future thing'. According to Alan, the school principal, the elective French class appears to attract more academically oriented students, those with 'tertiary aspirations ... the sort of kids you want to see in any class'. Aiden in Year 7 is less diffident. He will choose Chinese to study as an elective after Year 7 if it is available. Echoing John, he says, 'China's our future, like come on.' When asked if he knows anyone who is Chinese, he says 'yes' and then 'only you', nodding to one of the researchers.

We asked Pete, one of the parents, about his son studying Chinese. 'Yeah, it's fine with me if he wants to. I never got the chance when I was at school. It was only the kids in the top classes who studied languages. For me ... I tend to prioritise the reading, writing and arithmetic higher than the Chinese. But he likes it.' Later on, he comments on the lack of relevance of languages. 'We've been to Bali a few times and we only needed to speak English. Foreign languages are foreign to kids. They don't have to learn other languages. They don't necessarily hear other languages as such, unless your parents are foreign.'

John's Chinese classes are very interactive: student 'engagement' in the language and Chinese culture is fundamental to his purpose to make Chinese meaningful to their lives. He uses school excursions to Chinatown in Sydney, stories and photographs of his own experiences in China, and visits by native Chinese speakers. John was an experienced teacher of German who chose to retrain in Chinese and is now committed to that language with regular visits to China and a wealth of resources to draw on including interactive games (often computer-based) and brush painting (calligraphy). The classroom is full of productive noise. Chinese has its own homeroom with interactive whiteboard; walls are covered with pictures of ideographs and pages from Chinese stories. When we told John about Pete's comments, he replied:

> That's just the reason *why* we have languages. Studying Chinese gives the kids a chance to know about life and cultures outside Campbell; parents may not have had the chance to study languages but they're happy for their kids to have this opportunity. If you engage them in the language they see the purpose, they love it.

St Francis Primary School

St Francis is a Catholic primary school with 300 students (and growing) in a beachside suburb close to Sydney Central Business District (CBD). The school is in a high-SES area: 53 per cent of families are in the top quartile. Most children come from English-speaking backgrounds and have little access to languages other than English outside the school. Typical of many higher-SES primary schools, St Francis has a parent-funded languages program. The Italian teacher, Tania, was a grade teacher at the school and took on the position teaching Italian. In the beginning and when external funding was available, the program lasted for one hour for each class but dropped to thirty minutes when this funding stopped. The school values the program but both Tania and the principal, Sue, admit it is more language 'awareness' than language learning because of the limited time children have to learn each week. Languages are not a part of the primary curriculum and most children in mid- to low-SES government and non-government schools have little or no access to languages. Italian is not a community language at the school and only one of two students had any outside links with the language. Tania is realistic about what she can achieve.

> It's more the cultural awareness I'm trying to get through to the children, especially within the area that they're living in – turning off their blinkers. The little ones, more to become focused about who they are and also, bringing in the language of Italian, be able to converse with another person and know we don't have to just converse in English. We can converse in another language … In half an hour, it's more recognising the words so that if they do choose Italian in high school and have the option, they have a nice basis, a good foundation for it.

Because she is a qualified, primary-trained teacher in the school, Tania is accepted by the staff and tries to teach across the curriculum.

> I speak to the teachers and say, for example, what's our Science unit for next term, because sometimes there can be a swap and, like I said, Stage 3 are doing solar system. The Stage 1 had done the way we were, about families of today and the past, so we started working about families so they could go home and greet their parents in Italian and call their mother and father mum and dad in Italian, speak about the dog in Italian.

She tries to work in with other teachers' programs as she moves from room to room.

> I go into somebody's classroom, we do a lesson, but I keep my eye around the room and I think, oh they're learning about that. In the next lesson, as we're

working, I throw that in. It might be just the modification of my lesson for that half an hour…when it's oral work and on the board and smartboard work, there's a lot of chop and change.

George and Natalie are in a Year 3 class learning Italian. Tania has just sung some Christmas songs with them that they learnt in Italian. They then have a game revising the words they learnt: *Buon natale*, *auguri* and others. They then go through a series of pictures on the interactive whiteboard learning 'Twelve Days of Christmas' in Italian. The thirty students are sitting on the floor in a semi-circle engaged, participating and asking questions. Finally, Tania gives them workbooks she has prepared on Christmas in Italian with games, pictures and some writing. After the class they say how much they like learning words, playing the games and singing in Italian.

I like the Italian games…I like the Christmas ones and how you're supposed to guess what their names are from the pictures in Italian. (George)

Natalie's mother, Sandra, is positive about the program. She describes how Natalie tells her the words she learns every week. She was able to use the language when the family went on holidays to Italy the year before. Teachers, while echoing the parent responses, are also aware of the difficulties.

Thirty minutes is not enough. Once the kids get settled down it's more like 20. The curriculum is crowded. We have so many other things that the children need. It's not like state schools. They have more wriggle room. We have to cover religion too. (Jane, classroom teacher)

The school is typical of many mid- and high-SES primary schools that have parent- or school-funded programs generally for thirty minutes a week in languages such as French, Italian or Chinese.

Cheswell Primary School

Cheswell Primary School is unusual. Situated in the inner west of Sydney, the suburb, Cheswell, is classed as a low-SES suburb with high levels of unemployment and low family income. The school has grown in enrolment by 20 per cent to 760 in the past decade while all other schools in the area have declining enrolments. Nearly all students (97 per cent) come from language backgrounds other than English. The school has a bilingual stream taught in Korean for seven hours a week that is now in its third year. In addition, Chinese, Vietnamese, Arabic, Hindi, Indonesian, Greek, Spanish and Korean are taught

K-6 as community languages for two hours a week. In this way, all children can learn their community language plus one other. The program, one of only four in the state, is very much due to the commitment of the principal, Will, who worked to build the program with a staff who have languages skills and training in the languages the school offers. The government policy, *Local Schools, Local Decisions*, gave individual schools greater autonomy in terms of staffing and curriculum, and this has in turn led to most mid- to low-SES schools dropping languages. However, for Cheswell, it has enabled the principal to establish a lighthouse school in its provision of languages. Enrolments are increasing and the school focuses on languages for all students along with maintaining and developing heritage languages. Many staff have undertaken postgraduate languages and/or cultural studies.

> I can't just have three Chinese teachers. So I've actually got five. Three of them are mainstream teachers who've had language and I've recruited them. (Will, the principal)

Constant themes from parents and teachers were related to the cultural and cognitive reasons for learning languages. For example, Will explains:

> You're not really educated if you don't have a language. It doesn't matter even how well you do with a language but you're a different human being because you studied the language. So I think that will be a generally held – this is my view – I think that will be a generally held view here.

Concerns about the 'crowded' curriculum are addressed through lengthening the school day and by having languages and grade teachers collaborate to plan topics that achieve both languages and broader curriculum outcomes.

> We've had some good projects where we've done colonisation and you're meant to compare colonisation in another place as well as Australia. So in Indonesian they're looking at Dutch colonisation. So I would say they would have more empathy with Indigenous Australians with that sort of comparison. But last year we did a water unit where we were looking at water solutions in the Singaporean solution and Middle East and those sort of things as well. In Visual Arts we have been teaching calligraphy. We're only at the beginning of those things and of course we've adopted the national curriculum. We think that we can serve both things by the sort of examples I've just given you because you're getting the Asian perspective. (Will, the principal)

Proud of the work that he and his staff have put into providing thoughtful languages study for their students, Will laments the lack of continuity for languages study in high schools.

It appals me what happens with languages in high schools at times, you know, and so many primary schools have good languages programs and other things. They have the programs but they're not followed on with and it's such a waste. Learning a language is never a waste, but it could be so much better if they had the opportunity.

Paul, a parent we interviewed, has two children, Alanna and Eric, in Years 2 and 4. Alanna is learning Korean in a bilingual class for five hours a week and Eric is learning Korean for two hours a week. Paul has a German-speaking background (his grandparents were German-speaking and Jewish from Austria). He was born in Australia, speaking English at home, and his wife is of Greek background. Alanna and Eric attend Greek Community Language School on Saturdays and at home 'since they were born, they were spoken to in Greek every day by their mother and their grandmother'.

Well, they're 100 per cent Greek, 100 per cent Australian. I don't think they have a fully Jewish identity, although they do. But it's no different – the home and family experience of multi-faith, multi-religious, multi-identity, multi everything else is totally replicated in the school yard.

He reports that Alanna and Eric are too shy to speak Korean in local shops (though happy to speak Greek). But on a trip to Korea, people were surprised:

They were so amazed that these blonde-haired Aussie kids would be speaking and singing in Korean. (Paul)

Paul is very supportive of his children learning languages, 'the more the merrier'.

I want them to do it. I'd want them to do it because it really, really will help them with jobs. It opens their minds and memory, that's it. It helps them with memory. I think it's so absurd that it's not government mandated, compulsory in all schools and why we're even having the discussion. It should be enforced, legally, required curriculum. I mean no one debates whether kids should be numerate by the time they leave school.

Grace, another parent we interviewed, is Australian-born of Korean background. Her youngest daughter, Sunny, is also in the Grade 2 Korean program and Alice, her older daughter in Year 5, is learning Korean two hours a week.

I watch Sunny a lot. The way she thinks is different and amazing, 'Oh, you can think that way'? So I think it actually helps. There's a lot of progress. Alice is 10 but she doesn't progress as much. She just does the community language program two hours a week. Now Alice is asking Sunny, 'How do

I spell this?' Sunny is much better. I wasn't expecting it was going to be so good. She had no idea before. She's now reading. And also, she's interested in every single way.

The strong languages program at Cheswell is partly due to the government K-6 Community Languages Program, which funds five additional-to-staff community languages teachers at the school. It has been the initiative of the principal, however, to build Cheswell into a bilingual school for all students and embed languages in the curriculum.

The narrative of languages

How can four schools be so different in their provision and uptake of languages? These snapshots of four very different school programs raise issues which will be explored in this book: the inequity of access to languages study between high- and low-SES, urban and regional differences; the lack of continuity and achievement in study; the systemic difficulties in accrediting and developing heritage language fluency gained beyond the school curriculum; and the marginal role of languages curriculum, especially in a context of school-based management.

We explore these issues in NSW, Australia's most populous state. In NSW only 23 per cent of primary-aged students have access to learning a language at school, compared with 97 per cent of students in Victoria (Department of Education and Training, 2017). Both states have similar demographics: one-quarter of the population speaks a language in addition to English at home; 50 per cent are migrants or children of migrants; the population is urbanized with most living in the capital city; students generally attend government schools but there are strong Catholic and independent systems. The provision and uptake of languages, however, could not be more different. In Victoria one in five students studies languages to their final year of schooling, but in NSW fewer than 7 per cent take a language. In NSW only one in six children who start school as bilingual continues to develop their language skills; and only one in twenty children from a monolingual English background gains any level of fluency in a second language (Liddicoat et al., 2007).

This mosaic of provision and uptake has developed due to a range of historical factors which have been explored in depth by other researchers (Lo Bianco, 2009; Ozolins, 1993; Teese, 2013). During the 1950s and 1960s studying a modern or ancient language was required for students matriculating to Arts and other faculties of Australian universities (Teese, 2013). Languages were seen as an intellectual challenge for the brightest students and a marker of distinction. Over 40 per cent of final-year students, mostly in prestige-independent, Catholic and government selective schools, studied Latin, French or German. This requirement began to be dropped in 1968, and the percentage of students taking languages quickly fell.

The decline was masked, however, by the development of comprehensive schooling in the 1970s. There were rapid increases in languages enrolments, and by 2000 the numbers of secondary students taking languages had increased from the 1970s by 500 per cent, with most studying French. This rapid increase in numbers also camouflaged the inequities in access: language provision in rural, regional and lower-SES schools remained low (Teese, 2013). The discourse of 'languages for all' was central in the growth of languages in comprehensive schooling but it subsisted alongside traditional notions of 'prestige languages as markers of intellectual excellence' (Teese and Polesel, 2003: 89). Top-stream students in comprehensive schools studied French or Latin or German; lower-stream students tended not to have access to languages.

Growth of Asian languages

This shift was accompanied by a growing focus on Asian languages, firstly for reasons of diplomacy and then for career and trade, with the emphasis on Australia's position in Asia. Indonesian was introduced in the 1970s and there was a strong push for Japanese in the 1980s, as trade links developed, but particularly with a substantial increase of tourists from Japan (Lo Bianco, 2009). Substantial federal government funding was directed towards the study of Chinese, Japanese, Korean and Indonesian. In NSW and Victoria, students taking Asian languages increased by 10 per cent between 1995 and 2003 (Slaughter, 2009). The Asian language push, however, was ultimately a failure (Slaughter, 2009). No Asian language gained over 2 per cent of Year 12 student enrolments and students came mainly from high-SES schools with tertiary-educated parents (Teese, 2013). The key reason for this failure was structural.

Responsibility for education in Australia is divided between federal and state governments, with state governments responsible for curriculum, operating schools and teacher employment and federal government largely responsible for programs and policy. The impact of a top-down federal government push for Asian languages depended on the policy capacity and readiness of states to implement it. Victoria used the federal funding to build on existing language program capacity, whereas NSW used the funding to employ languages teachers and initiate new programs. When funding ceased in 2003, enrolments in Asian languages programs in NSW plummeted (down 78 per cent in Japanese and 77 per cent in Indonesian at primary level); falls in Victoria were much smaller (4 per cent at the primary level) in line with an overall decline in languages study (Slaughter, 2009). According to Slaughter, the differential impact was due to differences in 'the language policy of each state, along with appropriate support for structures that are designed to implement and sustain policy' (Slaughter, 2009: 7). Many teachers who retrained as Indonesian or Japanese teachers still remain in the NSW system, but are no longer teaching those languages.

From the 1990s neoliberal priorities and the role of career, trade and economics figured in every language policy. Reports in the 1990s directed attention to the intersection between education and the labour market; English literacy and language outcomes were priorities and languages other than English tended to be marginalized (Lo Bianco, 2009). The justification for languages study became couched in economic terms, typically referring to opportunities for jobs and careers. This discourse was much more common in languages than in any other subject. In these discourses 'diplomatic and trade elites have tended to advocate in favour of a select group of prestige, trade and security-linked Asian languages' (Lo Bianco, 2009: 25). The same economic rationalism also saw a devolution of responsibility and governance to individual school level but a centralization of funding and control. With the return to standardized testing and the focus on English literacy standards, languages tended to be squeezed out of the curriculum by other demands, as happened in the United States and UK (Rhodes and Pufahl, 2010; Tinsley and Dolezal, 2018).

The other key development in the late 1970s was the belated recognition of Indigenous languages and immigrant community languages. There are more than 250 Aboriginal and Torres Strait Islander languages in Australia (Marmion, Obata, and Troy, 2014). They were first identified as a priority for maintenance and support in the 1987 National Policy on Languages. There are now programs in NSW designed to support development of Indigenous languages, and programs have gained wide support (Singhal, 2018).

The rise and decline of community languages

Australia is a nation of immigrants, with just under 50 per cent of the population being migrants or the children of migrants. There are 300 'separately identified languages' spoken in Australian homes and over 21 per cent of the population speaks a language other than English (Australian Bureau of Statistics, 2016). The policy commitment to multiculturalism was realized in the many initiatives designed to promote community languages: in the 1980s community languages were first introduced to the school curriculum and grew to thirty-four community languages being accredited for Year 12 tertiary entry; community languages were funded in primary schools and grew to 243 programs; the Saturday School of Community Languages was established to provide access to community languages to Year 12; and government funding was provided for out-of-hours community languages schools where some 7,000 volunteer teachers across Australia now teach around 100,000 students one of sixty-four languages.

Community languages courses provided access to tertiary education for second-generation students: Modern Greek and Italian in the 1970s and then Arabic, which was introduced in the 1980s. The majority of students taking community languages were in lower-SES secondary schools (Teese and Polesel, 2003). A period of free tertiary education (1972–86) saw the rapid increase in equity of access for students from community languages background with over a third of tertiary students during this period speaking a language in addition to English at home (Teese, 2013). The immigrant parents of these students, from Greek, Italian, Maltese, Arabic and Turkish backgrounds, often lacked any post-school education and many had nothing beyond primary school (Teese, 2013). These conditions, however, did not last and the 2000s saw a decline in the number of languages programs in lower-SES schools and in the uptake of languages in the final years of schooling.

To understand the marginalization of community languages and this decline in languages in lower-SES schools, the system of tertiary entry in Australia needs to be explained. In Australia the final Year 12 examinations also count as tertiary entry. Examination marks are scaled according to an algorithm of ability across all subjects, called the Australian Tertiary Admission Rank (ATAR). When community languages were introduced, they were scaled according to French and German because enrolments were small and different languages were assumed to have been developed to equal levels of difficulty by the respective curriculum authorities. This worked in favour of students in lower-SES schools.

The ATAR algorithm differs in each state, but in NSW it involves a definition of ability reliant on how students perform in mass candidature subjects such as English and Mathematics. This has been criticized for resulting in students in lower-SES schools gaining ATARs of between five and sixteen points below the average.

> The model underpinning the ATAR scaling algorithm specifies that the scaled mean in a course is equal to the average academic achievement of the course candidature where, for individual students, the measure of academic achievement is taken as the average scaled mark in all courses completed. (Universities Admissions Centre, 2018: 7)

Complaints about the 'unfair advantage' of students from community languages backgrounds, however, led to policy shifts. It was argued that examinations were 'too easy' because proficiency was gained in the community and that this prevented other (i.e. non-background) students taking languages. From 1997 all languages, no matter what their candidature, were scaled individually with the consequence that all major community languages ranked much lower than French and German.

The second NSW government response was to introduce differentiated curriculum for students with 'first' and 'second' language learner syllabuses so that 'first' language syllabuses required much higher levels of fluency. The challenge was how to define 'first' and 'second' learners. Eligibility for different courses was defined by student background: in NSW students who had three years of study overseas in their home language had to enrol in 'first' or 'background' courses; students with parent/s from that background enrolled in 'heritage' courses. 'Beginner' courses were also introduced for students who had less than 100 hours prior study of the language in an attempt to pick up learners who had not taken elective languages; other students took a 'continuer' course. This attempt to address the challenge of community languages through differentiated curriculum led to five different syllabuses in some languages. Learners of Japanese, for example, were placed in Japanese Beginners, Continuers, Extension, Background Speakers or Heritage Japanese (Universities Admissions Centre, 2015).

The impact of these policies was a collapse in languages study after 2000 in mid- to low-SES secondary schools, especially those with students from community languages backgrounds. Both the shift in policy for tertiary ranking and the plethora of languages curriculum have resulted in the continuing decline of languages and the marginalization of community languages in the mainstream school system and a shift of those languages to the out-of-hours community languages schools.

Rhetoric versus reality

The resulting picture of languages is one of a gap between reality and rhetoric. There have been over seventy policy-related reports, investigations and substantial enquiries since 1972 (Lo Bianco and Gvozdenko, 2006). All major government declarations affirmed the central role of languages in school curriculum (Hobart Declaration 1989, Adelaide Declaration 1999, Melbourne Declaration 2008). The 1987 National Policy on Languages was acknowledged internationally as a landmark with its comprehensive recommendations for English, Aboriginal and Torres Strait Islander languages and a language other than English for all (Lo Bianco, 1987). In NSW only 21 per cent of students have access to languages study in their schooling (Liddicoat et al., 2007) and under 8 per cent take a language for the final year of schooling (Universities Admissions Centre, 2018). The issues highlighted in this brief summary are common to languages education in many English-speaking countries, but perhaps the lack of compulsory languages study and the marginal role of languages curriculum make them more evident. It is also the interrelationship of community languages and issues of SES that make the issues explored in this book more complex.

The following sections outline how we gained the data for our study, and the final section teases out some of the issues in the accounts from the four schools: issues which will be explored in this volume.

Our contribution to knowledge about languages study in schools

Finding out who studies languages to what level in what school is a problem that faces education providers. The only data normally provided by systems are the numbers and results of students taking languages for their final year of study. How policy can be developed and evaluated without consistent and coherent data collection has been the question raised by many reports (Liddicoat et al., 2007; Lo Bianco, 2009). Only one jurisdiction in Australia, the Victorian government school system, has annual language study data collection (Department of Education and Training, 2017). This compares with the UK where there are annual surveys in England and regular reports in Wales, Northern Ireland and Scotland, and the United States, where there are large-scale reviews (Board and Tinsley, 2014, 2015a; Pufahl and Rhodes, 2011; Rhodes and Pufahl, 2010). One reason suggested for this lack of data collection as the basis for policy development in Australia is the division of education between federal and state governments. The federal government is largely responsible for language policy and program development, and state governments and systems responsible for language teachers, curriculum development and implementation. Systems, thus, see their responsibility as ensuring curriculum implementation rather than evaluating the outcomes and the nature of language learning.

The accounts in this book come from a five-year study of the provision and uptake of languages in schools in NSW which collected three types of data: statistical data on K-12 language provision and uptake; survey data of language attitudes, skills and experiences of school staff; and school case studies of forty-two government, Catholic, independent and community languages schools.

The study

As a first step in the study, an online survey was used to collect the attitudes to languages study and the self-assessed languages skills of all school staff: principals, teachers, languages teachers and administrative staff, achieving a response rate of 11 per cent or 1,232 replies. At the same time, we collected all available language program data over a six-year period: at state and federal levels; from previous reports and studies; from Year 12 examinations; and from government, Catholic and independent schools. We aimed to build up a database for individual schools which included: details of grade level; numbers in languages classes; language/s studied; student cultural/language backgrounds; teachers' professional training and experience in languages; time allocated for study and type of course studied.

Our two research sites were inner-city Sydney (pop. 2 million), where almost 50 per cent speak a language other than English at home, and Wollongong, a regional city south of Sydney (pop. 300,000), where 15 per cent speak a language other than English at home. Together, these sites constitute 30 per cent of the NSW state population of 6.5 million. We interviewed languages and non-languages teachers, school principals and executives, parents where possible and languages/non-languages students individually and in focus groups. We found it difficult to interview a representative sample of low-SES parents, and the parents we managed to interview in low-SES schools were sometimes atypical. We also carried out observations of languages classes in the schools. Interview data were transcribed and analysed using NVivo and also content and thematic analysis.

The methodology draws on the *Multilingual Cities* project of Extra and Yagmur (2004), who conducted multiple case studies in six European cities. This slice or 'tranche' approach, combining large-scale quantitative and survey data with local case studies, provides a two-way process whereby local perspectives can highlight the impact of broader issues, and aggregated data can enhance the analysis of local school data.

Finding solutions

The chapters in this volume explore how the differential access to languages is constructed and played out at school level, drawing mainly on the qualitative case-study data. They also show ways in which schools have challenged systemic pressures and structural impediments to develop successful programs. The government policy discourses surrounding languages focus very much in the past two decades on languages of trade and diplomacy, languages study for career purposes and for Australia, the role of Asian languages in this mix. Government programs to expand the teaching of Asian languages with the injection of large amounts of funding have not so far been successful: 96 per cent of learners of Chinese drop the subject before Year 12 and no Asian language has managed to gain strong enrolments (Orton, 2008). The discourses in schools are mixed. Students and staff at Campbell High School have picked up the 'languages of the future' discourse: Aiden said, 'China, it's the way to go.' For students with home language backgrounds the reasons are different but clear. In other schools we came across what we called a 'cosmopolitan' discourse whereby parents spoke in terms of a world in which languages were needed for their children as citizens of the modern world (Wright, Cruickshank and Black, 2018). We also found that teachers argued most strongly for languages in cognitive terms. Our survey found that the importance of languages for cognitive development and thinking along with intercultural understanding and awareness were by far the main reasons for teachers supporting languages study. The discourses of language study are explored in Chapter 2 in the context of how principals view the teaching of languages in their schools.

In each of the case-study schools, languages had a high profile, which was largely due to the commitment of the principals and their executives. For example, Will, the Cheswell principal, and his deputy had worked to spread languages across the school staff, employing teachers who were trained in languages and supporting others to undertake postgraduate study. Eve, the Head Teacher Languages at Forster High School, was on the school executive and had a visible team of seven languages teachers. John, at Campbell, worked closely with the principal in building the languages program. The perceptions of principals of the value of languages study and their attitudes to supporting languages study in their schools are thus important elements in the future of languages programs. Chapter 2 draws on interviews with principals and school executives to provide insights into how the perceptions of the principals in our study affect languages provision and how this might differ for different groups of students.

Languages programs cannot be enacted without the support of teachers, both languages specialists and non-specialists. Since the curriculum and provision for languages in NSW are so different in the primary and secondary school, two separate chapters have been devoted to secondary (Chapter 3) and primary (Chapter 4) teachers' perceptions of languages and the constitution of their professional identities in relation to languages teaching. Parent attitudes emerge in many studies as key to whether children take or drop languages (Australian Council of State School Organisations, 2007; Coleman, Galaczi and Astruc, 2007). In Chapter 5 we explore the complexity of and reasons for family attitudes to languages.

Finally, it is young people who make the ultimate choice about whether to study languages and a specific language (when there are opportunities to do so). In our study most of the students we interviewed were in language classes, although the level of provision and their potential for further study varied considerably. All were clear about what they wanted from their languages study, but their expectations of learning differed depending on different stages of schooling, their different levels of fluency and the quality of languages teaching to which they had been exposed. These experiences and attitudes to languages study are explored in Chapter 6.

As pointed out above, in NSW languages are not a compulsory curriculum area and with devolution of responsibility to local schools there are great differences in provision. The following chapters look more closely at particular instances of provision: the situation of languages in primary schools (Chapter 7); the fragile existence in secondary schools, with particular attention to why community languages have become marginalized (Chapter 8) and lastly the singular case of Chinese in NSW and the complex reasons for students choosing or not to study this 'prestige' Asian language of trade and diplomacy, the language most spoken in NSW after English (Chapter 9). Chapter 10 explores the implications of the findings and compares these with contemporary developments in languages in the context of the UK and North America.

2

Principals' Perspectives on the Study of Languages

They all do it, that's the expectation. They all do a language. (Principal, Cheswell Public School)

Community language isn't necessarily a go for us. (Principal, Pennington Public School)

The above two quotes are from principals in two NSW public schools, and they are provided to illustrate the differing perspectives of school principals in the provision of languages in NSW schools. The two primary schools are less than 10 kilometres apart in suburbs to the south-west of Sydney. They have similar student numbers, similar middle-ranking SES ratings (ICSEA 1017 at Cheswell, 1046 at Pennington), and both schools pride themselves on their academic achievements with large numbers of students transitioning each year from Year 6 to academically selective high schools. And yet, in one important curriculum aspect they are different: at Cheswell PS, every student studies at least one of the many community languages taught at the school, and many participate in the school's bilingual program, while at Pennington PS there are no language classes. The reason for this curriculum disparity is primarily a matter of the personal attitudes towards languages of the respective school principals and their executive staff. At Cheswell PS, the principal was an avowed believer in students learning languages at school, claiming: 'You're not really educated if you don't have a language.' At Pennington PS, with the absence of a dominant community language spoken by students, the principal and deputy principal expressed the view that choosing a language to be taught at the school was problematic: 'I guess it's which language if you're going to only learn one.' In the absence of their promotion of languages, none were taught at the school.

This chapter examines the role and perspectives of school principals and their executive staff in the provision of languages programs in both primary and secondary schools in NSW. As the vignettes of schools in the introductory chapter of this book demonstrate, schools vary considerably in the type and extent of their languages provision, and in the discourses that have influenced perceptions of, and action in relation to, the role of languages in the school curriculum. According to Liddicoat et al. (2007: 153), the role of the principal in determining languages provision in individual schools is 'paramount', especially in this era of school-based management in which principals have considerable autonomy in deciding curriculum matters (e.g. Caldwell, 2005, 2008; Cranston, 2001; Cranston, Ehrich and Billot, 2003; Thomson, 2010). For decades since the 1970s in Australia, principals have expressed the desire for autonomy from interference from central authorities in the running of their schools (Thomson, 2010). Contemporary school-based management, however, is highly complex and requires principals not only to be active leaders and drivers of educational reforms, but, in a performance sense, to be accountable for how their school fares in competition with other schools (e.g. through NAPLAN[1] results, see Hardy, 2014; Thomson and Mockler, 2016), and in a fiduciary sense, to self-manage the financial resources of the school. Pervasive neoliberal ideology in recent decades has seen schools subject to competitive, market pressures from parental choice policies and massively increased audit and accountability requirements (e.g. Connell, 2013). The school principal is the linchpin at the local school level in this new business-oriented world of educational governance, and along with their new freedoms as autonomous leaders, they are expected to be entrepreneurial in promoting their schools. Whether these governance reforms have had a consistently positive educational impact, however, is debatable, and some have argued that they have increased educational inequalities and brought principals increasingly within the ambit of neoliberal governmentalities (Gobby, 2013; Keddie, 2017; Keddie, Gobby and Wilkins, 2018; Niesche, 2019). In the NSW context of this study, concerns have been expressed that the school-based management reforms, known as *Local Schools, Local Decisions*, appear to have been driven by economics and state politics rather than by stakeholders in NSW public education (Martin and McPherson, 2015).

While principals have an important role deciding curriculum matters in a school-based management system, curricular differentiation between Australian primary schools is generally quite rare (Perry and Lamb, 2016). Languages in NSW primary schools, however, are different because they are not mandated, unlike in some other states (e.g. Victoria and Western Australia), and thus

---

[1] NAPLAN is the acronym for the high stakes National Assessment Program - Literacy and Numeracy.

languages provision in an individual school depends largely on the principal's attitudes towards languages. Principals have long struggled to find curriculum space for languages in primary schools in various jurisdictions, and commonly they claim lack of time and difficulty in obtaining qualified staff as reasons for their absence (e.g. Baranick and Markham, 1986; Liddicoat et al., 2007). The 'crowded curriculum' often ensures that languages are located on the periphery of the primary curriculum, while high priority is accorded to improving standards in English literacy (Lo Bianco, 2009). This may account for why languages feature in the school curriculum of only between 30 and 40 per cent of NSW primary schools (Board of Studies NSW, 2013). At the secondary school level in NSW, 100 hours of languages are mandated in the junior high school years (either in Year 7 or 8), but again, which languages, and the extent to which they are offered beyond the 100 hours, fall primarily within the decision-making responsibilities of local principals and their executive staff. According to Perry and Lamb (2016), principals as curriculum leaders in secondary schools play a key role in differentiating the curriculum according to the SES backgrounds of students. Their decisions can be based on assumptions that have credence in popular discourse, such as only high-achieving students benefit from languages study, or on what is most likely to benefit their school in the market, rather than on student interest. For example, some students from low-SES backgrounds are counselled against studying more advanced academic subjects (such as languages) in the final two years of high school for fear of depressing the school's overall Year 12 results. A recent study in England indicates that school leaders, when deciding on the type and extent of languages provision, are driven primarily by concerns about student attainment in a climate in which languages 'remain a subject affected by harsh grading, and schools continue to operate in a climate of quantified accountability and exam-oriented success' (Parrish and Lanvers, 2019: 293).

There is some evidence that principals, in marketing their schools to (mostly middle-class) parents in this era of competitive school choice, recognize the value of languages programs in providing cultural capital as a marker of distinction (Smala, Paz and Lingard, 2013). For example, the rise in the number of schools offering the International Baccalaureate (IB) in Australia, of which languages are a key element, provides school principals with a 'point of difference' in the competition for students (Perry, Ledger and Dickson, 2018: 51). At the other end of the languages-valuing spectrum, however, as a recent submission to a curriculum review indicates, there are NSW secondary principals who would like to see even the mandated 100 hours of languages eliminated from the secondary curriculum, with responsibility shifted instead to primary schools (Baker, 2018).

In this chapter, as a way of helping to explain the diverse state of languages provision in NSW schools, we provide a discussion of the perspectives and actions of principals and executive staff through vignettes of their roles in individual schools. One of our key arguments is that the principals in our study perceived languages differently according to the socioeconomic status of students in their schools. Students from more affluent, middle-class families were seen generally to have access to superior forms of languages provision (in terms of cultural and linguistic capital) in comparison with more socially disadvantaged students (see Teese, 2013).

We begin with a focus on the perspectives of principals in the 'elite' government schools in our study – two academically selective high schools. Following the line of argument advanced by Teese (2013), we indicate how principals in these schools viewed traditional languages such as French, German and Japanese as part of a strong academic curriculum which has long reinforced their status as top-performing schools and the status of the students who study languages in these schools. We should make the point, however, that school principalships change over time as individual principals transfer to and from schools or retire. Given the 'paramount' role of principals in influencing language programs, schools can thus become subject to different leadership attitudes towards languages and languages may then become vulnerable as academic subjects. Our interviews and observations in schools were undertaken in 2013–14 and in the time since we have become aware of some formerly strong school languages programs being dismantled or left to dwindle through neglect due to changes of principals.

An academic tradition for the intellectual elite

Kids take to languages like a duck to water here. We've had some do three languages for the HSC and do exceptionally well at all of them. (Principal, Sherwood Selective High School)

The previous principal when we became a selective school, she could see that languages was an area that gifted kids would potentially want to follow. (Principal, Coolamon Selective High School)

Of the three academically selective high schools that participated in the qualitative component of our study, only two provided interviews with their principals: Coolamon and Sherwood. Both schools became academically selective following reforms in the late 1980s/early 1990s as part of the educational policies of a state conservative government. As selective high schools, the two schools were 'socially restrictive' (Windle, 2015) based largely on social class, featuring student populations with high SES ratings (Coolamon ICSEA=1168, 68 per cent in the top quartile; Sherwood ICSEA=1192, 74 per cent in the top quartile). Academically selective high schools increasingly cater to the most socially advantaged students in NSW (Ho, 2017a). Both schools also featured relatively high ratings for students speaking community languages at home (Coolamon 52 per cent, Sherwood 30 per cent), especially in view of the largely Anglo-Saxon-dominated local areas of the two schools. This was reflective of the higher concentration of Asian-Australian students in academically selective schools in NSW (Ho, 2017b, c; Watkins, 2017).

Languages featured strongly in the curriculum of both schools. At the time of the study, three languages were taught at Coolamon: French, German and Japanese. These languages had remained unchanged from the time the school became selective in the early 1990s, as had several of the long-standing teachers in the Languages faculty. All students in Year 7 undertook a 'taster' language program in all three languages (i.e. three × thirteen weeks). In Year 8, they chose to study one of the languages (as the mandatory 100 hours), and in subsequent years, they could elect to study one or more of these languages up to and including the HSC (Year 12). About a third of all students chose a language elective in Years 9–10. At Sherwood there were four languages offered – French, German, Italian and Japanese – and these languages were also unchanged since the early 1990s. As with Coolamon, these languages were offered as Year 7 'taster' courses, with students then electing to study one of these languages in Year 8 (though not Italian, which was later available to Year 11 students at Beginner level). Students could elect to take a language from Year 11 to 12, including at Extension level (the highest level of languages in the HSC). Annual overseas trips for languages students were a feature of both schools and were highly valued by the students. At Sherwood at the time of the research, Japanese was heavily oversubscribed as an elective in Year 9 in part because 'they all want to go to Japan in Year 10' (Principal). At Coolamon, trips to France had been a feature 'every year since I don't know' (Principal).

Through their commitment to languages as an essential element of a strong academic curriculum, and to the profile of their schools, the principals had ensured that the Languages faculties in their schools were strong with experienced, long-term languages staff, all of whom had specific languages teaching qualifications and extensive 'in country' experience. The provision of French, German and Japanese at both schools was no accident. French and

German in particular, since the decline of Latin, have traditionally conferred academic status as key curriculum subjects in elite schools. Teese (2013: 194) comments that learning these languages in a serious and demanding academic way, in particular with a heavy emphasis on grammar, is 'in the formal Latin tradition', so continuing the gravitas of traditional foreign language learning. As the comments by the two principals at the beginning of this section indicate, they saw a 'fit' (i.e. 'like a duck to water') between the formal study of languages and the 'gifted' students who attended their schools (see Chapter 4 on languages teachers for descriptions of how selective high school students are seen to comply with, indeed seem to have a predilection for, studying formal grammar). Teese (2013: 221) also points out that Japanese, as a traditional Asian language taught for many decades in Australian schools, can 'operate like the traditional European languages in translating cultural advantage into scholastic capital'. Japanese language studies grew considerably in schools in the 1980s and 1990s (the 'tsunami' according to Lo Bianco, 2000), overtaking German in student numbers as the Australian government focused increasingly on Asian languages and languages of trade (de Kretser and Spence-Brown, 2010).

At Coolamon, the principal explained that because he valued languages in his school curriculum, he deliberately privileged them through the provision of additional resources. He explained that for the Years 7–10 he had discretionary 'non-allocated' (i.e. non-mandated) teaching hours/periods available to him, 'and we choose to put four of those twelve into Year 7 languages. Now that's a big call'. In other words, he provided a strong languages program in Year 7 because he valued languages, which was in addition to the mandatory study of languages in Year 8. He also permitted small classes to run in senior school language electives.

Similarly, at Sherwood the principal structured the languages program (and also art and music) to provide continuity and depth of learning for Years 7 and 8. She decried and refused to run 'silly two period courses' because she believed they were not valued by students or teachers. Instead, she provided five periods a week and continuity of languages provision that extended way beyond the mandatory requirement. In the senior years, as with Coolamon, the principal allowed language classes to run with small student numbers, stating that in other schools 'they would can it'. She viewed languages to be important for students at her school:

> Language courses in a school like ours are really quite important, because a lot of our kids are going to live and work overseas when they finish. They're the sorts of kids who are going to get jobs with companies or seek international work.

Students at academically selective high schools are recognized as 'gifted.' As the later chapter on teachers explains, students are viewed differently from those in comprehensive high schools 'out there in the real world' (a comment by the French teacher at Sherwood). Selective school students necessarily arrive at their schools with strong academic skills, including English language skills, and they perform well in languages. In the case of Coolamon, over half of the students spoke community languages at home, but the principal nevertheless could claim that ESL was 'not a great need' at his school. Both school principals believed strongly that learning another language at school helped students with their English language skills. The Sherwood principal stated:

> The study of other languages actually helps you with your English, because it helps you with the structure of your grammar. It also helps you with the vocabulary that exists in English, which comes from all over the world in different language areas. So, kids will also benefit from learning a language and can have a lot of fun in doing that at the same time.

In saying this, the principal identified herself as one of the 'old school sorts' (in fact both principals had been employed at their respective schools since the 1980s), and as a later section of this chapter indicates, this view was not necessarily shared in low-SES comprehensive high schools. While not languages specialists, it is interesting to note that both principals learnt Latin as part of the regular languages program available when they were high school students.

As the comments by the two principals at the beginning of this section indicate, they saw a 'fit' between languages and the 'gifted' students who attended their schools, and this view was reinforced by comments from language teachers in the two schools who commented on the 'incredibly bright kids' and the way languages were so popular at the schools (see Chapter 4).

We conclude from these two selective high schools that this 'fit' between students and languages provision worked to differentiate selective schools from 'other' schools (i.e. comprehensive high schools) in the hierarchical and inequitable government secondary education system in NSW. Furthermore, students at the two academically selective high schools were differentiated from other schools according to social class (based on SES data), and by the languages curriculum which the principals actively promoted through their support for languages in areas such as curriculum structuring/prioritizing, timetabling and the maintenance of strong languages faculties. As Teese (2013: 223) writes of the role of languages for elite students:

> Languages are a recognised means of testing the capacities of children and outwardly declaring 'giftedness' through acceptance of a distinctive set of

academic tasks. The schools that are able to fill language classes also lay claim to a special status because it is through them that students are found who will take up the challenge of some of the most demanding work in the curriculum and teachers are found who are able to get good results. Modern languages are not only a vehicle of competitive individual advantage, but of institutional power and prestige.

The perspectives of the principals of Coolamon and Sherwood can be seen to be fairly typical of principals in academically selective high schools. These principals did not personally have languages backgrounds, but they recognized and responded to the prestige value of languages and saw them as a central part of the curriculum in catering to the needs of their students. In this respect, these principals' perspectives were also typical of those in the higher-SES independent schools featured later in this chapter, but they were atypical of low-SES comprehensive high schools, as we explain in a later section.

Language study as tokenism

We had lovely brie. (Principal, St Catherine's PS)

It's not like high school, we don't have specialist teachers as such. (Principal, St John's)

We now turn to primary schools, and in this section we consider the role of principals and languages provision at two high-SES Catholic primary schools. One of the schools, St Catherine's, is located in the inner city of Sydney and recorded the highest SES rating of any schools in our study (ICSEA 1227), and the other school, St John's (ICSEA 1126), is located in a middle-class outer suburb of the regional city of Wollongong. The attitudes and actions of the principals from both schools illustrate some of the issues confronting the study of languages in high-SES primary schools.

As in most primary schools, there were dilemmas over where and how to accommodate languages in the crowded primary curriculum, and the principals in the two schools approached this differently. At St Catherine's, every class from Kindergarten to Year 6 was timetabled for a single forty-minute French lesson one day a week (Wednesday). The lessons were conducted by a qualified French language teacher (secondary trained), but they were distinct from the regular school curriculum insofar as they were timetabled during the regular class teachers' RFF (release from face-to-face) teaching. Parents were also billed separately for the French lessons.

The decision to offer French was in response to a survey conducted some years previously with parents, and it was also a language that a number of the parents spoke. But while the principal personally thought that teaching languages was important at the school, and while it accorded with the wishes of parents, it was not a curriculum priority. It was funded and taught quite separately from other school subjects in a limited and defined curriculum space, and as the principal acknowledged:

> If we had to teach it ourselves, then it might get put on the back burner ... When you've got the pressure of performance in NAPLAN and all of this, that's where people put their money, to be quite honest with you.

Teaching French at the school, however, had some cultural positives. It appeased the middle-class and internationally well-travelled parent group, and in the year previous to the research study, the school had organized a trip to New Caledonia for a small group of five families. According to the principal, it also enabled some religious and cultural events 'which brought the staff together'. The French morning assembly, for example, was especially valued by the principal and teachers:

> We're incorporating it into our religion as well because we do – it's a French assembly on Wednesdays – we do a French good morning and then we just say the French Hail Mary. They're learning the French Our Father.

The principal also spoke glowingly of the annual French day held at the school:

> The children ... dressed up as anything from baguettes to – gosh, there was a Mary Antoinette came in one year. It was just wonderful ... All [staff] just sitting around watching a French film and drinking French champagne. It was really lovely ... we had lovely brie.

At this school every student had the experience of participating in French lessons, but given the limited time and resources made available for the program, it could be viewed more as a form of cultural tokenism than a serious curriculum subject. Classroom observations revealed that even after six years of lessons, most students had acquired little spoken French competency and only some basic knowledge of French culture. The French teacher herself concluded that while the principal and the parents liked the idea that French was taught, it was 'a bit of a posh thing to do' (see Chapter 4).

In the case of St John's, the principal was also personally supportive of languages, and in the broader school environment she played a key role on the Language Advisory Committee for the regional Diocese. She was herself an Italian speaker, having arrived in Australia as a small baby, and prior to her principal role she had taught Italian in schools for several years. She was conscious of the expectations of local middle-class parents in relation to languages:

> Look, St John's parents have very high expectations. They are generally well-educated people who come from a fairly, I wouldn't say affluent, but high socio-economic area who have been exposed to the opportunity of tertiary education. They really like their children to have had an exposure to language.

At first glance, the school appeared to provide a relatively broad languages program. Spanish was being taught in Kindergarten and Year 1, and Indonesian in Years 2 and 3. Italian had also been taught in recent years, and there had been an attempt to introduce Chinese at the school. But this number and range of languages belied some structural weaknesses that were also common in many other primary schools. First of all, there were no qualified languages teachers in the school. As the principal noted:

> The most common factor that makes primary schools offer a different language, or expose kids to a different language, is that they have native speakers on staff. Because it's not like high school, we don't have specialist teachers as such (though there were occasionally specialist PE teachers).

In other words, the only reason Spanish and Indonesian were being taught at St John's was because there were classroom teachers on the school staff who had some background knowledge of these languages and/or they felt they could teach these languages. None were qualified to teach languages. There was also the issue of language continuity, as some students experienced first one language, in this case Indonesian, then later another language, Spanish. Trying to enable some continuity in languages provision, however, was problematic because languages were not a priority subject on the curriculum timetable, and teachers were required, with the permission of the principal, to make informal timetabling arrangements among themselves in order to accommodate some continuity in languages. As a Year 2 teacher commented:

> We just say to the principal, look, this teacher would like Indonesian continued and I'm willing to do it at this time each week. We're willing to swap a lesson and do so. It's not been a problem. It can be done.

In effect, the languages program was ad hoc, relying on the language backgrounds of some teachers, their goodwill in wishing to teach a language and their informal organizational skills to enable programs to continue from one year to the next. Additionally, there was a lack of available language teaching materials and resources.

At one time, prior to our research study, the principal did try to introduce a language program using a different model based on her belief that Asian languages were going to be 'of high priority in Australia'. Chinese was introduced to Year 5/6 students by the Chinese teacher at the local Catholic secondary school in the hope that it might encourage them to later elect to study Chinese when they transitioned to the secondary school. However, this language experiment was discontinued when students were later found to resist Chinese as an elective in the secondary school. The principal also indicated concerns over the traditional pedagogy used in the program, commenting that her students 'aren't interested to be lectured at' and the lack of credibility of the Chinese teacher who was not a native speaker ('her expertise in using the languages was limited'). It was also difficult to fit Chinese classes within the existing 'crowded' curriculum, and one of the teachers commented that 'it was taking a big chunk of our teaching time out of HSIE ... we just couldn't fit it into the timetable. It was too much for us'.

In summary, while the principals at both St Catherine's and St John's expressed personal support for the teaching of languages at their schools, and both believed they were acting according to the needs and expectations of well-educated, middle-class parents, the languages programs they instituted at their schools were far from successful. At St Catherine's, the French language course was a forty-minute-a-week 'add-on' to the school curriculum for each class and lacked the legitimacy of other subjects as it was programmed while the regular classroom teachers had their RFF. At St John's, two languages (Indonesian and Spanish) were informally integrated with the regular curriculum by classroom teachers who had some background knowledge of these languages, but these teachers were not formally qualified to teach languages. When the principal attempted to introduce a new language (Chinese) in a curriculum space that made inroads into the timetabling of other subjects, and involved an external teacher, it proved problematic for both timetabling and pedagogical reasons. The principal at St John's did suggest that languages might have greater priority in the future, but as a high-achieving school, as with the St Catherine's principal, her stated main priority was for NAPLAN results to improve. We can conclude from these two primary schools that despite the personal support primary principals may provide for languages in an era of school-based management, unless languages are a mandated component of the school curriculum, they will be problematic to deliver effectively and will remain marginalized.

'It's not a priority for them' – A principal's perspectives on languages provision in a 'residual' comprehensive high school

Having considered principals' perspectives in secondary and primary schools that cater for mainly students from middle-class families, we now turn to languages provision for students from working-class families. In this section, we focus on the perspectives of principals in comprehensive high schools, a form of schooling that has long been implicated in social class inequities in Australia (e.g. Connell et al., 1982) and demonstrates a strong contrast to the 'elite' languages provision in academically selective high schools featured earlier in this chapter. We refer to low-SES government secondary schools as 'residual' comprehensive high schools, that is, local comprehensive schools with declining enrolments following the loss of students through the creaming effects of academically selective testing and local students attending private schools (Black, Wright and Cruickshank, 2018; Campbell and Sherington, 2013). In NSW, student enrolments in comprehensive high schools, that is, government secondary schools that provide 'education for all' in the local area, have been steadily declining since the late 1980s due largely to neoliberal educational reforms that have promoted specialist (i.e. selective) high schools and private schools (Campbell and Sherington, 2013). This has resulted in a 'class shift' as the SES of comprehensive high school populations (based on parental incomes and educational qualifications) has declined relative to those attending academically selective and private schools (Campbell, Proctor and Sherington, 2009).

    Metro High School is an inner-city school with a low SES (ICSEA 968) and a highly multicultural student population (84 per cent speak community languages at home). The school has seen its enrolments fall from around 1,200 students in the 1980s to fewer than 400 at the time of the study (information provided by a long-standing teacher at the school). The principal stated that one of the main reasons for this decline was competition from private and academically selective high schools:

> I'm surrounded by selective schools. Within 10 kilometres, I think there's five or six either partially or fully selective high schools, so they draw away the more academic students.

The principal perceived Metro HS to be an undesirable 'tough' school in the eyes of many local parents, especially with the increasing 'gentrification' of this inner-city suburb as many new parents to the suburb chose to send their children to more desirable (and often private) schools in other suburbs. The students who remained attended their local Metro HS.

Languages did not feature strongly in the school's curriculum. Italian was taught as the mandatory 100 hours in Year 8, and while Italian was available as an elective subject in Years 9 and 10, at the time of our research, insufficient student numbers precluded it being taught as an elective subject. There was just the one full-time qualified language teacher at the school. She was young and inexperienced (in just her second year of teaching), and she also taught ESL.

The principal, from a Greek family background and relatively new to the school (less than a year), was generally supportive of languages provision in the school, but despite her attempts, she had failed to develop it further. At one stage, using existing school funds, she introduced Chinese and Vietnamese classes as background languages for her international (i.e. fee-paying) Years 11 and 12 students 'more as a welfare thing just trying to support them'. But as international student numbers dropped, the classes could not continue, and students were instead referred to Saturday community language classes.

While the school population spoke a wide range of community languages at home, which according to the principal included Arabic, Chinese, Vietnamese, Greek, Spanish, Portuguese and many African and Creole languages, the choice of Italian as the mandatory 100-hour language taught at the school was entirely pragmatic. The beginning teacher appointed to the school by the state department of education was a teacher of Italian, so Italian was offered as the mandatory language. The previous language teacher at the school taught Indonesian for the same reason. This apparent randomness of languages provision at the school was the result of the state education department making decisions about appointments based largely on the availability of languages teachers on their waiting lists. We did, however, find that in some schools in our study, teachers of specific languages could be appointed following direct lobbying from principals. The appointment of a beginning solo language teacher at a comprehensive high school with little or no support from colleagues appeared to follow a pattern repeated at several other comprehensive high schools in our study.

The principal talked about the benefits of languages largely in terms of future travel and the ability to pick up other languages, but from her perspective, there was little active support from the school community for more languages to be taught in the school beyond the mandatory 100 hours. She had received no feedback from parents about languages and stated that some parents had other priorities for their children, such as 'getting through school.' It was the principal's experience at Metro, and also at her previous low-enrolment/highly multicultural schools (i.e. 'residual' comprehensives in south-west Sydney), that students were not choosing to study languages. When they elected to study subjects in Years 9 and 10, languages usually ranked poorly in competition with vocationally oriented or seemingly more attractive electives such as woodwork, metalwork, cooking, commerce, sports and computers. As the principal stated:

> They all want to be business – run their own businesses. But they're competing with more practical subjects too, so the kids that want to run around, want to do an extra sports subject. Or get the hammers out there. They're all really good with their technology and they think they're going to play games on the computers, so they pick computers, so that's what they're competing against. So, it does make it difficult.

For those few students who did choose to study languages as an elective subject, the principal believed it was not for academic reasons or because they loved the subject, but rather because they could relate to and personally liked the teacher:

> As much as we say to kids do something because you want to do it and you like it, it is those relationships that they have. If they like a person that's why they pick the subject and I think languages is the same.

Unlike in the selective high schools featured earlier in this chapter, delivering language classes as electives beyond the mandatory provision in comprehensive high schools like Metro was often problematic because there was a lack of critical mass of students. The Metro principal said she had to 'massage' the numbers in languages electives to try to stop languages from declining altogether in the school, and it entailed difficult compromises:

> We would try and massage it (i.e. the benchmark number for elective Italian classes to run, which was 10 students) – and because it didn't run last year – I'd be inclined to make it run and push some kids in that way for the following year so that we just … so it doesn't drop off … because we're a small school we can't run everything, so if it doesn't run for one cycle we try and have it run the next one round.

At Metro HS, languages provision existed primarily because it was mandatory for the 100 hours, but beyond that it had little support or status from the broader school community. The Italian teacher, for example, described her subject as 'more like a curriculum filler' in the eyes of other teachers at the school, and parents were seen to have other priorities. While few students elected to study languages and chose instead subjects they thought were more practical or enjoyable, Metro HS also lacked the critical mass of students that could enable specialist electives such as languages to thrive. Metro had about half the number of students as the two selective high schools featured in the previous section. The choice of Italian as the language taught at the school and the appointment of a beginning sole language teacher may also not have been ideal, but these curriculum and staffing issues predated the arrival of the principal at the school and she appeared powerless to change them.

Languages as a 'marker of distinction' in the school market: A principal tries to change the perception of a 'residual' comprehensive high school

Not all principals of low-SES comprehensive high schools appeared powerless to change the status of languages in their school. In this section, we consider a principal working closely with his one designated languages teacher to introduce a new language to students, Chinese, in the hope that it would change the community's perceptions about the school.

Campbell HS, as with Metro HS featured earlier, is a 'residual' comprehensive high school, catering for students remaining in the local suburb who do not attend private or selective high school. The principal referred to the local community perception of his school as a 'school of last resort'. The school is low-SES (ICSEA 917) and struggles with low student numbers (less than 350 at the time of the research). Only 13 per cent of students speak a community language at home, reflecting the demographics of the school's regional city location.

In the recent years prior to our research study the principal had introduced Chinese as the mandatory 100-hour program in Year 7 with the belief that students would later elect to study the language in Years 9 and 10 and beyond (at the time of the research, only a French elective was being run in Year 9, and there was also a small French HSC class, both taught by a designated 'generalist' teacher).

The principal at Campbell personally supported languages and he believed that all students should have a second language. But according to him, delivering languages well in his school was problematic in large part due to resourcing needs in a crowded curriculum and where the Australian curriculum prioritized subjects such as English, Maths, Science and History. As with Metro HS, Campbell did not have the critical mass of student enrolments to enable language electives to thrive. While the principal commented that he had the final executive power to decide on curriculum matters, 'the realities of the system' were that student numbers and departmental 'staff to student ratios' largely determined what subjects could be taught.

In a conscious bid to improve languages uptake and to increase the community profile of the school, and hopefully its enrolments, the principal introduced Chinese at the school:

> One of the things I deem to be important for the ongoing ability to change the community aspect of Campbell High School is to attract more students interested in studying Asian studies, including languages, to my school. Because my school has been seen, prior to me coming here, as being a refuge, welfare, school of last resort, and I'm trying to change the perception of the school and the clientele we have coming into the school. I also see Chinese as being one of those drivers as well, so I'm very supportive of it for that reason.

The key to the success of this initiative was the principal's support for a highly skilled and enthusiastic languages teacher who had retrained in Chinese (he formerly taught German) and who could work in tandem with the principal to promote Chinese. A contract had been signed with the Confucius Institute and the Department of Education to encourage the teaching of Chinese at stage 4 level (Years 7 and 8), and it was part of the principal's school plan to extend Chinese beyond stage 4.

The principal expressed his view that Chinese was important at the school 'to meet the future-proofing needs of our students out in the employment force ... it would set them up for employability over other people and that's important'. Thus, the principal promoted Chinese largely as a marketing opportunity relating to its human capital benefits – future employment opportunities for students. For him, Chinese was potentially a 'marker of distinction in the school market' (see Smala, Paz and Lingard, 2013). As the Chinese teacher noted further, 'it's looking for a niche' in the educational marketplace.

The principals of the two low-SES secondary schools we have highlighted, Metro and Campbell HS, were confronted with similar issues of declining student numbers and the 'realities of the system', which made it problematic to deliver languages electives in their schools. At Campbell, the principal's proposed solution was to introduce the study of Chinese to capitalize on an Asian studies discourse which he hoped would resonate with community expectations and revive not only languages but the reputation of the school more generally. This promotion of Chinese was premised predominantly within the human capital discourse of improved job and career prospects for students and the implied implications for upward social mobility. It stood in contrast to the perspectives expressed by the principals in academically selective high schools where languages were seen to fit the strong academic needs of high-achieving students and where international travel was a feature of their middle-class family lives and future aspirations.

'Languages are the core fabric of the school'

In this final section, we consider the perspectives of principals and executives in four schools in which languages have a central place in the curriculum. Three of these schools incorporated bilingual programs in various forms. Two of the schools are private, and of the two government schools, one is primary and the other secondary. Principals played a key languages advocacy role in each of them.

The first school, the Sydney International School (SIS), is an independent, secular, co-educational school for students from pre-school to Year 12. It is in the inner city, and unsurprisingly as a private school, its ICSEA score indicates that it draws students from relatively affluent families (ICSEA=1154, 71 per cent in the top quartile). The school's website refers to its 'globally focused bilingual education', and music also features strongly in the curriculum. From the time students commence at the school, usually in pre-school or at Kindergarten level, they must choose to study one language, either French, Italian, German or Japanese, in a 'partial immersion' program based mainly on social science curriculum content. In the primary years, students receive eighty minutes/day of their chosen language, and they must continue with the same language through to Year 10. In Year 7, an additional language is introduced for all students, either Spanish or Chinese. All students spend time overseas on school trips and language exchanges.

The principal of the school and his executive staff advocated strongly for bilingual language programs taught within the core school value of 'diversity' and the vision of 'a community of global citizens'. These formed a major part of the school's marketing platform (e.g. the school's website) designed to attract fee-paying parents who tended to live in 'cashed-up' (principal's term) areas in the inner city, inner-west and eastern suburbs of Sydney. The principal was himself a language specialist, having been brought up with Greek-speaking parents, studied Italian at university, and prior to becoming principal at SIS he had taught at an English–French bilingual school. He was one of few principals in our study with a specialist languages background and he considered this background to be important for the school:

> I know that being a languages head of school has had an enormous – brought an enormous symbolism to the study of languages in the school. Irrespective of the quality or otherwise of my leadership. But do you know what I mean? Just being a languages head has been important.

It meant that he had strong opinions on languages and how they should be taught, and on occasions he was happy to expound his languages philosophy when he acted as a replacement teacher in the classroom. He recalled one class in which he debated with students the merits of a deeper understanding of languages:

> I remember the particular unit I had to teach them, the counterpart grammatical concept, it's the subjunctive. I said – and I say to them if you can use this well, it – if you can use an irregular it's a really – and one of the kids said to me in a fairly irreverent way: Oh, but you just want to make this James Ruse [the highest performing selective high school in NSW] and you just want us to do well. I said, no, actually, doing well is a by-product of a sophisticated understanding of the language. Once they understood that – understood it in terms of well, it's just about having a deep knowledge of the subject. It's not about impressing the examiner with the subjunctive, there were mindsets at work there.

The principal acknowledged that not all executive staff, including his predecessor (who was not a language specialist), and some members of the school board, shared his perspective that languages were the 'core fabric of the school'. He indicated that there was a tension between 'some who say, oh well languages is just something we do' and others (himself included), 'who say, languages *is* what we do'.

Several members of his school executive had been at the school since the early 1990s and had been largely responsible over the decades for continuing to promote the school values of diversity and global citizenship through languages. So strong was their commitment to these values and beliefs that they had often enrolled their own children in the school (this was a feature of many teachers in the school). For example, the head teacher of the primary school, who also taught her first language, Italian, enrolled her son in Japanese from pre-school to Year 12. She commented: 'He said the best thing he ever did was learning Japanese. He's been to Japan so many times. He loves it, speaks it, writes it.'

The principal referred to the school 'as a sort of linguistic nirvana' due to the level of languages proficiency displayed by languages teachers and students, and that for teachers, 'you wouldn't want to set foot into a classroom here unless you could run your class in the language. The kids would slice you up'. In working with parents, the principal had no problems in promoting the primacy of languages, claiming 'I don't have to go to any parent meeting and convince anyone'. And in working with the school's extensive alumni, the principal attested to the results of the school's approach to languages, pointing to their 'openness to the world' and varied professional careers that demonstrated not only linguistic gains, but high levels of intercultural understanding as well.

This valuing of diverse languages and cultures at SIS accorded with the multicultural ideals that were prevalent when the school was first established in the early 1980s. It appealed to well-educated, middle-class parents for whom languages provided a form of 'civic multiculturalism' (e.g. Resnik, 2009; Wright, Cruickshank and Black, 2018) as a means of understanding 'the other'. The principal was a key driver of languages and he was supported by similarly minded executive staff and linguistically diverse parents which he typified as 'mum's French, dad's Canadian, mum's Chinese, dad's German, we've got scores and scores of those'. These parents were generally educated, mobile and international in their outlook (e.g. 'mum's an academic and she's got a sabbatical in Freiburg').

The second school where languages occupied a central place and were embedded in the curriculum was the Dante Bilingual School (DBS), where the primary aim was fluency in Italian language and culture. DBS is a small (101 students), independent, co-ed primary school established by Co.As.It., an organization that promotes Italian language and culture in Australia. In recent years, the school has moved from its original Australian/Italian suburb in Sydney's inner-west to one fifteen kilometres away. Students are taught exclusively in Italian for half the school week, integrated with the regular school curriculum. School trips and exchanges to Italy are an integral part of school life. According to the principal, while fluency in Italian takes the students a while to develop, by grade 4 it becomes automatic, and by grade 6 'they just click'. Not surprisingly, many students have an Italian background and travel from their inner-west Australian/Italian suburbs each school day. By the same token, many students have no Italian family background, and the principal stated that these parents were often the strongest believers in bilingual education because they made a conscious choice to send their children to the school, 'rather than someone who has some Italian background and [they] say, okay, keep the family language going'.

The principal was Italian and arrived in Australia in her mid-thirties as a qualified secondary teacher of history and philosophy. She then qualified as a languages teacher at Sydney University and subsequently gained employment as an Italian teacher at a Catholic primary school, before teaching Italian at DBS for four years. She became the principal during the period of our research study. All the Italian language teachers in the school had extensive experience of living, working and visiting Italy. The school's motto was 'una faccia una lingua' (one face one language), which for the principal and all teachers of Italian on the staff meant speaking to the students only in Italian as a means of encouraging students' use of Italian. One language teacher commented that to be discovered speaking English 'is like the end of the game'.

The principal indicated that the approach to languages at DBS was different to many schools insofar as the primary purpose of the school was for students to learn Italian:

> When children come here they know that they have to work in Italian. It's not like do I like it, don't I like it, it's all a different mentality, so a different thing altogether because they come here for this.

She was highly critical of the Australian primary school curriculum which focused on topics and did not enable students to engage with 'real, real deep learning'. She viewed the most recent national curriculum on languages to have 'zero' usefulness for the immersion program at DBS, in particular because of its focus on translating:

> because young kids don't have the concept of translating at all. In fact, if you get one of those kids and you say, how do you say this and this and this in Italian, they look at you, they can't answer, but they know, oh ... So if they know their science in Italian, that's great, they know the concepts. Why do they have to focus on translating it all the time?

The principal and her staff had devised their own assessment benchmarking system for Italian based on the Common European Framework because the bilingual students at DBS were too advanced in their language skills for the NSW syllabus ('our kids are miles far away', i.e. above the level). The principal expressed frustration with departmental language policies and their officials ('why we are so behind?'), claiming that Australia was not capitalizing on the many languages spoken in the general community. She felt very strongly about the priority of Italian in the school and sometimes had to defend it against claims by parents and some teachers that because we lived in Australia it did not need to be a priority:

> I fight this with all my heart and soul because really, what they can get from this school, they can't get it from anywhere else. So I guess, if you decide to send your

child to a bilingual school, you know then you send it for this, not for English. English is everywhere else.

The principal understood, however, that sending students to this bilingual school could be perceived as a risk for some parents and that not all families were receptive to bilingual education. She made the comment that:

> I don't want to sound bad, but sometimes it's because this, around here, is a lot of working class. It's difficult, they have other things to deal with every day, rather than thinking about having a bilingual child. You know what I mean? They have to battle in their life.

She appeared to be suggesting that parents in the area in which the school was now located (fifteen kilometres from the founding Australian/Italian suburb), which was relatively low SES, had different educational priorities. The quote is telling. Small, private bilingual schools such as DBS (and also the larger SIS) are sought after primarily by well-educated, middle-class parents with the financial capacity to purchase linguistic and cultural capital for their children's futures. From the principal's perspective, parents who are less well educated and less financially secure (e.g. working-class parents who may have to 'battle in their life') may have less propensity and opportunity to send their children to a private bilingual school like DBS.

Languages at SIS and DBS had a central place in the curriculum and were taught well. In many ways they could be considered pedagogical exemplars. Both schools at the time of the research were led by principals with specialist languages backgrounds and strong opinions on the value of languages and how they could best be taught at school. But both schools were also independent and largely comprised students from middle-class families. To conclude this chapter, we consider the perspectives of principals at two government schools, one primary and one secondary, where languages also had a central place in the curriculum taught, but where the students were from lower-SES families.

'You're not really educated if you don't have a language'

Cheswell Primary School is located just thirteen kilometres south-west of the centre of Sydney: a traditional working-class suburb whose demographics have been transformed in recent decades with the arrival of many Asian background families. Nearly all students at the school (97 per cent) spoke a community language at home, and the principal made reference to his local '95 per cent

Asian-Australian community'. As we outlined in the introductory chapter, Cheswell PS offered a Korean bilingual program, and also a wide range of community languages funded under the Community Languages Program (CLP), including Chinese (at several levels), Vietnamese, Arabic, Hindi, Indonesian, Greek and Spanish. This focus on bilingual and community (mainly Asian) languages was seen by the principal to be largely responsible for increasing enrolments at the school from the low 500s to 740 in recent years.

At the time of the research study, the principal at Cheswell was about to retire after a long career in school education, including the past twenty-five years as a principal. He was not a language specialist, but a strong personal believer in the value of learning languages. The extensive languages program at Cheswell was testament to his philosophy on languages and his desire to meet the cultural and linguistic needs of the local community. Unlike principals and school executives in many other primary schools which focus their efforts on improving English literacy standards, often at the expense of subjects such as languages (many primary schools offer no languages), the Cheswell principal argued that 'the stronger the first language the stronger the English'. This was reflected in what he referred to as the school's 'sensational' NAPLAN scores and the high number of Year 6 students who gained entry to academically selective high schools ('we've more than tripled the number of kids who get selective here'). According to the principal, *all* students at the school were required to study languages, including 'special needs' students:

> Any child who studies a language is going to get something out of it, some idea of another part of the world, its culture, its history, geography, the way they view the world. So, we wouldn't take a child out of a language because of any learning difficulty and we don't.

His promotion of Asian languages and Asian educational approaches more generally accorded not only with his desire to meet the needs and demands of the local school community, but with his own experiences of visiting schools in Shanghai and Singapore. He spoke, for example, of 'trying to replicate the Singapore idea of collaborative time' between class and language teachers, and of his belief in the 'classic view of a broad curriculum' in these countries that featured not only strong languages provision, but also music and traditional arts. To accommodate the extensive languages program, the principal made many adjustments to the school program and had even lengthened the school day: 'Our school week is 26-and-a-quarter hours because we've added a quarter-hour to the length of the day, plus we've taken a quarter-hour off our breaks.'

The success of the school's languages program depended on having supportive teaching staff, and the principal specifically promoted Asian-focused professional development activities for his staff:

> Eleven of the staff here did a Graduate Certificate in Teaching Asia and I was one of them, so I think I modelled that. So yeah, and there's a lot of interest in that. Five of my staff decided to have themselves trained as Korean teachers when we adopted the Korean language program and they've done well.

Actively recruiting teachers with Asian language backgrounds was also a major factor:

> If you want to run a comprehensive program like that, I can't just have three Chinese teachers. So, I've actually got five. Three of them are mainstream teachers who've had language and I've recruited them. I've recruited three of them.

As a result of these actions, all the staff appeared to be in agreement with the Asian perspective: 'It's been happening for nine years and they're all onboard with it. I've never had any resistance, I've never had anyone stand up and say I'm not going to do it.'

The principal at Cheswell was significant for providing the driving force behind an extensive community languages program, including a bilingual program, at a state primary school. Bilingual programs are a rarity in Australian schools, especially for students from minority language backgrounds (Harbon and Fielding, 2013). In responding to the cultural and linguistic needs of the local Asian-Australian community, the principal had taken on the Asian languages and Asian literacy discourse that Australian governments and leading political figures had been promoting for several decades (e.g. Garnaut, 1989; Rudd, 1994), and most recently following the Australian government's White Paper *Australia in the Asian Century* (Australian Government, 2012). The literature to date has shown that implementing an Asian literacy policy in Australian schools has been difficult, referred to by one researcher as 'a wicked policy problem' (Halse, 2015a), although the personal efforts of the Cheswell principal clearly provided an important exception.

The 'equity thing': Languages in a girls' high school

To complete this chapter, we now turn to the role of the principal and executive staff in providing a substantial languages program at a low-SES state secondary school. This, too, is a rarity, especially in view of earlier discussions in this chapter about languages provision at 'residual' comprehensive high schools.

Barnsley Girls High School, 17 kilometres to the south-west of Sydney CBD, has a mid–low SES rating (ICSEA 989) and a very high percentage of students who speak a community language at home (96 per cent). Five languages were taught at the school: French, Italian, Arabic, Modern Greek and Chinese. The latter three languages were spoken quite extensively in the local community, with 40 per cent of students having an Arabic-speaking background (principal's comment). The structure of the languages program was similar to those in the selective high schools featured at the beginning of this chapter insofar as all students undertook a languages unit in Year 7 which briefly introduced them to all five languages. Studying at least one of these languages was then mandatory in Year 8, followed by languages electives in subsequent school years. The school also had overseas trips to Italy and a sister school arrangement with a school in Tuscany.

As a state high school, Barnsley Girls differed from the 'residual' comprehensive high schools outlined earlier in this chapter (i.e. Metro and Campbell) not just in gender composition but in school enrolment numbers. There were over 1,000 girls at the school, and demand for places was high. The principal explained that the school had a good academic reputation and was especially popular with parents from Arabic-speaking backgrounds who wished their daughters to receive a single-sex education in a state secondary school. Unlike the 'residual' high schools, there was the critical mass of students to enable languages electives to be maintained, although even at this school some language electives were under threat.

The languages program survived in large part due to the advocacy of both the current and previous principals and the school's long-standing (more than twenty years) head of languages, one of the few remaining in NSW high schools. The current principal had been at the school for more than a decade (seven years as deputy head, four as principal), and though he inherited the strong languages program, he was concerned to maintain it:

> I like having languages in the curriculum ... I think it adds another dimension to what schools can meaningfully offer kids. I mean, we're a high language background other than English school. We're at over 90 per cent now.

Not all languages at the school were thriving, however, with some electives experiencing declining student numbers. The principal's challenge was justifying the relatively low enrolments in languages courses in comparison to other subjects. He referred to this challenge as the 'equity thing':

> I've got to make a stand when I've got classes of 25 in maths and class of 11 in Italian ... I mean it's not huge numbers of kids choosing the [languages] courses

and that therefore becomes an equity thing for me in balancing the number of students taught by languages teachers as against the number of students taught by other teachers, so that's a perennial discussion we have with the head teacher each year.

For the principal, managing these issues was 'a struggle' and, through consultation with the head teacher of languages, often resulted in 'creative and flexible' responses designed 'to preserve languages in the curriculum':

> So for instance, in the one classroom you might have beginner's Italian and continuers Italian. Now that is not ideal, but we can't run a separate class of three kids doing beginner's Italian and a group of six kids doing continuers, so we put them together.

Maintaining the position of a head teacher of languages in the school was viewed by the principal as essential 'to keep the faculty going' in the face of declining languages enrolments. The principal explained that without the head teacher, languages could fall within the supervision of any other head teacher, 'let's say head teacher admin or head teacher teaching and learning'. As was the case in other schools that we studied, the danger was then that the languages' Key Learning Area 'loses that impetus … because [these non-language specialist head teachers] don't have a particular love of languages necessarily or a particular emphasis on the value of languages in the curriculum'. The long-standing head teacher of languages retained his passion for languages. He talked of his battles over the years to maintain languages in his school, in a context where there were few remaining head teachers of languages in state secondary schools:

> When I became head teacher [of languages] twenty years ago all the surrounding schools at Barnsley had head teachers. All of them have collapsed. Mine's the only one that hasn't. It's been through fighting the principal. Not introducing Japanese but introducing community languages, doing things like dangling overseas trips to the kids to attract the kids, employing – hand picking staff by employing native speakers.

In relation to community languages, the head teacher's passion for and strong advocacy of languages transcended the idea that students should necessarily have backgrounds in the community languages they studied at school:

> Some schools are saying you're of that background, you have to do the language. Or you're not that background, you can't do the language. I said well hang on, what about free choice? What about the kids? Let them choose. How dare you say, oh you're Chinese you have to do Chinese. Or you're not Chinese, you can't do Chinese. You have to do French. What if I want to do Chinese? In my school

I've got Arabic kids who want to do Chinese because they want to do Chinese. Good luck to them. And vice versa. There should be choice.

Barnsley Girls HS was an example of a strong languages program surviving at a low-SES high school while in many other similar schools they had declined. This was largely because the principal was personally supportive of languages and prepared to be 'creative and flexible' with school resourcing, and the head teacher of languages, one of the few remaining in the state, was a strong and competent advocate for his subject area. But as the principal acknowledged, 'whether it [languages] stays that way into the future is another thing' and he claimed it depended largely on when the current head teacher retired and whether enrolment numbers in languages courses could be maintained at a viable level.

Summary

To conclude this chapter, we have indicated that in this era of school-based management, principals, along with their executive staff, have a high degree of power and autonomy in all aspects of school governance, including decisions about what is taught – the curriculum. For the study of languages in NSW primary schools, this has particular implications because languages are not mandatory, and as this chapter has shown, languages can feature as a key curriculum subject, or they can be ignored altogether, which is the case in the majority of primary schools in the state. As the opening vignette to this chapter demonstrates, it is largely down to principals and their executive staff to decide whether languages should be studied and/or the form this may take. Thus, languages provision in primary schools can be rendered fragile and subject to the vicissitudes of recruitment practices for principals and their executive career trajectories. In several of the schools we researched, both primary and secondary, successful languages programs have subsequently been weakened as key principals have transferred to other schools or retired.

As leaders in the highly competitive, performance-driven school 'market', principals need to demonstrate accountability in a quantifiable form such as NAPLAN results to school stakeholders, parents in particular. In some schools, as at Cheswell PS, the principal successfully argued that languages performed a 'value-added' role insofar as the school's NAPLAN results improved following the introduction of languages programs. In some other primary schools, however, principals adopted a different argument and felt the need to deliver a restricted languages program (30–40 minutes per week) in order not to hinder a more important function, which was to maximize NAPLAN results. As one principal noted, NAPLAN results were where 'people put their money'.

In secondary schools, we found that principals in high-SES schools, including independent and selective high schools, strongly promoted languages provision. In large part this was because they shared with parents the value of languages for both cultural and economic capital. In these schools, students generally performed highly in languages, which reinforced the exam-oriented success that the research suggests is needed to meet accountability standards (see Parrish and Lanvers, 2019). In low-SES secondary schools, while at a personal level principals declared they perceived the value of languages in the curriculum, there seemed to be recognition that students struggle for academic success in languages and that more vocationally relevant subjects may be more appropriate. There was also recognition of systemic factors that limited their autonomy as principals to deliver languages programs in their schools. Low school enrolments meant that no matter how hard principals tried to 'massage' the numbers, it was very difficult to maintain languages electives beyond the mandatory 100 hours. The 'realities of the system' in the form of departmental 'staff to student' ratios effectively limited their autonomy. As the principal at Barnsley Girls HS indicated, there was a constant balancing act, what he termed the 'equity thing', in trying to maintain language electives while also trying to act in the interests of other school subjects and other school stakeholders. To some degree, supportive principals and executive staff could, through various promotional activities and timetabling compromises (such as mixing different languages classes), maintain languages provision. But for how long in low-SES secondary schools often depended on the continuing employment of individual principals and executive staff who believed in the value of languages and had sufficient agency and power to keep them alive.

3

Secondary School Language Teachers' Identities and Experiences

Teacher identity is integral to the teaching of languages; indeed, prominent researchers in the field of applied linguistics make the claim that 'language teaching is identity work' (De Costa and Norton, 2017: 8) and, more generally, that 'learning to teach is an identity making process' (Beijaard, 2019: 1). In this chapter, to better understand teachers of languages we focus on and explore how they and others view their professional identities.

Research on identity in the field of applied linguistics has grown substantially in recent years. Norton (2016), for example, explains how she contributed to a lone chapter on identity in a handbook of applied linguistics in 2002 (Toohey and Norton) and yet by 2016, a substantial handbook had been devoted entirely to language and identity (Preece, 2016). It was mainly from the mid-1990s that identity studies in this field moved beyond narrow views based on linguistics and cognitive psychology. Prior to this time, a language teacher's identity was viewed largely as a matter of being either a native speaker or a non-native speaker. As part of what some language researchers have termed the 'social turn' (e.g. Block, 2003; Gee, 1999), identity research has increasingly been undertaken within poststructuralist framings which see identity not as something fixed for life, but as fragmented and contested in nature (Block, 2007). Norton is a key researcher in this area with her work on identity and investment (2001; Norton Peirce, 1995). She indicates, for example, that a learner may be highly motivated, but nevertheless have little investment in the language practices of a given community if they are not consistent with the learner's expectations (especially if the classroom is racist or sexist and/or not consistent with learners' expectations of good teaching). Norton (2001, 2013) argues that an imagined community assumes an imagined identity, 'and a learner's investment in the target language can be understood within this context' (2013: 3). Norton (2018) draws on the theoretical work of Bakhtin (1984), Bourdieu (1984), Weedon (1987) and Lave and Wenger (1991) to indicate the complex relationship between social structure and human agency. In the process of successfully learning a second language, she points out that learners

> need to struggle to appropriate the voices of others; they need to learn to command the attention of their listeners; they need to negotiate language as a system and as a social practice; and they need to understand the practices of the communities with which they interact. (Norton, 2018: 240)

While much of Norton's identity work is based on second language learners, usually marginalized individuals and groups, it applies also to a more privileged group, teachers, and identity in language learning and teaching has become a 'fast evolving research area' (Norton and De Costa, 2017: 90). Specifically addressing language teachers' identity, De Costa and Norton (2017) provide an update of theoretical developments in the field, and in particular they draw on the work of a collection of researchers (including Norton) known as the Douglas Fir Group (2016). This transdisciplinary group of researchers has developed a broad framework for the field of second language acquisition, which includes as a fundamental theme (one of ten such themes): 'language learning is identity work'. Language learning (and thus identity work) within this framework is complex and occurs along three interrelated levels of social activity: micro, meso and macro, with the latter level involving 'ideological structures' (Douglas Fir Group, 2016: 36).

As we suggest in this chapter, the macro level of ideological structures, drawing on the work of critical researchers such as Block (2014, 2017) and indicating the influence of neoliberal ideology and social class, plays a role in influencing how the teachers of languages featured in our study understood their work and their professional identities. As previous chapters, and in particular Chapter 2 on principals, made clear, several decades of neoliberal reforms in NSW schools, and in Australia more generally, have produced, particularly at the secondary schooling level, a hierarchical schooling system in which children from higher-SES groups have access to a different and more privileged academic curriculum in comparison with children from lower-SES backgrounds (e.g. Ho, 2017a; Perry and Lamb, 2016; Perry and Southwell, 2014; Teese, 2007; Tranter, 2012;). Not only does this set up different knowledge and resource contexts, but there is also research indicating that teachers view their professional roles differently according to teaching context, including whether their students are high achieving or low achieving (Ben-Peretz, Mendelson and Kron, 2003). To date, however, research studies have not focused on the experiences and sense of identity of languages teachers in the teaching contexts of the highly differentiated schooling system in NSW. This chapter is based on semi-structured interviews and presented as vignettes of language teachers' backgrounds and experiences. We begin, as we have done in previous chapters, with examining teachers' perspectives in academically selective secondary schools that feature students from high-SES backgrounds, where languages as academic subjects are valued, and where languages teachers enjoy high status. We follow this with the perspectives of teachers from an independent school which specializes in languages and where students have similar SES backgrounds to the selective high schools. The perspectives from the languages teachers in the high-SES secondary schools are then contrasted with teachers in low-SES comprehensive high schools.

Teaching languages in academically selective high schools

As indicated in other chapters, the academically selective high schools in our study valued languages highly, and in particular, traditionally taught European languages such as French and German, and Japanese, popular in Australian schools since the 1970s and 1980s. At the time of the study, each of the three academically selective schools in the study had a head teacher of languages, a rarity in NSW high schools today, and a relatively large complement of permanent languages teachers (usually five or six) plus part-time teachers, all well qualified, and in many cases long established in the schools.

One of the characteristics of the languages teachers in the academically selective high schools was their career stability, demonstrated by their length of tenure at individual schools, and with a number of those we interviewed, not planning to leave their school until retirement. At Coolamon, for example, the German teacher had taught at the school continuously since 1989. The French teacher had begun teaching at Coolamon even earlier, in her first year as a qualified language teacher in 1983, although she had a ten-year break from 1989 for family reasons, before recommencing at the school part time and then again full time. At the time of the research both teachers were very close to retirement. Similarly, at Sherwood the head teacher of languages commented that 'there's only been one change in 20 years in the Japanese staff'. The German teacher at Forster also commented that she had previously spent twenty years teaching languages at a nearby selective school of similar status.

From selective high school languages students to selective high school languages teachers

In addition to their career longevity in particular schools, several teachers indicated they had themselves attended selective high schools as students, which they had typically followed by studying languages at university, gaining teaching qualifications and then returning to selective high schools as languages teachers. The longstanding French teacher at Coolamon explained how this apparently seamless process worked for her:

> I went to a selective high school in Newcastle and it was basically compulsory to do languages there ... So I just went along with the flow and did French all through. Then when I was in Year 12 I got a teacher scholarship ... to do French and German at university ... I did prac teaching and I really loved it, so then I decided, okay, this is really good. So I decided that I would go into it and I was just really lucky. I came out of university, like a month into the new year, I got this job, it was my first year out [in 1983].

Her Japanese teacher colleague at Coolamon followed the same career pattern, although in her case she returned to the very same selective high school in which she studied Japanese as a student. These teachers, in their transition from languages students to teachers of languages in academically selective high schools, appeared to have experienced a high level of investment in their chosen careers with a clear prior understanding and appreciation of the professional community they wished to become a part of as languages teachers. These transitions could also be considered a condition of class privilege, befitting the career trajectory of students from mainly middle-class families. An example from the literature is Mizoshiro (2013), who, in a study of Australian language teachers' narratives of practice (Harbon and Maloney, 2013), provides a personal account of her own seamless transition from Anglo middle-class background and private school education, to university language studies, to teaching Japanese at an academically selective girls high school in Sydney.

In-country experience

The languages teachers at the selective schools were privileged in other ways that contributed to their passion and credibility with their students. The teachers in our study, for example, could be considered not only proficient teachers of languages, but proficient users of languages as well, mainly through having extensive 'in-country' experience. As the head teacher of languages at Sherwood explained:

All of us have had extensive experience in country, which is unusual for a school with five language teachers. All of us have spent years and years and years in our respective countries. I think the kids can see that it's relevant to us. We've got friends in those countries, we've got relationships and it's made a big difference to our lives.

As an example of in-country experience, this head teacher described how several years ago her principal 'very reluctantly' released her for a year to work in Japan when she was 'head hunted to work in Tokyo as the learning and development manager for Travelex, the foreign money people'. Several other teachers spoke in detail of their in-country experiences. The German teacher at Sherwood, who had chosen to teach part time as she moved closer to retirement, explained that, following her honours undergraduate study in French and German in Sydney, she gained a scholarship to study languages in Vienna, and also classical singing. Later, interspersed between teaching languages in Wollongong and Sydney high schools, she went to Germany as an assistant teacher, and then on another occasion to Bavaria 'for a year teaching French and English to German children up to year 12'. Again, Mizoshiro's (2013) personal narrative also indicates how she travelled to Japan on several exchanges before moving to Japan to teach English following her university graduation. Several years later, and married to a Japanese man, she returned to Sydney where she commenced teaching at an academically selective high school.

The teachers in our study, like Mizoshiro, seemed not to have moved far beyond a narrowly defined education career as they transitioned from high school students of languages to teachers of languages in selective high schools. There were some exceptions. The Japanese teacher at Forster, for example, explained that he was working in Japan in the early 1990s with a company 'that kind of did exhibitions for the Government of Japan', but when the 'bubble hit', he decided to return to Australia where he worked for a Japanese trading company for a few years. He then studied at Macquarie University to become an ESL teacher and taught adults for a couple of years. He said he was 'basically 40' when he decided 'I wanted to teach Japanese more than I wanted to teach ESL'. He had spent a total of twelve years working in Japan, had married a Japanese woman and spoke mainly Japanese at home. The essential point from these in-country examples was that they provided legitimacy and status; the teachers were recognized by their school communities and beyond not only as proficient teachers of languages, but as users of languages, indeed as expatriate role models for their students considering living and/or working overseas using the target languages.

Few native speakers/overseas trained

Despite their fluency in their second or third languages, few of these academically selective high school language teachers were native speakers or trained overseas. Of those interviewed, one native speaker was a part-time French teacher at Forster. She was born and educated to university level in France and trained initially to teach English. On moving to Australia, she obtained a postgraduate teaching qualification in languages at a NSW university and managed to secure part-time work at Forster after she covered for the French teacher who was on long service leave. The other native speaker taught Mandarin at Forster. He was formerly involved in business in China before arriving in Australia, where he studied for a four-year double degree in linguistics and education. It was unclear whether the relative absence of native speaking/overseas trained languages teachers in the three academically selective high schools in our study was part of a general trend for such schools, although, as Cruickshank (2015) notes, such teachers are often marginalized in employment contexts and tend to teach in disadvantaged hard-to-staff schools.

'We all love teaching the language here'

The teachers had a demonstrable passion for their work and for inspiring their students to 'love' languages like they did. At the risk of sounding glib, the word 'love' featured prominently in the interviews with teachers in contexts ranging from their experiences of studying languages at high school, at university, in-country and as languages teachers. For several teachers, and this was a narrative affecting some languages teachers in non-selective school contexts as well, their inspiration for studying languages could be traced back to how they were taught languages in their high school days. For example, the Japanese teacher at Sherwood explained: 'My Japanese teacher was really cool at high school. It was my best subject at school. I really enjoyed it. It was kind of like an escape from all of the other work that I was doing.' The Japanese teacher at Coolamon similarly commented that she 'had a couple of really good Japanese teachers that I really liked in Year 9 and 10, so then I decided to carry on with it'.

There were teachers in other types of schools who also expressed their love for teaching languages, but we argue that the conditions for teaching languages in academically selective high schools were particularly receptive to such an emotion, and this had much to do with the nature of the students. It was easier to love teaching a subject when students were academically accomplished, well behaved and enthusiastic learners. At the very least, these students would do what they were told in the classroom, and at best, they might begin to reciprocate their teachers' love of languages. This describes the generally privileged students (in SES terms) who, through their success at highly competitive entrance exams, had gained entry to these academically selective high schools.

'The kids [at this school] are just so different from teaching in a mixed-ability environment'

Without exception, the languages teachers at the selective schools viewed their students highly for their academic accomplishments and positive attitudes towards academic work, and this clearly affected their own professional identities. It was a pleasure to teach such students. The French teacher at Sherwood, for example, indicated that she was fortunate, indeed 'lucky', to teach at the school rather than 'out there in the real world' because

> the ones who choose a language, they love it and they work hard and they are good students. We have very good numbers. From what I hear from other schools it is not the same. So, I think they enjoy it, and I do too – we do too, we all love teaching the language here. But I have been told by many of my colleagues, you will not enjoy somewhere else.

The German teacher at Sherwood commented that after having taught German to students at Sydney University:

> it was like teaching university coming here. The kids are just so different from teaching in a mixed-ability environment because in a normal school in an elective class you get kids that can't write their name right up to kids that are going to do medicine; everything.

It was quite a regular occurrence at these selective high schools to have students topping the state in some HSC languages, and teachers explained that part of the reason for the high academic achievements in languages was the students' attitudes towards learning. The German teacher at Sherwood, for example, explained that 'doing lots of basic grammar' with students generated the feeling of 'wow, I've got somewhere' and that this was more motivating for students than activities 'like making a film … even though that sounds like fun and having eating days and all that sort of thing'. She stated that 'with incredibly bright kids like I teach now, it's also about success'.

It should be no surprise to find languages teachers celebrating the academic accomplishment of students in selective schools and enjoying teaching them. The fact that selective school students had academic dispositions that enabled them to thrive on learning grammar, the basic foundation of languages as an academic discipline, could be viewed as a fairly predictable outcome of a differentiated schooling system that rewards some groups of students at the expense of others 'out there in the real world' (i.e. in non-selective high schools). It is the broader 'ideological structures' of neoliberalism that have encouraged this differentiation. Considine (2012), for example, explains how the ideology of parental school choice took hold in NSW from the late 1980s and has resulted in a highly differentiated secondary school system which influences how teachers' work has changed and differs between types of schools. At academically selective schools she found that teachers 'worked with many more students who were academically gifted, and who enjoyed attending class and school' (p. 289). These teachers were satisfied with their work and careers, disinclined to want to leave their schools, and reported improvements in their own experiences of teaching.

Social class plays a significant role in this differentiation of secondary schools, with academically selective high schools in NSW featuring the most socioeconomically advantaged students in the state, more so than prestigious private schools (Bonnor, 2019; Ho and Bonnor, 2018). As Ho (2017a) indicates, academically selective high schools are

> designed to cater for gifted and talented students with superior academic ability and high classroom performance... But these public schools are increasingly bastions of inequality, rather than simply havens for the gifted and talented.

Many of the selective high school students in our study were formerly in so-called 'gifted and talented' streams in primary schools. Differentiated learning in its various forms has increased and flourished in schools in recent decades with increased accountability/audit measures and evidence-informed agendas and policies such as NAPLAN (e.g. Mills et al., 2016; Spina, 2018). In this era of neoliberal educational reforms, practices such as ability grouping/streaming are increasingly seen as 'natural' (Spina, 2018), despite their long established and continuing inequities, especially for children from low-SES backgrounds (Macqueen, 2013; Mills et al., 2016).

We thus draw links between 'ideological structures' in the form of neoliberal reforms which have resulted in the concentration of higher-SES students at academically selective schools and the professional identities of languages teachers that are largely positive as a result of teaching highly motivated and academically accomplished students. It could be argued, based on social-class backgrounds, that the selective high school teachers and their students shared similar cultural values regarding education. Certainly, as we have indicated, for some languages teachers in the selective high schools there appeared a seamless transition from high school students of languages to selective high school teachers of languages. As later sections of this chapter indicate, this contrasts with the greater social distance and cultural dissonance experienced between teachers and their students in low-SES comprehensive schools.

So far in this chapter, a very positive picture has been presented of teachers in academically selective high schools enjoying (loving) teaching languages, and in many cases, students reciprocating this enjoyment. But there were some challenges, and they came from within their own schools and related to the value ascribed to languages as a disciplinary subject from various school community members – students, parents and teachers.

'There's no room in their timetable for languages'

The academic and career aspirations of the high-SES students in the selective high schools mirrored those for high-achieving students more widely with preferences for studying subjects in their final years of high school, such as advanced Maths, which would provide entry into 'prestigious' university programs including medicine and engineering (e.g. Polesel, Leahy and Gillis, 2018). Despite academic languages such as French and German qualifying as traditional elite school subjects (Teese, 2013; Teese and Polesel, 2003), in the senior schooling context, languages were often not a priority because scaling procedures for university entrance (i.e. ATAR scores, see Chapter 1) diminished their appeal to students. Thus, for students intent on maximizing their ATAR scores for entry to highly competitive universities and courses, it was often a rational decision not to study languages at this level. As a result, the languages teachers lamented the loss of many of their best language students in the senior years. As the Japanese teacher at Sherwood pointed out:

> There's no room in their timetable for languages. They know that they want to do – a lot of them, it's medicine or something science-based, like sport science and – different forms of science and medicine. A huge number of kids from here go off to study that. But they get into Year 12, and they're doing maybe three or

four units of Maths. Two units of English or sometimes three units of English, because they're bright kids here. Chemistry and Physics. There's no space for anything else.

The German teacher at Forster, who was also a careers adviser at the school, claimed that for many parents, maximizing their children's university entrance scores (ATAR) was the aim and they often had the incorrect perception that the students who did well in languages at this level were native speakers, thus making it difficult for non-native students to achieve high ATAR scores. These views on the relative value of languages as an academic subject in the senior school years had likely implications for the professional status of languages teachers, who were down the informal pecking order in terms of teaching a prestige subject.

'It's a sissy subject'

Teachers of languages also faced a challenge to their status in schools relative to other-subject teachers because of perceptions based very largely on a lack of understanding and particularly experience of languages and language teaching. Whereas every teacher in a school was familiar with English, Science and Mathematics through their own learning experiences, many in Australian schools would never have studied languages or studied them only in the most tokenistic way (Liddicoat et al., 2007: 33, for example, indicated that in NSW government schools in 2001 and 2005, only 27.6 and 23 per cent respectively of students had enrolled in a languages course). This made it possible for non-languages teachers to make comments like the one experienced by the German teacher at Sherwood. Describing her prior experiences of working under the supervision of a head teacher who did not specialize in languages (he was science-based), she said:

> So the science teacher first day to me said, oh well, I think you should retrain as Chinese, and he told all the boys in his science classes who were doing a language that it's a sissy subject, drop languages, get into your sciences boys, if you're real men. Now that's the sort of thing we need to combat.

This type of attitude affected languages teachers in schools more generally, and languages teachers believed that they had to work harder than other subject teachers to maintain their positions on staff. As the Sherwood head teacher of languages said, 'they've got to fight for their job all the time. Maths teachers don't have to fight for their job.' For example, they often had to counter comments that they had it easy because they had small numbers in their classes.

Teaching languages in an independent school specializing in languages

An overall sense of positivity and 'love' of teaching languages was also reflected by teachers at the Sydney International School (SIS), the one designated language school in our study that taught to Year 12 level. SIS had a very similar, though marginally lower, student SES compared with the three selective high schools in our study. As we mentioned in the previous chapter, the principal at SIS spoke of his school being a 'linguistic nirvana' for languages teachers.

Many of the professional themes we have outlined at academically selective schools were also apparent at SIS. For example, career longevity in one school was a feature for a number of the languages teachers that we interviewed. One Italian teacher had commenced at SIS when the school was first established in 1984, and another Italian teacher commenced in 1989. By the same token, at the other end of the teaching career trajectory, SIS was actively pursuing the recruitment of young languages teachers who had demonstrated their worth at the school during their professional experience as pre-service teachers. As a private school, the school had greater flexibility in its recruitment practices compared with the more bureaucratized government schools. A Spanish teacher, for example, with a double major in French and Spanish in her undergraduate degree, described how the school had made considerable concessions to ensure that they were able to eventually add her to their staff:

> So I did my prac here in 2009 and then got offered the job the day I finished. I said oh well, I want to go off and do honours, so they offered me part time. So I did part time. Then I said that I'd want time off to write my thesis and so they said well why don't you work part time for a year and then take the following year off and that's what I did. For my thesis I needed to travel to Bolivia for research.

For the teachers we interviewed at SIS, languages had always been an integral part of their lives because, unlike the predominantly 'Anglo' backgrounds of the languages teachers in academically selective high schools, most of these teachers grew up in families where English was not their first language. Two teachers, for example, while born in Australia, spoke only Italian within their families, and the French/Spanish teacher stated that she grew up in a bilingual home where she spoke French with her mother and English with her father and she attended a French bilingual school. These teachers had family connections in Europe, valued their heritage languages and had spent lengthy periods in their parents' countries of origin.

In a number of respects, teaching languages at SIS seemed to be even more professionally rewarding than in the academically selective high schools. In addition to loving their teaching, working with high-performing students and participating in annual overseas exchange trips, the SIS languages teachers comprised a department with a critical mass of twenty-five teachers, most of whom had desk space in one large purpose-built office area. This context indicated the considerable standing of language teachers relative to other subject and class teachers, and any resistance to the primacy of languages at the school from non-languages staff was 'not a question' in this school (Italian teacher's comment). As a French/Spanish teacher noted, 'there's more of us than them', and besides, the 'whole ethos of the school' was based on languages. There was also recognition that 'using another language doesn't reside just with the language teacher', and non-languages staff who spoke another language were encouraged to 'come in and use that language with us' (Italian teacher). Such a scenario contrasted with the relative lack of status of languages expressed by some other-subject teachers (often science-based) noted earlier in this chapter in the academically selective high schools. SIS languages teachers did not have to fight for their subject.

The large number of languages teachers in the one office space enabled a strong community of practice in which ideas and resources were shared extensively. An Italian teacher commented: 'It's great because we share, we talk, we see a [resource], we go, we can do that in Japanese. Can I borrow? Can I have that? That's what it's all about.' There was also a strong professional development program for languages teachers involving three or four faculty meetings a term and often guest speakers. The only other teaching context in our study that resembled such a supportive community of languages teachers was the School of Languages, a government school which provided individualized languages tuition by distance mode to students who were unable to study their chosen language at their own high school. All teachers at the School of Languages were languages teachers, and like SIS, they were physically located together in the same building and similarly enjoyed the sharing of ideas, resources and a languages teacher identity.

In summary, the languages teachers at SIS, perhaps even more so than those at the academically selective high schools, enjoyed strong professional status and subject/career affirmation. In both types of schools, languages teachers loved their work and often remained at their schools for many years. A key attraction in both types of schools was high-achieving and motivated students who regularly topped the state in a language. Highly supportive and well-resourced parents were also a factor. Many of these teachers, however, understood and were thankful that they worked in these schools and not in others where they may not have been held in such high esteem. For example, an Italian teacher at SIS who started at the school in the late 1980s recounted her prior experiences as a first-year teacher in her early twenties at a working-class comprehensive school in Sydney's south-west, where she was one of only two language teachers on the staff and was located within the Art department. She commented on the physical violence in the classroom and that 'I didn't know how to stop them … I couldn't control them, basically'. Teaching languages in this school was not particularly valued:

> [It] was no more/less-regarded than anything else in that school. It didn't have the clout of some of the big departments, of course, and what parents might have wanted, but then a lot of parents didn't care or know what they wanted in this environment. The kids were just at school.

Our reason for including this teacher's anecdote is that similar issues for languages teachers in working-class comprehensive high schools were apparent nearly thirty years later, as our next section explains.

Teaching languages in a low-SES comprehensive high school

By way of contrast with the experiences and identities of languages teachers outlined in the first part of this chapter, we now consider languages teachers in low-SES comprehensive high schools, beginning with one teacher in the inner-city Metro High School. As we outlined in Chapter 2 on principals, low-SES comprehensive high schools, in particular those in urban centres, have been referred to as 'residual' schools following neoliberal school choice reforms that have decimated enrolment numbers at some local comprehensive schools, with the drift of many students to private and selective schools (Black, Wright and Cruickshank, 2018; Campbell and Sherington, 2013). School choice reforms have resulted in a 'class shift' (Campbell, Proctor and Sherington, 2009) as selective high schools and private schools, and also the better-performing comprehensives, increasingly comprise students from a higher-SES background, while the remaining students in low-SES comprehensives end up consolidated 'in a class of their own' (Bonnor, 2019; Ho and Bonnor, 2018). These residual high schools have a 'tough' reputation in the eyes of many parents, and they struggle to maintain elective subjects such as languages in large part because they lack a critical mass of student enrolments.

We focus on the experiences of one languages teacher at Metro High School because there was only one at the school. This appeared quite typical of languages staffing at other low-SES comprehensive high schools in NSW because one qualified teacher was the minimum to enable the mandatory 100 hours of languages to be taught in the junior high school years. The teacher was in her third year of language teaching, and Metro was her first school appointment. She replaced a teacher of Indonesian, and because she did not speak Indonesian, she changed the language taught at the school to Italian, her main language. While her primary role was to teach the mandatory 100-hour language program to Year 8 students, she also taught Italian electives at Years 9 and 10, but these electives were irregular as many students chose instead to study more 'vocational' electives such as woodwork, ICT or Design & Technology. She also taught ESL, her second teaching subject, because her Italian classes were insufficient for a full teaching program. She was located within the English/ESL faculty at the school.

Lack of status and support for languages

This teacher's experiences at Metro HS and the effects they had on her identity as a languages teacher were in marked contrast to those of the languages teachers described earlier in academically selective high schools and SIS, the independent specialist language school. As the sole languages teacher, she perceived a lack of disciplinary support from her teaching colleagues, stating that they viewed languages in the school as 'more like a curriculum filler' and that talking with them about languages 'would be a very one-sided conversation'. While passionate about languages (Italian was her home language and she was also qualified to teach Spanish), she struggled to inspire the same enthusiasm for Italian in her students. She commented, for example, that if students chose to study Italian as an elective subject, they did so 'not for academic reasons, for social reasons, like my friends are doing it, or that teacher might not yell at me as much as that teacher'. To some extent, she herself saw problems with teaching Italian. She suggested that the reasons for learning a language these days were 'very much business-driven' with Asian languages in demand, 'killing out the Latin ones'. Hence, while she personally saw Italian as 'great for opening doors and just knowing there's a world outside our boundaries', she perceived that others in her school saw little value in it. She had discouraged those of her students who took the Italian elective in Years 9 and 10 from continuing with their language study because she believed they would struggle to be competitive in the HSC in a system in which they would be required to study the Italian Continuers course (i.e. not Beginners, having studied the language beyond the mandatory 100 hours). Thus, they could be competing against students who spoke Italian at home (as she did) as well as studying the language for most of their secondary schooling. She viewed this situation as

> just not a fair playing field … there's absolutely no amount of teaching or learning that could take place in those isolated lessons that could make them as proficient as someone who's been speaking it from birth.

Perceived structural determinants and student academic underachievement

As an inexperienced and relatively isolated teacher in a working-class comprehensive high school perceived by the local community to be 'tough' (according to the principal), and with falling enrolments, this Italian teacher tapped into a commonly held educational discourse which sees academic underachievement caused largely through disadvantaged home circumstances. She commented, for example, that many parents were uneducated in a formal sense and that they lacked access to resources and knowledge. She described students as 'not particularly studious' and not prepared for the kind of commitment that languages study required: 'Languages is just something that you have to constantly, constantly expose yourself to and engage with.' Furthermore, she felt that the students' English skills were 'not strong to begin with', which was seen to limit their ability to learn Italian.

Her experiences as a languages teacher may have been typical of many in low-SES comprehensive high schools and contrasted with the languages teachers in the high-SES selective and independent schools featured earlier. There was no 'community' of languages teachers within the school to work with, and it was difficult to love teaching languages in a context in which languages lacked curriculum status with teaching colleagues, parents and students. Moreover, this lack of 'core' status in the school's curriculum may have accompanied the view that languages were only taught in the school because they were a mandatory requirement. The school's main curriculum focus was on 'the basics', Maths and English, and elective subjects perceived to have direct vocational relevance. The generally low academic achievements within the school fed into a discourse of socioeconomic disadvantage.

Social separation

While this Italian teacher professed a love of languages and she was well qualified to teach both Italian and Spanish (a combined degree, Bachelor of Education/Arts, Humanities), she felt her background and training had left her ill-prepared for the teaching context at Metro.

> At that stage, how could I have any idea what sort of context I'd be teaching in? Because I went to such a – quite a priv – a public school, but a very privileged one. I just thought everyone, all students came into the classroom, sat down and waited to learn without being naughty or anything. But there are so many other things you're just completely unaware of that inhibit that dream or hinder it.

These comments indicated that she imagined her professional identity as a languages teacher to be much different from what it turned out to be in practice; there was a disconnect between her expectations and educational values and those of her students. In terms of class background, qualifications, proficiency in and passion for languages, this teacher was no different to those teachers featured earlier in selective high schools and the independent school; it was simply the 'luck of the draw' in the state departmental recruitment process that saw her offered an initial languages teaching position at a 'residual' comprehensive school. In some respects, her perspectives on students at Metro resonated with the work of Connell et al. (1982) several decades ago in their seminal study of working-class comprehensive schools and ruling class private schools. In the former, teacher–student relationships signified 'the social separation between teachers as a group and the working class as a group, which embodies a profound disconnection between knowledge and social life' (p. 196). It is likely, moreover, that several decades of school choice policies have increased this social separation between teachers and working-class students in residual comprehensive high schools.

Pedagogy in the Italian classroom reflected the teacher's view that students would struggle with academic tasks in a subject they would be unlikely to study beyond the mandatory 100 hours. Thus, her focus was on topics that might spark some interest from students, but within an overall framework of maintaining control. Lessons were teacher-directed using interactive whiteboard and worksheet exercises. Her classroom practices included what she termed 'spoon-feeding' students with structured activities designed to keep them on task as 'a sort of discipline thing'. This pedagogy accords with observations of classrooms in other working-class school contexts (e.g. Lupton and Hempel-Jorgensen, 2012).

'The way to go': Teaching Mandarin at a low-SES comprehensive high school

The languages teacher at Campbell High School, another low-SES comprehensive high school located near a regional city, enjoyed a very different status. He was the sole designated languages teacher at the school, and he taught Chinese as the mandatory language for Year 7 students. French was also taught at the school as an elective subject, but by a designated 'generalist' teacher who nevertheless had language teaching qualifications. What was different in the case of the Chinese teacher was that he enjoyed a very positive language teacher identity in the school, and this was due to several factors, including the perceived significance of Chinese as a school subject, which received strong support from the school principal, and his own agency as an experienced language teacher.

Chinese as a marketing opportunity

The choice of Chinese as the mandatory 100-hour language at Campbell High School was a deliberate decision made jointly by the principal and the Chinese teacher to enhance the profile of the school, with the hope that it might be the first step in establishing the school as a designated specialist languages school. In other words, Chinese was seen as a marketing opportunity for the school (see Chapter 1). By the same token, languages teaching at Campbell also experienced some of the same precarious issues facing languages at Metro and other low-SES comprehensive high schools. These included the 'numbers game', with insufficient students electing to study Chinese beyond the Year 7 mandatory hours, and many choosing electives such as sports and industrial arts instead. It was also unclear that many parents supported Chinese beyond their priority for basic skills in Maths and English.

Teacher agency and teaching Chinese

The Chinese teacher managed to overcome the above negative aspects and retain a positive professional identity because it was shaped through his own experiences with languages and his attitude towards and promotion of Chinese. He studied languages and Asian Studies at undergraduate level and initially taught German at secondary school level (he had a German background), but he realized that German was not as 'usable' compared with Chinese, which he considered was: 'the way to go. I think it's definitely the language of choice we should follow and we should push'. He based this view on the prominence of China in world affairs, and that in Australia, Chinese was the fastest growing language ('the numbers, the numbers speak for themselves'). And while the local Campbell school catchment area did not have a strong Chinese community representation, he believed that Australian life had changed: 'You walk up to Hurstville or you go up to Eastwood or Chatswood and the whole dynamic has changed, it's been flipped on its head.' Within this new dynamic, he perceived there were future work opportunities for people who could speak Chinese.

The Chinese teacher also had considerable 'in-country' experience in China, having travelled there many times, and as a non-native Chinese speaker, he believed he could be a role model for students at his school, enabling them to imagine that they too could learn to speak Chinese: 'I think my advantage here is because I'm not a native speaker the students can go oh, but you know how to say that or you know how to write that, oh, you're like us.' His positive identity and extensive experience as a languages teacher were reflected in his pedagogy, in which he aimed to create student interest and skills in Chinese with the hope that they would continue with the subject in later school years and beyond. One of the researchers commented, following a classroom observation, that the classroom atmosphere was 'fun, engaging, collaborative, supportive'. There was a focus on communicative tasks in Chinese and a range of activities including interactive games (often computer-based), brush painting (calligraphy) and school excursions to Chinatown. Engagement in the language and Chinese culture was fundamental to his purpose to make Chinese meaningful to their lives.

Teaching languages in low-SES comprehensive schools – A struggle for legitimacy

As we have seen from the perspectives of the languages teachers at Metro and Campbell, the factors that influenced their professional identities were varied. They included their own backgrounds as languages teachers – one being an inexperienced beginning teacher of Italian, the other an experienced languages teacher of many years, firstly of German and then of Chinese. But of considerable impact were the broader ideological structures that influenced the nature of the student populations and enrolment numbers in both schools and, in turn, the teaching contexts under which both languages were taught. It was largely neoliberal reforms, and in particular school choice, that had resulted in both schools becoming 'residual' schools for working-class students ('a school of last resort' according to the principal at Campbell). These neoliberal reforms had served to differentiate school populations according to social class, with academically selective high schools and private schools catering increasingly for students from high-SES families, and correspondingly, comprehensive high schools for students from low-SES families. It was thus no surprise to find languages teachers in the former schools enjoyed teaching students in a highly academic teaching context, while languages teachers in the comprehensive high schools struggled for legitimacy in a teaching context that was mandatory, and within an educational discourse where academic underachievement was seen to relate to socioeconomic disadvantage (see Black, Wright and Cruickshank, 2018). And while the situation varied at Campbell due to the promotion of Chinese and the individual agency of the languages teacher, it was nevertheless significant that neoliberal ideology was at the centre of the promotion of Chinese as the salvation for the school's reputation. Chinese was perceived primarily as a product that would sell well in the educational market.

Adding to and reinforcing the languages teachers' struggle for legitimacy at Metro and Campbell were the perspectives of other teachers we interviewed in the course of our study who either were, or had previously worked as, languages teachers in low-SES comprehensive schools. As with the languages teachers at Metro and Campbell, they often found themselves working as the sole designated languages teacher, or possibly with just one additional colleague, and their primary role was to teach the mandatory 100 hours of languages to Year 7 or 8. Lacking numbers, these teachers were invariably required to work under the supervision of another faculty in the school, with teachers who may have had little understanding of their work as languages teachers. For example, one languages teacher at a western suburbs comprehensive high school taught Spanish and she had a colleague who taught French. Both teachers were located within the Maths faculty in the school, and the Spanish teacher expressed frustration at the lack of status and subsequent lack of material resources available for languages:

> The school doesn't value languages. I'm with the faculty of Maths … where my head teacher knows nothing about it and she doesn't want to be involved. There's a Spanish and French teacher. I realise we don't have much. We were the last ones. Our faculty doesn't have any smart boards. The rest of the faculties, they have the smart boards.

Employment as a languages teacher in low-SES comprehensive schools was also quite precarious with constant battles over student numbers for elective classes and even which languages to teach. One Italian teacher, for example, reflected on her previous experiences:

> It was a constant battle in the numbers. You get nine students, they want 10, you get 11 they want 12. Taught many combined classes for many years, 11 and 12 together. Italian's not the flavour of the month so we're going to teach something else.

Another languages teacher described how school executives and teachers from other subject areas seemed to assume that a languages teacher could speak and teach *any* language that was required:

> The unfortunate thing is … you get into a school and they'll say you're a language teacher. I could offer Italian and Spanish and ESL. But can you teach French, do you think you can take the French class? How about next year, do you want to do German? They have this thing that you're a language teacher. (Italian teacher)

This teacher in fact decided that to continue her passion for teaching she needed to discontinue teaching Italian at high school and retrain as a TAS (Technological and Applied Studies) teacher instead, although she continued teaching Italian at a Saturday school of community languages. It would be difficult to envisage languages teachers in academically selective high schools or independent schools experiencing such precarious professional roles and lack of status as the teachers in the above examples.

This chapter has provided the perspectives of languages teachers at different secondary schools and has indicated how their experiences and professional identities varied largely according to teaching context, and in particular, whether they were teaching high-achieving students in high-SES academically selective or independent schools or underachieving students in low-SES comprehensive high schools. The differences in the teachers' experiences and professional identities were marked, and yet, in terms of their personal socioeconomic and educational backgrounds, including university and teaching qualifications, they were very similar. We have argued that this differentiation of schools according to SES factors has increased in recent decades following the implementation of neoliberal reforms such as parental school choice, ability grouping/streaming and the purchase by middle-class parents of private academic tutoring and places at private schools to ensure their children excel at school at the expense of others. Thus, we make the link between macro 'ideological structures' and the professional identities of languages teachers. This is not to deny that human agency can play a role, as with the experienced Chinese teacher at Campbell High School, although, as we have noted, his rationale for teaching Chinese was driven by the market – a neoliberal belief (shared by the principal) that Chinese would become a selling point, a competitive market 'niche' for the school.

4

Being a Languages Teacher in NSW Primary Schools

In this chapter, we continue to discuss the experiences and professional identities of languages teachers, though with a focus on those who teach in primary schools, where teaching contexts and professional identities differ from those of the secondary teachers in the previous chapter.

Employment contexts for primary school languages teachers in NSW are diverse and often limited. Unlike in secondary schools, languages are not mandatory in the primary school curriculum, and they are not always valued in a crowded curriculum (e.g. Curnow, Liddicoat and Scarino, 2007; Lo Bianco, 2009). According to Jones Díaz (2014), the legitimacy of English has been secured at the primary school level at the expense of other languages. It has been estimated that only between 30 and 40 per cent of NSW primary schools have a languages program, and most are in metropolitan Sydney (Board of Studies NSW, 2013). By the same token, as this study illustrates, some independent primary and K-12 schools have made languages their raison d'être, and similarly some government primary schools prioritize languages when they are promoted by principals and their leadership teams. Other primary schools in our study offered languages along a continuum ranging from languages as a key curriculum subject with two or more hours per week, which the NSW Department of Education (2016) maintains is the minimum for community languages programs, to more tokenistic provision of thirty minutes or less each week. While NSW is the most populous state and the largest provider of public education in Australia, it provides considerably fewer languages programs at the primary school level than Victoria, where languages provision is legislated for all Victorian schools (Department of Education and Training, 2017).

In addition to diverse and often limited employment opportunities, few primary school teachers have university degrees that include specific languages teaching qualifications and training (Board of Studies NSW, 2013), and to become qualified usually requires additional studies in languages and/or languages teacher education. The number of these courses offered by Australian universities has decreased in the past decade (Asia Education Foundation, 2015). Most qualified languages teachers have been trained for secondary and adult teaching contexts, where there are more employment opportunities. The role of languages teachers in individual primary schools is also different to most of their generalist teaching colleagues. Languages teachers are often employed part time as 'specialists', along with teachers of subjects such as music and physical education, and they may teach across a number of classes and school grades in the one school and/or, as 'itinerant' teachers, they may teach in several schools. 'Generalist' classroom teachers on the other hand are usually full time and teach the one class throughout the year. Often the specialist languages teachers are timetabled to teach when generalist teachers are on their RFF (release from face-to-face), and indeed specialist teachers are sometimes defined as RFF teachers (e.g. Ardzejewska, McMaugh and Coutts, 2010). This demarcation of roles can affect the professional identity of languages teachers, who may be regarded by primary school executives and generalist teachers as not only a separate category of primary school teachers, but with reduced professional status. The research literature has long indicated that languages teachers in primary schools, 'itinerant' languages teachers in particular, are often marginalized with a lack of support and resources and career paths (Kleinhenz et al., 2007; Nicholas et al., 1993).

As with the previous chapter on languages teachers in secondary schools, we begin with languages teachers who enjoy high professional status in teaching contexts where languages are valued highly. We follow this with an in-depth look at teachers of community languages in several government primary schools, and then languages teachers within several different models of language provision.

Equality of status: Integrated pedagogy at an independent bilingual primary school

At the Dante Bilingual School (DBS), teachers of Italian enjoyed a very positive professional status that was at least commensurate with, and possibly greater than, that of other teachers in the school because, after all, learning Italian was a key reason why parents sent their children to the school. As a Year 4 English teacher commented of the students: 'Italian is part of the life that they have here.' The teachers of Italian were fully integrated into all aspects of the school's teaching program and approximately half of the teaching program was delivered in Italian. In addition to teaching Italian as an academic subject, Italian teachers taught across other subject areas through the medium of Italian, as one of the Italian teachers explained:

> So the way the school works is that every class has got an Italian and an English teacher. The English teacher teaches Maths and English, and the Italian teacher teaches all the other areas, like Science and Technology, HSIE, PHPD, Creative Arts, all in Italian.

This dual focused educational context involving the teaching of curriculum subjects through the medium of an additional language (i.e. CLIL programs, Content and Language Integrated Learning; see Chapter 7) effectively eliminated the traditional distinctions between specialist languages and generalist teachers. Some of the Italian teachers explained that in their previous experience of teaching languages in primary schools that were not bilingual, they often felt separated and marginalized from generalist classroom teachers, and that they had to fight for recognition and justify their role. One of these teachers explained how languages teachers had to be proactive within the school to counter this marginalization:

> First of all, you need to be part of the staff, meaning you have to be at all the staff meetings. You have to have the courage to present things. You have to educate the rest of the staff about the values of understanding and using a different language.

At DBS it was different; the Italian teachers had equal, if not higher, status than the generalist teachers. One of the Italian teachers commented: 'I love this place because I don't have to fight to be a teacher. I am a teacher, that's the end of the story.' Other teachers in the school, for example, English or Maths teachers, were completely on-side with languages and some had themselves previously studied and taught Italian in schools.

All of the Italian teachers had native-speaking proficiency and, without exception, they spoke only Italian with the students. Several of the Italian teachers interviewed were born in Italy, while others had spent considerable time studying and living there. Some had previously taught Italian in NSW schools in 'Insertion programs' funded by Co.As.It. (the Italian association that also owned and operated DBS). They all had university qualifications in languages and teaching and they were passionate in their beliefs about the value of languages. They described their students as enthusiastic, and even those with non-Italian backgrounds quickly achieved good levels of language fluency through the language immersion model. One of the Italian teachers, for example, described her delight at overhearing an informal conversation between two Year 3 students which validated both the language immersion model and her role as language teacher:

> They were having the best conversation and it was just lovely because it was natural, it just happened to them. Whatever the situation was it's something that made them think of something and the conversation just happened in Italian, just naturally.

The point needs to be stressed however that while teaching languages at DBS in some ways presented as an ideal and served to reinforce a positive language teacher identity, it was nevertheless atypical. At the time of the study there were no other Italian bilingual schools in NSW, plus the school was small, independent (charged fees) and drew its students from mainly out-of-area middle-class suburbs in the inner west of Sydney. Many of the students were 'bussed' to the school each day. As we noted in Chapter 2 on school principals, DBS was not considered by the principal to be an appropriate kind of school for local area students from 'struggling' working-class families.

Teaching community languages for linguistic and cultural pride

In NSW government primary schools, languages are often funded under the NSW government's Community Languages Program (CLP), designed to promote the first (home) languages and cultural identities of students in local communities (NSW Department of Education, 2016). The program was established in a policy era of multiculturalism in the 1980s in which minority community languages were promoted in schools as language rights that reflected local community demographics (e.g. Lo Bianco, 2003, 2009). In Australian schools generally, researchers (e.g. Liddicoat and Curnow, 2014) have indicated that community languages struggle for space in the curriculum.

In this section, we provide vignettes of teachers of community languages in several government primary schools to indicate the diverse range of themes and issues that affected their experiences and professional identities as language teachers. Most of these teachers were native speakers and trained overseas (Cruickshank, 2015). We focus on schools in highly multilingual/multicultural suburbs of Sydney that traditionally have accommodated working-class, migrant communities. We begin with languages teachers at Clarke Public

School because the school provided a particularly strong program of languages including Chinese, Arabic, Greek, Macedonian, Indonesian and Maori. The majority (92 per cent) of Clarke PS students spoke a community language at home, and the languages offered at the school reflected these languages, except in the case of Indonesian, which was provided for those students who did not have a community language. Languages classes were programmed for two hours per week at a time when classroom teachers were having their RFF.

Becoming a primary school languages teacher

Teachers became languages teachers at the school through a variety of ways, ranging from deliberate shifts in teaching roles to almost accidental recruitment circumstances. For example, some teachers were initially generalist teachers in primary schools before specializing in teaching languages. At Clarke, the Greek teacher had been a K-6 teacher for about ten years and had been teaching some afternoon Greek classes. As a proficient Greek speaker (born in Australia of Greek parents, attended afternoon Greek classes at school, studied Greek for two years at university), she subsequently undertook the language proficiency assessment and was recognized as the teacher of Greek at the school. Similarly, the Maori teacher had been employed as a generalist teacher at the school for eleven years, having transferred from the New Zealand primary system where she had taught in a 'total immersion Maori' context. Due to the high number of Maori and Pacific Islander students at Clarke, she was asked by the principal 'to put a Maori program together'. She subsequently became the first and only Maori school teacher in Sydney, which she reflected on with pride: 'I feel really good. It's something not for myself but for the language and for my people and, yeah, it's a great achievement.' Both Arabic teachers at the school were also initially primary-trained classroom teachers, having qualified at a NSW university, but in seeking work they found they were in demand primarily as Arabic teachers, and following their proficiency test, they became exclusively Arabic teachers in primary schools prior to settling at Clarke. With few trained Arabic teachers in primary schools, they gained permanent positions very quickly ('straight away, the first year I was out').

In contrast, other languages teachers at the school were qualified initially as secondary language teachers before gaining employment as primary school language teachers. These included both the Chinese teachers at the school. One of these teachers was a Kindergarten teacher in China before arriving in

Australia, where she later qualified at university to teach Chinese and Japanese in secondary schools. After working as a casual languages teacher in secondary and Saturday community schools, she obtained full-time work at Clarke PS. The other Chinese teacher obtained a Bachelor's degree in China before arriving in Australia, where she did a Master of Teaching course and qualified as a secondary Chinese teacher before teaching at Clarke PS.

The two Indonesian teachers provided examples of the common phenomenon of the almost accidental nature of how teachers could find themselves teaching languages in the primary school. Neither of them had previously imagined themselves in this role. One of the Indonesian teachers was born in Indonesia but moved to Australia at the age of eight. At school she enjoyed learning French, and later at university she obtained a Bachelor's degree in English and psychology and then a Master of Teaching. As a qualified primary teacher, she was seeking work at Clarke as a casual generalist teacher but was subsequently offered work as an Indonesian teacher because her application form indicated that Indonesian was one of her special skills. As she commented, 'I kind of fell into this job... They said, well, we actually need an Indonesian teacher.' At the time, she said that a primary qualified Indonesian teacher was a job she 'didn't even know existed... I didn't actually realise that primary schools taught languages'. These comments could be seen as a reflection of the relative lack of recognition and status of primary school languages teachers. The other Indonesian teacher was born in Australia and studied Indonesian at an academically selective high school in Sydney. He said he was attracted to the subject by his 'excellent' Indonesian teacher, and also 'Bali, surfing, that sort of thing'. He later studied psychology at university, then social work, and then teaching, ending up after five years of study with a Master of Teaching and qualifications in TESOL, Indonesian and special education. He travelled to Indonesia initially as an interpreter and went back and forth many times, including living and working in Sulawesi for extended periods as a teacher. He obtained his Indonesian teaching position at Clarke when a friend emailed him an advertisement while he was travelling overseas. He applied for and won the position via a Skype interview. He did not expect to be offered the work because he was secondary trained and had no prior experience or training in primary education. He commented: 'As soon as I got there I was thrown in the deep end. I think my first class might have even been a kindy... It was hilarious. I had no idea.'

While these vignettes indicate the variety of ways teachers in one school successfully became community languages teachers, what they fail to show are some of the difficulties that native speakers/overseas trained teachers sometimes have to overcome in the process of becoming languages teachers, including difficulties with recognition of their teaching qualifications and accessing permanent teaching positions (Cruickshank, 2015). For example, at another NSW primary school in our study a Hindi teacher recounted how, as an experienced primary school teacher from India, her teaching qualifications were not recognized in NSW. After initially giving up the idea of teaching (she worked in a bank, which she found unsatisfying), she then undertook four years of additional study for a teaching qualification, only to be informed close to graduation that her Indian qualifications were now accepted (see Cruickshank, 2015). Following her appointment and work as a generalist teacher at Cheswell PS, the principal asked her if she would instead teach Hindi at the school.

The vignettes of teachers' experiences in this section have indicated that becoming a primary school languages teacher was often not a deliberate career choice but came about through a range of circumstances that were not always straightforward. Not one of these teachers followed a defined career pathway with the express intention of becoming a primary school languages teacher.

The status of community languages and teachers' professional identities

Although there were ten languages teachers in total at Clarke, which formed an important teacher bloc in the school, neither they, nor the languages they taught, should be viewed as having similar or equal status. Each language program had its distinct characteristics and was viewed differently within the school community, and this affected the ways the languages teachers experienced their varied professional identities. The two Chinese teachers, for example, enjoyed a very supported role with a critical mass advantage as they had over 300 students attending their classes (out of 780 students at the school), with numbers rising in recent years with increased migration from mainland China, Hong Kong, Taiwan and Vietnam. Demand for Chinese classes was sufficiently strong for two classes to be offered at each grade level, and the program was well resourced. Although Chinese was considered a community language, many of the students spoke Cantonese and a range of dialects at home. The Chinese teachers described the parents as being supportive of Chinese because of its potential human capital benefits as 'an extra language ... something very practical in the future'. In this sense, Chinese was valued by parents for both pride and profit (Duchêne and Heller, 2012).

The Maori teacher, by contrast, experienced much less demand for her classes, and her student base was waning as Maori families moved out of the area. She suggested that for cost of living reasons many were returning to New Zealand or seeking work in the mining regions of Australia. As a consequence, her largest class had eight students, her teaching program had been reduced, and she was concerned for her future at the school ('I might even lose another day next year'). Compounding her difficulties, this teacher was trying to establish Maori identity when her students tended to be a mixture of Maori, Tongan, Cook and other Islander groups falling generally within the 'Pacific Islander umbrella'. Many families (about one in four she estimated) had only one Maori parent, and in one family she recounted that the other parent was Greek, and the student subsequently went to the Greek classes at Clarke. The teacher noted that not a lot of Maori was spoken at home, mainly English, but Maori parents wanted their children to learn Maori for reasons of cultural identity: 'They just wanted kids to know who they are and where they're from.' Few Maori parents attended parent–teacher functions ('I don't get a lot of parents, just four. Chinese will have a lot'), which she believed was in part because many parents were working. An additional role that she seemed to have acquired as the Maori teacher was the welfare of Pacific Islander students and, in particular, responsibility for dealing with student behaviour: 'The teachers would say to me, oh so and so, he did well today ... You've done something to him.'

Another language in decline at the school was Macedonian, although this language began from a much large population base. The Macedonian teacher had been at the school for twenty-two years, and she started at a time when one-third of the students had Macedonian backgrounds. Most Macedonian-background students in recent years were third or fourth generation, and little Macedonian was spoken at home beyond the occasional communication with grandparents. With few students attending outside community classes, much of her teaching role involved promoting Macedonian cultural identity and pride at the school with celebrations, concerts, dancing and food days.

The Indonesian teachers on the other hand were teaching in a very different context; rather than teaching a community language for cultural identity and pride, they were teaching a language for the sake of interest and enjoyment. According to the female Indonesian teacher, this had positive implications for her professional role as students seemed particularly motivated to learn Indonesian:

I don't know what it is with just learning a new language that you don't have to do that's not a community language, because I've had teachers come up to me and say, you know, your kids are the only ones who want to go to languages.

Both Indonesian teachers stated that they loved teaching Indonesian at the school, and the feedback from students, other teachers and parents was generally positive. Despite this, both teachers resisted identifying themselves professionally as Indonesian teachers and did not imagine the role would dominate their future careers. The male teacher stated: 'I don't see myself as a primary Indonesian teacher, but while I'm here I do love it.' He said he had no sense of a specific career and would probably drop in and out of teaching during his working life and at times follow other areas that interested him, such as social work. The female teacher also declared her love for teaching Indonesian, but again, it did not define her professionally as she was concerned not to lose her connection with generalist classroom teaching:

> I love languages and primary teaching so I'd love to do [both] – I've done Indonesian for three years now. I'd love to do primary teaching next year, just so I don't lose that part of my qualification.

What was clear from Clarke PS was that languages teachers were not equal in terms of how they and others perceived them professionally. As we have illustrated, languages such as Chinese were on the rise, and the Chinese teachers enjoyed a largely positive role, while other languages, such as Maori, were on the wane, with the Maori teacher experiencing a correspondingly depressed role. These trends were largely a reflection of how languages were valued differently in this and other primary schools according to the numbers of students speaking community languages, and these varied as government migration policies and local demographics changed over time. In another school, Keswick PS, for example, the Greek teacher had lost classes and students as the majority Greek population in the area since the post-war period (especially in the 1960s and 1970s) had been replaced by Chinese-background families in recent decades. As she explained:

> Chinese has become the main language now. Greek has taken a step back. Before I started they used to have a full-time teacher here in Greek five days a week, and L1s, the background speakers, were separate from the non-background speakers.

She spoke of the depleted number of Greek students in her classes these days: 'being honest … the only Greek thing they have about them is their name, that's about it'. The Chinese teachers, on the other hand, were grappling with high numbers of students wanting to study Chinese, and they indicated their concern that classes were getting too big, with infant classes of twenty-seven or more students. Chinese was also promoted strongly by the school executive and the Greek teacher perceived that school resources promoting Chinese were much greater than for Greek. Unsurprisingly, the Greek teacher felt some concerns at her reduced status as a languages teacher.

On being a second-class teacher: 'other staff will talk, why should you get the same wage as they are'?

In addition to the effects of local demographic shifts, staffing dynamics within primary schools could also result in languages teachers experiencing inferior status. For example, an Indonesian teacher at Clarke PS alluded to the differential status of languages teachers when she commented on a perception among students and generalist teachers regarding 'real' teachers: 'Yeah, go to your real teacher, not your language teacher', and she conveyed the idea that there were different 'levels' of teachers in the school:

> Over the years we've had some tension and I know last year there seemed to be just lower morale, if I can call it that, where I think just it's kind of like you've got your classroom teachers up here, then you have your ESL and language teachers.

Her fellow Indonesian teacher at the school also thought that some languages teachers (but not him) were not always highly regarded by generalist teachers:

> I think there's probably some sentiment from other staff that's maybe not so positive towards some of the other language teachers that maybe they don't feel they're as qualified or as connected to the rest of the school.

One of the Chinese teachers at Keswick PS elaborated on the perceived distinctions between languages teachers and generalist teachers. She said that historically, generalist teachers understood languages to be 'games and songs and things' and that both types of teachers had different roles in the school:

> Because they [language teachers] felt like you're only teaching one subject, but a classroom [generalist] teacher, they had multiple subjects. In the playground in the morning I see it with my eyes, they have to deal with the parents every morning and I don't really. I do get parents come to me but compared to them it's less.

She also commented on the fact that languages teachers were in a minority (only three at Keswick PS), that they formed a separate department and they reported only to the school executive. Thus, for generalist teachers there was a 'mysteriousness' about what languages teachers did, and in some cases, there was a perception that they were not 'pulling their weight'. She provided an example which related to a discussion she had with a school executive over the allocation of extra (non-teaching) duties:

> I said how come I have so many [duties], and this executive said to me, I don't put you on camps and all this like other classroom teachers, so that's how it works out. This particular executive even said to me that you need to pull your own weight or else other staff will talk, why should you get the same wage as they are?

The Greek teacher at Keswick PS felt particularly aggrieved at the lower status of languages (Greek in particular) in the school and believed the languages learning area was not a priority as a core curriculum subject. As a result, she felt 'isolated sometimes because I don't belong in the mainstream'. She outlined a series of grievances about the status of languages, including: students were sometimes withdrawn from her class in order to catch up on another subject; the limited time for some of her language classes ('by the time I get the Kindergartners upstairs and settle them, I really have only ten minutes to teach'); often students studied Greek 'by default' because parents had not indicated a language and Chinese classes had few vacancies; and that once every three weeks she was required to take her classes to the Confucius classroom because the introduction of the Confucius classroom had added to timetable problems and 'it was decided to take that hour from languages'. She concluded with a poignant anecdote which indicated a generalist teacher's negativity towards the speaking of languages other than English:

> I don't know if I should say this – I was in the staffroom and one of the ladies, one of the cleaners, spoke to me in Greek because she comes from a Greek background, and her English is not that great. But then I had a comment afterwards, one of the teachers said I hate it when people speak another language in front of me. I thought, gosh, you are teaching in a school… You're teaching in a school that is multicultural and you're telling me this. What do you say to that?

As a rejoinder to this anecdote, one of the researchers spoke to a classroom teacher in the playground (probably the same one as above), who commented that learning Greek was of limited use to students unless it was to 'talk with the cleaner'. This teacher, long employed at the school, thought the curriculum was too crowded and there was not enough time to focus on the 'basics'.

The structure of community languages programs and its impact on teachers' professional identities

Teachers' professional identities and their capacity to teach languages well were also affected by the structure of the languages program. According to the NSW Department of Education (2016: 2) guidelines for community languages programs, 'effective programs are characterised by the integration of the language into the curriculum activities of the school rather than the teaching of the language as a separate subject in isolation'. In schools where languages were fully integrated with the school curriculum and taught in a bilingual program, as described earlier in this chapter at DBS, and also the Korean bilingual program at Cheswell PS, the status of languages teachers was high in relation to generalist teachers. For example, there were minimal differences between them in terms of curriculum planning, access to resources, professional development opportunities and professional recognition. However, in the many more schools that provided a languages program of just two hours per week or less, integration was interpreted more in terms of the languages teachers providing support to generalist teachers by focusing their lessons on the vocabulary used in the curriculum content areas. As the Greek teacher at Clarke noted, it was: 'consolidating what they're already doing in their classroom and we're just sort of backing it up with a different language, but it's the same work'. With this interpretation of integration, it could be argued that languages teachers occupied a role of secondary importance in providing support to the curriculum content work of the generalist teachers.

In most of the primary school languages programs in our study, languages were integrated with the HSIE (Human Society and Its Environment) key learning area. This was seen by the languages teachers to have both positive and negative consequences for their professional identities. On the positive side, the whole team of languages teachers planned and worked together, often with generalist classroom teachers, to agree on HSIE topics and vocabulary to be learnt. This helped to break down divisions and to some degree equalize the professional status of both languages teachers and generalist teachers as they were working on and sharing the same curriculum content. The Macedonian teacher at Clarke favourably compared this form of integrated provision to a previous era when she withdrew students for Macedonian classes from mainstream classes, which had caused some animosity with classroom teachers. She claimed, as a result of integrating languages with HSIE: 'The mainstream teachers love language [teachers] at Clarke.' The languages teachers generally seemed to manage to adapt the mainstream HSIE curriculum content to fit within the cultural contexts of the language in which they were teaching. The Chinese teachers, for example, linked the topic of natural disasters to earthquakes in China, and the Indonesian teachers managed to adapt the topic of gold: 'We're going to do spices, because that's Indonesia's gold because that's how the Dutch came into that … I don't want to be teaching about gold.'

On the negative side, however, for some languages teachers, trying to fit in with the existing HSIE curriculum constrained their teaching because it reduced the time available for focusing on other important aspects of languages pedagogy. In response, some teachers felt the need to try to find space to do their 'own thing'. One of the Indonesian teachers, for example, stated: 'We deliberately do a small unit so in terms of a ten-week term, with Antarctica, it might only last six weeks so that the last three weeks we can just do more conversational stuff.' Some of the technical language in the study of Antarctica was found to be too obscure and inappropriate, and he lamented that teaching units on different subjects (such as animals, body parts) provided few opportunities to teach everyday conversational Indonesian. The Chinese teachers at Clarke also found the HSIE content vocabulary to be too difficult for Kindergarten and other beginning groups. One Chinese teacher claimed 'it's so hard for us', and when asked what changes she would like to make to languages if she were the principal, she stated: 'I think I will let the language teacher teach whatever they think is better for children, not follow the HSIE program … it's not really suited to our language.'

The relative pros and cons of integrating languages with the HSIE curriculum and their implications for how languages teachers perceived their professional role were reflected in other schools. One of the Chinese teachers at Cheswell PS, for example, with its large community languages program, valued the fact that because languages were integrated and compulsory, her teaching of Chinese was seen to be on par with the work of generalist teachers:

It's a good feeling. Here they put a language position it's really the same as the other KLA. It's the same, very important. [Unclear] everyone to go to learn language; it's kind of compulsory in this school. So that makes a big difference. So the kids know that's an important thing.

By the same token, other languages teachers in the same school felt constrained in their professional role in ways similar to those expressed by teachers at Clarke. The Hindi teacher, for example, found that teaching about the planets was problematic for beginning Hindi students and it was necessary 'to explain it to them in English so they understand and then I tell them, okay this word is called this in Hindi'. As a designated languages teacher, this Hindi teacher, along with others cited in the above paragraphs, felt her professionalism was compromised to some degree through having to provide a vocabulary support role to the curriculum work of generalist teachers.

In summary, from the many comments from community languages teachers in just a few government primary schools, it was clear that their teaching experiences and professional identities varied. The picture was complex and depended a lot on the language a teacher was employed to teach. Community languages were provided in schools to meet local community needs, and these varied according to local demographic changes. For this reason, Chinese teachers often enjoyed positive professional status following the large influx of Chinese-background families in local school catchment areas. But teachers of other languages, such as Greek, Macedonian and Maori, experienced reduced professional status as these population groups had declined in some local areas and there was a lack of critical mass of students. The differential nature of languages work vis-à-vis generalist teaching could also result in tensions due in part to a lack of understanding of the work of languages teachers (i.e. 'games and songs') and the perception among some executive and generalist teachers that languages teachers might not 'pull their weight'. In most schools, languages were integrated with the HSIE curriculum, which to some degree reduced the separation between languages and generalist teachers insofar as both groups worked on common curriculum content. The downside for the languages teachers, however, was that this limited their ability to teach languages as a discipline, and in some cases, HSIE curriculum topics and vocabulary were unsuited to languages teaching, especially for students beginning a language.

Professional identities within different models of language provision

We conclude this chapter with three case studies of languages teachers in primary schools with different program models for the teaching of languages. A common feature in each school was the limited time that was made available for languages in their crowded curriculum, and in each of the languages programs, the teachers experienced varied professional identities. The primary schools were all Catholic, high SES and featured students who were less culturally and linguistically diverse than the government primary schools outlined earlier in this chapter. The main languages taught in the three schools were: Italian (very popular in Catholic schools), French, and in the third school, Spanish and Indonesian.

Integrating languages: 'It's the only way'

The languages teacher at St Francis taught Italian in thirty-minute lessons to each class in the school on one day each week. Several years previously she taught one-hour lessons to each class for two days a week with funding provided by Co.As.It. Subsequently, 'the Italian government cut back a tremendous amount of funding', and it was this 'money issue' that caused the program to be reduced to one day per week and thirty-minute classes, and the program was instead part funded by the school's Parents and Citizens Association. This funding arrangement meant that the Italian teacher's tenure was insecure. As the principal noted: 'It's a year by year situation [and] it all comes down to money.'

But despite job insecurity and minimalist thirty-minute lessons, the Italian teacher at St Francis managed to develop a program that she felt was valued by the whole school community – students, other teachers and parents. She enjoyed this value and the accompanying status in part because she was not only a qualified languages specialist, but a trained and experienced primary school teacher. This made a difference to how she was regarded as a languages teacher, because languages specialists in some other schools often did not have primary teacher training and were required to have the classroom (i.e. 'generalist') teacher present in a supervisory role during lessons. In this Italian teacher's lessons, however, her additional training and experience as a primary classroom teacher meant that the students 'keep their eyes focused on me', and behavioural problems were not an issue. Another reason she was valued in the school was because she worked with classroom teachers and integrated her Italian lessons with mainstream curriculum work, not because of a policy directive, but as part of her own deliberate pedagogical philosophy ('it's the only way', she claimed). However, in the absence of the joint planning time which was available at some government primary schools with large languages programs (e.g. Clarke PS and Cheswell PS), her approach to integration was undertaken informally through discussions with classroom teachers:

So I'll speak to the teachers and say, what's our HSIE and science unit for next term? The stage one had done the way we were, about families of today and the past, so we started working about families, so they could go home and greet their parents in Italian and call their mother and father mum and dad in Italian, speak about the dog in Italian.

Her approach meant that she was always alert to what the students were learning in their regular classrooms and she tried to build on that:

I go into somebody's classroom, we do a lesson, but I keep my eye around the room and I think, oh they're learning about that. In the next lesson, as we're working, I throw that in. It might be just the modification of my lesson for that half an hour.

Unsurprisingly, classroom teachers were very receptive to this approach, and the Italian teacher was accepted fully as part of the teaching staff working on common curriculum content:

and not, you're the Italian teacher, there's your corner, that's all you can do … like I said, I'm fortunate here with the staff because I can walk in, and they go, Teresa, by the way, I've got some pictures for you. I found some spare solar system pictures. Did you want them labelled? I can get the kids to do it if you like?

Thus, at St Francis, despite the minimal time available for languages, the Italian teacher felt she was valued and respected by other teachers, and her role in the school was also acknowledged by parents. She mentioned, for example, that when she was on 'afternoon duties' (as students leave at the end of the school day), parents would often engage with her: 'I've got people that drive past, beep, buon giorno and ciao. Isn't that lovely?'

'They don't really care what the kids are doing'

The overall positive identity of the Italian teacher at St Francis was not so evident in the case of the French teacher at another Catholic primary school, St Catherine's. In a timetabling sense, French at St Catherine's was taught within a similar structure to Italian at St Francis insofar as the French teacher taught only on one day per week, during which time she taught every class in the school. Lessons were between thirty and forty minutes long and they were all located in a small, sectioned off part of the school's library. This meant that students were continually moving to and from this one location during the school day, which differed from the Italian teacher at St Francis who continually moved to different classrooms. This program structure enabled the French teacher to have good access to her own materials and resources, but it did also mean that she had less interaction with classroom teachers and may have contributed to the perception that French was a separate, add-on subject. French was timetabled during classroom teachers' RFF time, and it was billed separately for parents, which reinforced a view that it was an extra-curricular activity, even though it was compulsory for all students.

After studying for a degree in French (BA, Dip Ed, Sydney University) and then spending a year in France, the French teacher taught English and French at a secondary school for fifteen years before taking time off for family reasons. She then returned to teaching part time and had occupied her current position at St Catherine's for two years. While the French teacher believed that learning French might provide students with 'a head start' in later high school years, she felt that the school community, in particular, executive staff and other teachers, was not completely supportive of French. She commented, for example, that 'the school likes the idea of it, but on an academic level they don't really care what the kids are doing'. She felt the subject was a little tokenistic and played to the demands of parents:

> I don't really have any contact with the parents. I imagine that the parents here, like a lot of parents, would like the idea of their children learning French, yeah. I think it's quite a – it's a bit of a posh thing to do almost, and people like that idea [laughs]. I mean when I tell other people what I do here they all say oh, my gosh, I wish my children learned French, I wish we had French in our school. People often say that.

Undoubtedly the timetabling of French classes contributed to her perception that French was not really valued highly at the school. One lesson per week was limiting, and the day itself was 'a bit rushed and the class sizes are too big' (thirty-four students was the norm). She commented further that while the students seemed to enjoy the lessons, 'they don't take it terribly seriously on an academic level. I mean I don't think they think of it as very important', which reflected, in a sense, the prevailing attitude of the school executive and other teachers.

The classroom teachers we interviewed indicated they had concerns about French and how it was taught. Comments included that: the priority should be ESL and not the introduction of 'yet another language system'; an Asian language would be more appropriate; and forty minutes per week made little difference 'in the long haul'. Several classroom teachers suggested the need for collaboration (e.g. 'we're studying celebrations and I asked her maybe if she wanted to tie in you know how to say balloon or clown or something in French'), but the issue invariably came down to lack of time. One teacher commented that 'being able to sit down for five minutes with the French teacher, that would be a great luxury'. Teachers commented on the already-crowded primary school curriculum, and especially in Catholic schools where 'you have half an hour at least of religion a day'. The only place where French was integrated in mainstream school activities was the Wednesday morning assembly – the 'French Hail Mary', which teachers thought was 'amazing', 'brilliant'.

The reasons why the Italian teacher at St Francis and the French teacher at St Catherine's experienced a different professional role and status, despite similar timetabling structures at the two schools, appeared to relate to the extent to which they integrated their teaching with the work of the generalist classroom teachers. The French teacher's program at St Catherine's was more clearly viewed as a program separate from mainstream school activities and she had little interaction with classroom teachers and no interaction with parents. It contrasted with the Italian teacher at St Francis who took it upon herself personally to integrate with the work of classroom teachers. Individual teacher agency and professional backgrounds (one was primary trained, the other secondary) may also have played a role in these differences.

Native speakers and teaching languages as a component of being a generalist teacher

In this final case study, we examine some of the identity issues for generalist teachers who, as native speakers, also taught languages at a primary school. As the principal at St John's Primary School indicated, many schools drew on the existing resources and skills of their classroom teachers: 'The most common factors leading to a school offering languages are the native speakers on the staff, and those staff members qualified to teach languages.'

At St John's, on the northern fringes of Wollongong, Spanish was taught at Kindergarten and Year 1, and Indonesian was taught at Years 2 and 3, both by existing generalist teachers at the school. The Spanish teacher was born in Spain and arrived in Australia when she was five years old. She spoke Spanish at home in her childhood years and rated her level of conversational Spanish as 'still five and a half to six years of age'. She qualified as a primary school teacher but without a language specialization. She began teaching Spanish to her Kindergarten class following a successful presentation she gave to the staff on languages. She managed to incorporate the teaching of Spanish into her regular Kindergarten class work on a daily basis, often for just ten minutes each day, and focused on songs and movement ('I always start my lesson with a song, a welcome song') and Spanish conversational greetings. Further, in order to provide Spanish to the other Kindergarten class at the school, she had an informal arrangement with the other Kindergarten teacher in which they swapped lessons – one taught Physical Education while the other taught Spanish. In Year 1, there was another classroom teacher who also spoke Spanish and so there was some continuity with Spanish over two years of schooling.

The informal swapping of classes among classroom teachers was also how Indonesian was taught across Years 2 and 3:

> What happened was my class would go up and the teacher might say to me, look I'll take your PE class, if you take my class for Indonesian. A couple of teachers did that to me, and they said, oh look, I'll do say your Religion once a week or something, if you take my class for Indonesian … We just say to the principal, look, this teacher would like Indonesian continued and I'm willing to do it at this time each week. We're willing to swap a lesson and do so. It's not been a problem. It can be done. (Indonesian teacher)

The Indonesian teacher had been a generalist primary school teacher for nearly forty years. She had always been interested in languages, having multilingual parents (their main language was Hungarian), and she studied German, French and Japanese at high school. In the mid-1990s, she applied for and was successful in obtaining a position to teach Indonesian as part of the policy push for introducing Asian languages in schools. The program was based on broadcasts from Indonesia, and as she described it in the first year: 'I was only a few lessons ahead of the children.' Since that time, she had incorporated Indonesian in her role as a classroom teacher, and she modelled her pedagogy on a native Japanese teacher with whom she had worked previously in the school which involved conversational work in the target language and constant repetition.

For all these teachers, however, their foremost role at the school was generalist teacher. Teaching languages comprised just one component, albeit an important one, of their role as generalist teachers, although in a limited way they could become more of a languages specialist at the school through informal timetabling arrangements that enabled them to teach languages to classes in other year levels. Their professional identities, however, were related primarily to being a generalist teacher. Lacking professional qualifications to teach languages, it was highly unlikely that they could imagine a professional role in another primary school as a languages specialist.

For the school executive and generalist teachers at this school and other similar primary schools, there appeared to be a dilemma for languages teaching. It was considered to work well when taught by existing classroom teachers, practised daily and not encroaching on the already crowded primary curriculum. But the downside was that the classroom teachers were not specialist language teachers, and the only languages that could be offered were those that featured within the skills of existing generalist teachers. And even then, who taught what language seemed to be almost a lottery. One generalist teacher, for example, explained that she was not teaching her first language (Spanish) at St John's because at a staff meeting: 'Maria put her hand up first, and I was new to the school, so...'

Summary

This chapter has illustrated how being a primary school languages teacher can be complex. If languages teachers are well-qualified specialists working in a bilingual program in equal partnership with generalist teachers, then they are likely to experience a strong, positive sense of professional identity. But these roles are rare in primary schools, and more often generalist or secondary-trained languages teachers, through a range of recruitment circumstances, become primary school languages teachers for classes of no more than two hours per week, and sometimes as little as thirty minutes. Their status within the school community and their professional identities depend on a range of variables, including: the perceived value of the languages they are teaching in the local school community, the available funding, the timetabling structures of the school, and the professional qualifications, teaching skills and individual agency of the languages teachers. The comments of many of the languages teachers in this chapter indicate that teaching tenures are often insecure, and teachers may feel they have little influence in the power hierarchies within individual schools compared with their generalist teaching peers. A key issue is that languages are not always viewed as a core academic subject in a crowded primary school curriculum, necessitating in some cases, local improvisations, drawing on the skills and experiences of existing generalist teachers.

5

Parental Perceptions and Attitudes to Language Study

Introduction

Many studies indicate that the family is a key domain for the shaping of children's attitudes to languages and that parental perceptions and attitudes play a major role in children's choices to take up or drop languages in schools (Kenner, 2004; Spolsky, 2012; Wright, Cruickshank and Black, 2018). The majority of studies indicate positive parental attitudes to their children's study of languages; the same studies, however, indicate little support among parents in general for languages study (Australian Council of State School Organisations, 2007; Bartram, 2010). Several factors have been identified in these studies. For example, several studies point to lower-SES parents tending to see less relevance in the study of languages and middle-class parents as more supportive (Bartram, 2010; Gayton, 2016). Parents who have a home language other than English, however, are generally positive about their children's maintenance and study of languages (Francis, Archer and Mau, 2010). There is some evidence that parents' knowledge and personal experiences of language learning affect attitudes: parents in lower-SES schools, for example, have fewer opportunities for travel and fewer experiences of language learning – two key motivating factors in children choosing to study languages (Carr and Pauwels, 2006; Gayton, 2010). To this end this chapter focuses on the perceptions and attitudes of the parents in our project to language study, and how these attitudes are influenced by social class, cultural background and perceptions of the purposes of education.

The data from this chapter come from interviews with over eighty parents of children in the case-study schools involved in our project. We interviewed parents who had and had not studied languages, and we made every effort to interview parents who were not necessarily favourable towards language learning. Parents were also interviewed individually or in small groups in their homes, at the schools, or at Parents and Citizens meetings. The parents we interviewed, even those parents from lower-SES schools, were likely to be middle-class or aspiring middle-class parents with an interest in languages, so this is a limitation to the scope of our analysis. Interview questions covered: parental perceptions of languages; attitudes towards their children's language learning; when they believed children should best begin studying a language; which language(s) parents thought were important for their children; reasons for taking up or dropping language study; and the role of the community language schools. Our access to parents was through school authorities, and parents who were nominated or volunteered to be interviewed were generally those favourable to languages study, a possible limitation of our study.

Analysis of our interview data indicates that parents felt there was little support for languages in the wider community. We found a construction that parents in lower-SES schools see no value in languages study. This confirmed staff perceptions of the broader community but it also makes for a paradox. Our interview and survey data indicate strong support for languages study from nearly all parents and school staff we interviewed. This chapter explores the extent to which this negativity to languages is a perception or a reality, a reason for schools not offering languages or a post hoc justification. This leads us also to question the greater emphasis on parental perceptions in school-based decisions about languages provision than in other subject areas. We would argue that parents' attitudes to languages study depended in large part on their own cultural and language backgrounds, previous access to languages and views on what it means to be a citizen in today's world. Given Australia's history of migration it is not surprising that many of the parents had histories of other cultures and languages in their backgrounds. For some, this was many generations ago, and language was no longer spoken in the home; for others, migration was recent and the family language was still spoken in the home. Other parents valued languages because they identified with a more cosmopolitan approach to culture and regarded languages as a valuable asset in the contemporary world.

Perceptions of language learning

As indicated in Chapter 1, languages in Australia struggle to find a place in the school curriculum. This is not helped by the widespread popular and scholarly perception that the broader Australian community does not support language learning in schools and that parents see languages as less important, less useful and more difficult than other subjects (Clyne, 2005). Some school principals in Clyne's study reported that 'parents say I don't want my child to learn a second language because they find it boring or too difficult' (Clyne, 2005: 355). One study found that only 15 per cent of parents agreed with the statement that 'most people think that languages form an important part of the school curriculum' (Australian Council of State School Organisations, 2007: 7). This construction of language learning has been defined by Clyne as 'monolingual mindset', that is, seeing everything in terms of a single language (Clyne, 2008: 348).

Findings from our study confirm that school personnel expect little respect for languages study on the part of parents and the community. For example, in the survey we conducted in 2012, only 25 per cent of school staff felt that languages were valued in the Australian community. In many of the lower-SES case-study schools, there were comments from staff, such as 'parents are not interested', and 'there's no need for languages here'. Alice, a deputy principal of a selective high school, encapsulated this when explaining why languages study was not common in mid- to low-SES schools:

> In comprehensive schools they're [languages] hard. That's not a perception. They *are* hard. Parents know there's no job prospects. In a comprehensive school, given the choices that you can get to choose journalism, you can get to choose visual arts, textiles, design and technology, hospitality, are you going to choose a language? I don't think so. We're in Australia. We're isolated, culturally and geographically. So, unless their parents are bilingual, it's not something that's on their agenda. (Deputy principal, Forster HS)

While this perception that parents were not in favour of languages was echoed by some parents when asked about others' attitudes, most of the parents in our study were strongly in favour of the inclusion of languages study in the school curriculum. Their disparaging comments about others' more negative positions were often related to assumptions about Australia's monolingual cultural cringe in relation to countries unlike their own or to Australia's apparent isolation from the rest of the world, particularly Europe and European languages:

> They [Australians] are fairly – they're also a bit complacent. They just expect when they go overseas that everybody will speak English, that everybody can speak English to them. There just hasn't been that culture of learning. (Parent, St Benedict Boys HS)

The comparison with the European case where 'you have to speak three languages' was often made:

where we are demographically situated in the world doesn't help. I mean if you live in Europe you have to speak three languages. English is your first language you learn after your native tongue and then you might learn another one or two depending on whether your country borders. So for us it makes sense that I can see why there's a push for Asia per se but I don't know how you push people into the European languages. How do you push them there? I don't know. (Male parent, Quentin HS)

The parent's comments below are typical of many parents whose own cultural and languages background led them to see children gaining fluency in another language as 'the norm' and the Australian case as divergent:

> Coming from a European background, it's like it's just the Aussies who … expect the whole world to speak English. Dutch five-year-olds are speaking six languages and if it happens, if an Australian speaks five languages, they think that they're the Secretary-General of the United Nations when it's just normal everywhere else. Well I guess the migrants would be saying, no, you've got to do brilliant at English so you can be a brilliant doctor. I guess the Aussies who … aren't outwardly looking would go, what good is a foreign language when you should be doing a job, studies that will get you a job, like engineering or law or something. Then there'll be a third component for whom, regardless of the vocational implications, they're just not attracted to the language per se. (Parent, Cheswell PS)

Another parent, a linguist herself, remarked on the concern of other parents about the lower profile of languages in comparison with the high profiles of Mathematics and Science, and the negative effect learning languages would have on their children's English literacy, Mathematics and Science:

> I think there's a big cultural shift, too, that's happened, like I think if you look back to the heyday of multiculturalism, there was a real embracing of multiculturalism. But now we've moved into a different era where it's all about measurement and literacy and numeracy. People are worried that if their kids take languages it will detract from the literacy and numeracy and from the subjects that have a high profile like maths and science. … I think the measurement and the whole focus on reading, writing and numeracy is partly to blame. (Parent, Sherwood HS)

For some parents, social class was a factor influencing support for language study and for which language should be studied. As one of the parents pointed out: 'There's certainly a socio-economic status or a social class thing [for not wanting languages study]' (Parent, Pennington PS). This view was shared by a teacher at St Catherine's, where French is taught:

I imagine that the parents here, like a lot of parents, would like the idea of their children learning French, yeah. I think … it's a bit of a posh thing to do almost, and people like that idea [laughs]. I mean when I tell other people what I do here they all say 'oh, my gosh, I wish my children learned French, I wish we had French in our school'. (French teacher, St Catherine's PS)

Maintaining a language: Cultural capital, identity and heritage

In the literature on social class and languages, the concepts of cultural and social capital (Bourdieu, 1991) are invoked to explain the value of language to particular groups of people, such as cultural communities and/or students (and their parents), as they make decisions about taking up second language study (Francis, Archer, and Mau, 2009, 2010; Smala, Paz and Lingard, 2013). The ways in which language can be understood as capital vary between and within these groups. For example, Francis et al. (2010: 527) use the term 'ethnic capital' to distinguish between 'the mobilization of a minoritised community language and the mobilization of foreign languages as capital more generally'. Other scholars point to the ways community language contributes to the education capital in relation to mainstream schooling (Zhou and Li, 2003; Zhou and Kim, 2006), cultural capital and identities (Francis et al., 2010) and global citizenship (Wright et al., 2018).

In their study of parents' construction of the purpose of Chinese complementary schooling, Francis, Archer and Mau (2010) found that the parents encouraged their children to study Chinese because they believed that perpetuating Chinese language and culture and maintaining a Chinese identity would benefit their children in the future, particularly in relation to China as a global economic force, were the three main purposes for encouraging their children to study Chinese. This finding is useful in understanding broader notions of cultural and social capital in relation to the complexity of identity. The two quotes below exemplify how many parents in our study tried hard to maintain the heritage and cultural identity even if their children did not speak the language of the culture and they themselves were born in Australia.

My children love saying they're Greek, we're Greek, it's like, well, you are but you're also … it's funny how your kids feel about their background. I think they're very proud of their heritage, very proud and I think they like to know that they've got something. Isn't that funny? … I like the fact that they have some background and understanding of where my family came from. (Parent, Keswick PS)

The motivation is to keep the children connected to the Polish culture because when they come here they not only learn the language, they get that from us at home, but also as part of the classes they often do Polish traditions. Around Easter time, they concentrate around the painting of the Easter eggs and where all that comes from, so I think it's really important for them to have that, and Christmas time, of course, we celebrate in the Polish way, so it's all the events they're doing now concentrate around that. So it's a lot of cultural heritage. (Parent, Polish CLS)

The theme of inter-generational communication was often mentioned in the parent interviews. In many cases families were second- or third-generation Australian but the children had access to languages through grandparents and extended family. Dona, for example, was fluent in Greek and sent her children to Greek afternoon school. She and her parents are Australian-born but they have maintained the language through three generations.

When I was little too, how could I communicate with my grandmother because they came from Europe to Australia and my grandmother couldn't speak a word of English. She could still say hello to someone and all that, but for me to communicate with her and take her grocery shopping when I got older, I have to learn how to speak Greek otherwise how am I going to tell my grandmother what … when she asks me something. (Parent, Dante Bilingual School)

My grandparents were here in the '20s. They were the only token Greeks in these country towns so they chose to speak English rather than Greek, there was no-one. Because of the Greek background. Both of Elliot's sets of grandparents are born in Greece. My husband and I speak Greek and we really wanted him to learn as well. (Parent, Greek CLS)

The diversity of languages through marriage was also a common theme. Parents who had married or partnered into a family with a language other than English were also enthusiastic about their children learning languages. For example, John and Dianna are both Australian-born parents and so their daughters are seen as coming from an English-speaking background. James is from a German-speaking background, although English was the language spoken at home. But his grandparents are from Austria. His wife Dianna is from a Greek background. John, who learnt to speak Greek fluently in order to speak to his in-laws, was very pleased that his children were immersed in Greek from birth.

Yeah, I learnt it at the workers' centre, the Australia workers' centre in the city when I fell in love with a Greek woman. I thought the best thing to do – I couldn't buy a diamond, like, that big – so I thought I'd learn Greek. It worked with my mother-in-law ... Whereas the kids have been exposed to Greek every day from the day they were born. We never worried too much about their English because we ... first of all that was ... I mean I knew I was going to speak it and second of all we knew they were going to be exposed through life.

The children now attended Greek Saturday school and John had chosen to send the children to Cheswell Primary School because of their Korean bilingual program.

> Plus they learn Korean here in the special, not the community language, but the specialist program here. So that's specialist Korean here, plus Greek language on Saturdays. Plus at home since they were born, they were spoken to in Greek every day by their mother and their grandmother. (Parent, Cheswell PS)

Access to languages through extended family was also common. Brittany grew up in Ireland learning Gaelic and had close contact with her family who were fluent in Gaelic.

> Look, when you're at school in Ireland, Gaelic is still the official language of the country. So you actually have to learn, the idea is you're actually supposed to be educated through Irish, though in practice that doesn't usually happen ... So there's actually been a great upsurge in Irish-speaking schools. So a lot of my nieces and nephews go to Irish-speaking schools. (Parent, St Benedict Boys HS)

Our data indicate that multilingual parents generally had very positive attitudes to their children's language learning. This applied not just to learning the heritage language; rather, these parents were very much in support of their children learning other languages. The intersection of community language background and SES then raises questions about simplistic constructions of language attitude and socioeconomic status.

Expressions of regret

One of the reasons the Chinese parents in Francis and her colleagues' (2010) study supported their children's languages learning was their regret at losing their family language. In our study this also emerged as a theme, with parents expressing regret for relinquishing opportunities for language study in their early years and/or losing fluency in their family language. They lamented the missed opportunities that being bilingual or multilingual might have afforded them in a global world.

> I did Italian, French and German at school in Year 7. And I totally screwed it up. I wasn't interested. I wish someone had slapped me and said, this could be good. But like I was really hopeless at the languages. So like I said when my father and I then went off to try and learn Italian at TAFE I thought yeah, I don't think I imagined it like I really … Well as I said I decided because I'd been travelling and I was just so in awe of people that could speak other languages. I thought … and yeah I felt guilty really that I could get by on English whereas many people with many other languages need one of these other major languages. (Parent, St Benedict Boys HS)

For some parents, languages study was outside both sociocultural expectations and possibilities.

> I was exactly the same as you [speaking to another parent]. Because I wasn't introduced to it [language] in primary school. We didn't have anything when we were going to school. Then I was in a country town. Then I sort of moved and I think at that point I wish my mother had said do French. But my mother was the era of no, go and do home economics and sewing. You know? So I look back and I just go, you know, it's a huge regret of mine. Then we moved three times so I had three different high schools. (Parent, Metro HS)

For those parents with languages other than English in their backgrounds, there was a sense of nostalgia or regret for lost opportunities to continue learning their community language or to recover it through studying their language at school. For example, Marcia was born in Australia but raised by her grandparents. She described how she lost her fluency in Greek because of negative attitudes to community languages when she was growing up and was determined her children would not have the same experience and so sent her children to a community language school to learn their heritage language, Greek. The following quotes indicate a common phenomenon of immigrant lives, where community attitudes, busy parents and the push to learn English contribute to early loss of the heritage language.

> I used to go to Greek school after school when I lived here, when I was little, when I was at primary school. I can't read and write now, I forgot all that. I used to go after school. My grandmother took me. For me to read now, I can't read Greek and write Greek, but I can still speak it, but to write it, I can't. My husband still can. He can still read a little bit of Greek, but I can't, I've forgotten all that. (Parent, Keswick PS)

> I was born here, went to school here but my mum was working when I was young, before I went to school, and my grandma pretty much raised me. My grandma only speaks Greek, she doesn't know much, a few words here and there of English, so I went to school only knowing how to say the word toilet. I could

tell the teacher that I needed to go to the toilet. But then there was this big push for me to learn English at school. I was doing the extra aide of learning to speak English and all of a sudden I forgot my Greek. Like I'm not as fluent in my Greek. I can't…I knew everything in Greek and now I struggle. (Parent, DBS)

Monolingual schooling, especially in low-SES Australian primary schools, has contributed substantially to children's loss of their home language. As Curdt-Christiansen (2009) points out, in combating language loss an immigrant family also has to compete with mainstream ideologies, children's popular culture and peer influence on children's social values. In our study we found that parental access to languages, even when linked to loss and failure, accounted for positive attitudes that cut across SES lines.

Languages for global citizenship and/or intercultural understanding

We agree with other studies that languages, usually a marginalised subject area in English-speaking countries, are gaining 'elitist' ground as part of the 'value-added' marketization of schools and the parents' desire to gain positional goods through schooling. (Smala, Paz and Lingard, 2013: 380)

In a report, 'Attitudes towards the Study of Languages in Australian Schools' (Australian Council of State School Organisations, 2007: 6), a teacher commented that 'Australians think of educating their children for local, not global capacities'. However, in our study, parent imaginings of their children as global citizens were often part of their explanations for the appeal of language study. While parents did talk about the advantages of languages in the labour market, they were more likely to invoke a broader construct of languages as providing the dispositions needed for growing up in a more globalized world, what Resnik (2009) describes as 'civic multiculturalism' and Singh and Qi (2013), citing International Baccalaureate documents, 'international mindedness'. This latter position was also more evident in the ways in which languages were promoted by some of the schools in our study, particularly the schools marketing themselves to a middle-class population (see Chapters 7 and 8). For some of the parents, 'international mindedness' was mostly associated with learning about a non-English-language-based culture. For example, in the following quote, the parent of a child in a low-SES secondary school suggests that learning a language will facilitate acceptance by other cultures.

I don't really have any expectations. I just think that when you learn a different language it does open your mind, your eyes and your ears to other people. You are not restricted, you can go to that country and not be a total stranger. If you try to embrace the language, then people will embrace you as well, I think. (Parent, Campbell HS)

For the parents in the following exchange, who shared several languages and cultures, learning languages was about being what Resnik (2009) describes as 'a civilized person'.

Male parent: Well, I think to learn a language you learn a culture as well. That seems to come along with it. I think for one thing that it's a great thing to learn because another culture is another viewpoint, another way of looking at the world in some ways.

Female parent: Yeah, I do too. I just think end of the white-bread Anglo – why wouldn't you want to learn another language? It feels like would you choose a smorgasbord or one meal? It just broadens and enriches your life speaking other languages. (Year 9 parents, Sherwood HS)

Another parent, speaking at a community languages school, also pointed to the importance of learning a language to becoming a global citizen.

Look, I think it helps with general learning to be able to speak a second language ....I think basically the little bit of overseas travel I've done, I just feel Australians must feel so inadequate, you know. When I meet children from overseas who have been immersed in second languages, I just think their ability to travel the world and be part of what's happening is so much easier for them, than our children. I'm a really big advocate for pushing towards a second language. (Parent, CLS)

Other parents were more specific, strongly supporting the teaching of Chinese as a language widely spoken in Australia and in Asia as a global citizenship/trade language.

Oh, very, and Mandarin in particular, because of Australia being where it is located and our proximity to countries that use that language more frequently than the northern hemisphere, I think. It's very, very important. (Parent, Campbell HS)

Parental attitudes to language learning were linked to contact with languages through travel and work. Many parents had accounts of travelling when they were younger or travelling with their families. These early experiences seemed to have shaped their attitudes to languages study.

I travelled with one of my girlfriends who is of Italian descent. She spoke the language when we were in Italy. It was good, that. I would love to be able to do that. I think it's really good. (Parent, St John's)

Others envisaged the work opportunities that a second language would open up.

Yes, and especially, like I said, for when our kids travel when they get older, the job opportunities would certainly be more open to them, I would think, if they had a second language. (Parent, St Catherine's PS)

Oh everything, travel, work. I mean like society today – everything, buying globally. We're all becoming… everything's all done internationally now. Not many things are staying within the country, it's all dealt with overseas from various countries so if they've got one or two languages up their sleeves that's just giving them that extra head start. (Parent, Dante Bilingual School)

The notion of languages as providing a form of transnational human capital (Gerhards, Hans and Carlson, 2017) is exemplified in the following example. The mother speaking is a middle-class parent, who herself enjoyed a privileged schooling – an overseas exchange, later work in Europe and so on – and her wish to reproduce that privilege for her own children now at Sydney International School (SIS). She explains below how learning a language changed her life:

The real point for me that sealed it for me was when I went on exchange at the end of Year 11 when I was 16 to Germany for two and a half months and it just changed my world. It changed the way I looked at the world. It changed the way that I saw myself. It changed the way that I saw my relationships with my parents… It just – … you are a fish out of water and you learn so much about the way life is different and it just opens your eyes up to that… I just thought, this is such an amazing experience that I would want anyone and everyone I know to have and I want my children to have it. Because I want them to see that there is a world outside what you do in your everyday, which as a child you don't get that exposure necessarily. (Parent at SIS)

This parent strongly supported her three children learning three different languages, one was studying Japanese, one French and the other Italian. She said the purpose of language learning was for her children's future careers and travel.

The accounts of contact with languages through travel, through work and through family were common in our interviews. The accounts of such contact with languages were from parents in high-, mid- and low-SES schools. This is not to discount negative comments: for example, one parent commented that, 'foreign languages are foreign to kids. They don't have to learn other languages. They don't necessarily hear other languages as such, unless your parents are foreign'. Another suggested that in the best interests of her son, her curriculum priorities lay elsewhere, 'as I said, I tend to prioritise the reading, writing and arithmetic higher than the Mandarin'. The access to languages through travel has often been seen as a marker of SES. In one study of lower-SES schools no families had travelled abroad, and none anticipated doing so (Carr and Pauwels, 2006: 124) supporting the comment that 'young working class people have not historically seen language study as having relevance to their lives' (Gayton, 2010). Such comments, however, were also reported in the same studies by middle-class parents of English-speaking backgrounds (Gayton, 2010, 2016). In our study it was parent from a low-SES school (Campbell HS) who made the comment that learning languages 'does open your mind, your eyes and your ears to other people'.

Languages for cognitive development

The association of languages learning with cognitive development has recently become a key trope in the promotion of languages study (Baker, 2006). This idea was picked up by some of the parents, who suggested that learning a modern language would facilitate their children's cognitive skills and brain development. In this case, it often didn't matter what language was learnt.

> Because it works a different part of your brain and when you've got more of your brain working it sort of filters through so the English comes into place, the Maths comes into place, everything comes into place. That's my understanding, I could be wrong. (Parent, Dante Bilingual School)

Another parent pointed to how his child's facility with both his heritage language and English seemed to have facilitated his learning of other languages, 'he's a natural'.

> It's a fantastic tool for developing your brain, just grasping different languages, how they work, and being able to switch from speaking Polish to me and speaking English to his friend, just like this, easily just swapping. So his brain is functioning on many levels, and therefore his Italian teacher is so impressed, saying oh, I must have him – because they had to choose electives – I must have him in my elective class because he's just a natural. And I said, 'oh, it's just that he's so multilingual', so … (Parent, Polish CLS)

The same parent who commented on 'foreign' languages being 'foreign' to children then reported his own son's learning of Korean.

They started a Korean program at Tarra Public School. They implemented now from – I think it is Year 1. They started with … I can't remember if it was Year 3, 4, 5, 6, but Kevin was in it for two years, which I thought was excellent. They need to start it in primary school. They really should be starting there and mould their brains to understand that there are other languages. (Parent, Campbell HS)

A linking factor on the cognitive and learning benefits of languages was often parental experience of their children's learning.

Learning languages should start early

The report on 'Attitudes towards the Study of Languages in Australian Schools' (2007), compiled for the Australian Council of State School Organisations and the Australian Parents Council, indicates that 86 per cent of parents support the statement, 'Learning a language should start in the early years of primary school.' In addition, there were forty-eight written responses which advocated this position. The strength of this finding supported the MCEETYA Taskforce prioritizing the early years of schooling as a base from which to progressively expand the provision of languages education. These findings were echoed by the parents of primary-school-aged children in our study, who indicated they wanted their children to learn languages early, and again, it often didn't seem to matter what language. For example, although the following comment comes from a parent with a Greek background, she is impressed by how her cousin's early start with Chinese has influenced her fluency.

There's a school up the road my cousin goes to, I'm just not sure if it's a city public [government] school, they're learning Chinese and my cousin is speaking unbelievable Chinese but she has wanted to do it because they started it when she was like Year 1. They're not doing any other language but that and she's really embraced it. She's actually speaking it better than she speaks Greek. (Parent, Dante Bilingual School)

Other parents commented on the more common phenomenon that children were rarely exposed to languages in primary school:

I think it's a shame that they don't learn. I think it is imperative. If they want to get kids to learn languages they have to start in primary school. That is really a big thing. Because learning in Year 7, it's too late, really too late. (Parent, Campbell HS)

In the policy literature the question of which language should be taught and in which contexts is a thorny issue (Hornberger, 2005). When we asked parents whether there was a particular language they would like their children to learn, their responses depended on their own cultural and language background and/ or their perceptions of the value of a particular language for their children's future in contemporary society. For those parents from a language background other than English, learning their heritage language was their preference, though some, like the parents below, accepted (sometimes pragmatically but with less enthusiasm) that another language (e.g. Chinese) might have more utility:

> [I want my children to learn] Danish. But it's not really very useful in one sense for them, because there are only five million Danes. It is not a big pool, but then you can understand people from Sweden to a degree, depending on where they come from, and Norway. So you are getting a bigger pool. But it's just very different. Ian is learning Chinese, which … I can't really help him because I never learnt Chinese. He says he is going well. I don't know how well he is going. He tells me stories, so I can't tell. (Parent, Campbell HS)

> You are in the right region where it should be either … most likely Chinese. They were learning Korean, which I thought, how much do you need the Korean compared with Chinese? But I don't know. It was an opportunity because one of the parents was Korean, and that's how I guess it all came in, which is excellent. Any language really, I think, they would benefit from learning something new – different cultures. (Parent, Cheswell PS)

Attitudes to HSC and ATAR

In our study we found that parent attitudes were also affected by other factors such as the instrumental value of languages in terms of tertiary entry. Pachler (2007) indicates that choices in language education at the individual level are directly linked to the conditions set at the macro and meso levels. At the macro level we refer to the global world discourse for positive attitudes towards language learning. At the meso level our data show that parents made their decision for their children's language learning based on the practical scaling system for languages at HSC level made by the NSW Board of Studies. When language has some capital/exchange value in terms of credentials and potential careers, it is more likely to be valued by parents who value those credential and careers. In Europe, for example, a second language is necessary for acceptance into a university. In Australia this is not the case, and as pointed out in Chapter 8, other subjects have far greater status for higher education entry, particularly for high-status professions/careers. While parents of children in the elite schools of NSW might recognize the potential value of language for 'global careers', our data suggest that many of the parents in our study saw languages as displacing a focus on subjects such as Science and Mathematics and so to be encouraged up until Year 10, but not for HSC study. As indicated in Chapter 8, the whole process around ATAR, and the scaling of languages in NSW, further renders language study unappealing for parents who have high-status careers in mind for their children. For example, a high-achieving Year 11 student at a Catholic girls' college described how her father discouraged her from continued study of Italian for the HSC (a luxury 'that she could pick up at any time'), because it clashed with a Mathematics subject which would enhance her chances for acceptance into medicine, engineering and so on at university. In this case the young woman's passion for Italian won over, but because it was timetabled against Extension Mathematics she had to study the language externally. Another parent explained how her husband disparaged languages study as a study 'only for girls', presumably because girls would not need to compete for high-status careers.

> Well, that's funny because my husband, who's from Queensland, is only a little more Australian than me, he says languages is only for girls [unclear] ... So I mean, he's very encouraging with our children. But it's very much a cultural thing. They [Australians] don't see any value in it, given the fact that it's so competitive and don't see any monetary value in it. (Parent, St Catherine's PS)

The considerable confusion over the scaling process and definition of categories (beginning, heritage and continuing) around the assessment of languages in the HSC was also a deterrent for some parents (see also Chapter 8). The anxiety over competitive entry to university, particularly for the more prestigious programs, meant that anything that might work against the highest possible score was likely to be discouraged by parents, despite students' interest in and often facility for studying a language. The following quote exemplifies how the ATAR score influences parents' reluctance to encourage their children to study languages in Year 11.

> I think what impacts on our decision is the ATAR score, whether they're going to be marked down because they're doing a particular language. There are all these conversations that parents have and often it can be misinformation as well. (Parent, Cheswell PS)

For the parents of some Chinese-background students, again like the parents in Francis and her colleagues' (2010) study, learning their community language (or least Mandarin) was important for its prestige and utility as a trade language. According to one Chinese-background student, Chinese parents at the school 'almost force' their children to learn Chinese in the early years, so that they have a 'basic knowledge of Chinese'. However, in the final years of school, what mattered were subjects that would result in a high ATAR and entrée to prestigious professions. For these students this meant dropping Chinese because of their classification as 'background speakers'. The ATAR scaling process results in Chinese (as well as other community languages) being scored far lower than the actual mark achieved in the HSC. This had a powerful impact on the decisions of the Chinese students and their parents not to continue with Chinese beyond Year 10 into the two preparation years for the HSC.

Summary

We found a conflict between parental views of language learning and their perceptions of general community attitudes. Most parents felt that languages study was not valued in the broader society and by parents in lower-SES schools. This reflects the traditional status of languages as a marker of prestige and it also runs counter to policy discourses on the relevance and value of languages (Teese and Polesel, 2003).

For the most part, parents in our study had positive attitudes towards languages, often formed through their own family and cultural/language background, and/or experiences of study or travel. As Rhodes (2014) points out, parental influence is one of the most important factors in maintaining multilingualism for the future. However, the picture is far from simple. As in many studies, our sample could have been biased because we relied on school and parent self-nomination. However, studies by Gayton (2010, 2016) confirm the link between socioeconomic status and parental attitudes to languages study in Scotland: the lack of access to travel correlated with lower-SES parents' negative attitudes to languages study. She found, however, that many middle-class parents also held similar beliefs. Our findings suggest that arguments on SES are not an adequate justification for a divide in attitudes to languages. Parents of heritage language backgrounds were strongly supportive of languages, no matter what SES background.

A key factor in our study could be this link of parental access to languages as an explanation of attitudes. Many of the parents from English-speaking backgrounds had experiences of languages study and learning languages through travel, work or further study; economic constraints, however, limit these experiences. We need to question the ways in which these perceptions of a class divide are used to justify the provision or not of languages. In many primary schools in our study, programs needed to be funded by parents or individual schools; funding tended to be more readily available in mid- to higher-SES schools. Exploring parents' attitudes in terms of their own and their children's experiences of languages means that we must take a more contextually based approach to attitudes. This was evident in the shift in parent attitudes between junior and senior secondary school. Although most parents want their children to learn languages in primary schools and junior high school (Years 7–10), they were much more ambivalent about languages in the senior school, with some actively discouraging their children from studying languages for Year 12.

What we found interesting was the range of parents' reasons for supporting languages study: for their children's cognitive development; for intercultural understanding and for global citizenship; for more instrumental reasons such as travel and future work and study; for family, cultural and heritage reasons. These were mixed in a coherent not contradictory way. There is a need for further research into parent attitudes to languages study which takes the complexity of these factors as the starting point.

6

Student Attitudes to Languages Study

While parents and teachers are clearly influential in students' choices of subjects in schools, ultimately it is the students' perceptions of how languages study works for them or not that makes the difference in what they choose when there is no obligation to study languages in secondary schools beyond the mandatory 100 hours. In this chapter, we examine students' perceptions of and motivations to study languages. We focus on secondary schools because, firstly, all students will have experienced some form of languages study as part of the mandated provision in Year 7 or 8, and, secondly, given the highly differentiated nature of languages provision in NSW covered in previous chapters, we would expect this to be reflected in students' comments.

According to one Australian study, while there is the perception at a more general community level that knowing more than one language is a good thing, languages nevertheless are considered hard to learn, and only 'clever kids' learn to speak a language (Curnow, Liddicoat and Scarino, 2007: 8). This same study, which included student perspectives, also outlined the following range of attitudes that are specific to learning languages in schools:

- Other subjects are more important
- Languages are scaled down/too hard to get a good university entrance score
- Students will not continue through to Year 12
- Languages are not popular
- Learning a language is boring
- Languages are a girls' subject
- You can only learn a language properly/well in-country
- You don't learn anything in class except colours and numbers.

A more recent study of student motivations to study languages at the senior secondary level in Australia (Kohler et al., 2014) found some of the same attitudes, as well as students having low expectations for achievement in languages, and the perception that languages hold limited utility.

In research studies in the UK based on large-scale surveys, school students (and undergraduates) were asked why they chose to study languages (Canning et al., 2010; Gallagher-Brett, 2004, 2012). The key reasons related to personal benefits such as communication and travel and the enjoyment they experienced in learning languages. While future employability gains were an important factor, they were considered less important than the personal satisfaction of learning languages.

Much of the theory relating to why students do or do not study a second language(s) has developed from individual-psychological studies of motivation, and researchers often cite the classical theory of Gardner (e.g. 1985) who distinguished between integrative motivation (willingness to engage with the target community and culture) and instrumental motivation (usefulness of languages for jobs, travel, etc.). Motivational theory for learning languages has since developed extensively. Dörnyei (2009), for example, a prominent researcher in this field, suggests three primary sources of motivation for learning languages: the learner's internal desire to become an effective L2 user (*ideal L2 self*); social pressures coming from the learner's environment to master the L2 (*ought-to L2 self*); and the actual experience of being engaged in the L2 learning process (*L2 learning experience*). Research on student motivations/attitudes to learning languages in the past two decades has become increasingly complex as research approaches have broadened beyond psychological theories to incorporate various studies of identity, and in particular, sociological approaches, including those from a poststructuralist perspective (e.g. Norton, 2001, 2013; Norton and Toohey, 2011). Norton, for example, developed the term 'investment' as a sociological construct which sees languages learners having complex identities 'which change across time and space, and which are constructed on the basis of the socially given, and the individually struggled-for' (Norton and Toohey, 2011: 420). Norton (2001, 2013) provides examples of students who were motivated to learn a language, but not invested in a language class because of the methodology and attitudes of the teachers. There was a disjuncture between the students' imagined identities in their affiliation with imagined communities, and those of their teachers, which in turn affected their participation (or not) in the language classes.

To date, most studies of motivations to learn languages have been based on learning (global) English, leading some researchers to focus instead more on languages more generally in the contemporary multicultural world (Ushioda and Dörnyei, 2017). Duff's (2017) comments on the work of authors who contributed to a special edition of *The Modern Language Journal* indicate how the field of motivation to learn languages has become so complex:

> The authors collectively raise awareness of the importance of understanding language learning motivation in multifaceted, multilingual ways in the diverse linguistic contexts represented by each research site – with indigenous, immigrant, global, and national languages that students may (or may not) want to learn or may be required to learn through the curriculum. How students and adults reconcile their own linguistic identities and aspirations, as well as local, familial, sociopolitical, and educational discourses surrounding them, and the perspectives of others that bear on their decisions and dispositions, continues to be a critical topic for educators and applied linguists. (Duff, 2017: 605)

Despite this complexity, issues of social class remain largely absent, as they are more generally within the field of applied linguistics (Block, 2014). Recent research in the UK, however, highlights the 'social divide' and increasing elitism in languages learning in English schools which is 'unrivalled in any other subject' (Lanvers, 2017: 520). Basing her research largely on the work of Board and Tinsley (2015a), Lanvers (2017: 520) summarizes how language choice is influenced by social class:

> There is strong evidence from England that students from more affluent socioeconomic backgrounds choose to study languages (beyond the compulsory phase) much more willingly than those from poorer backgrounds, suggesting that they are more easily enthused to study languages.

Lanvers (2017) indicates, citing Board and Tinsley's (2015a) data, that low-SES schools in the UK, measured by indicators such as the provision of free school meals, provided much reduced languages provision beyond the age of fourteen years. The type of school also mattered, with a high percentage of independent schools (76 per cent) making languages compulsory for all students 14–16 years, compared with 18 per cent of state schools. Furthermore, schools that controlled their own admissions (i.e. academies, free schools) had more students studying languages at 14–16 years than schools that did not select students. This was seen to be due in part to competition between schools that led to situations in which successful schools may 'cream off' the most able students (Lanvers, 2017: 519). These findings are significant, because while there are systemic differences between schools in Britain and Australia, there nevertheless appear to be some parallels with the SES factors identified in the schools in our own NSW study (see Black, Wright and Cruickshank, 2018; Cruickshank and Wright, 2016; Wright, Cruickshank and Black, 2018).

Another UK study by Coffey (2018) described how languages were valued by fourteen-year-old students at four London schools, two of which were independent. Drawing on Bourdieu's theories on class and social practice and Foucault's notion of discursive field, Coffey suggests that motives for languages study should not only be seen in terms of instrumental goals such as future employment or travel abroad, but as a form of cultural capital often reinforced through parental models. In middle-class families, this form of capital may comprise personal qualities for a desirable metropolitan ideal – an educated citizen in the liberal, humanist tradition. This work resonates with a recent study of transnational human capital (Gerhards, Hans and Carlson, 2017), also drawing on Bourdieu's class theory. In an increasingly interconnected globalized world the possession of transnational human capital, defined as the acquisition of foreign languages, cross-cultural competences and the knowledge and skills that enable individuals to act in social fields beyond the nation-state, is viewed by the middle class as a means to obtain distinction in the ongoing positional competition between social classes. Transnational human capital can be acquired in part through participation in early bilingual schooling and international student exchanges, both of which are largely the preserve of students from middle-class families (Gerhards, Hans and Carlson, 2017). As our study (this volume) indicates, working-class students have little opportunity to participate in these learning opportunities (Black, Wright and Cruickshank, 2018).

Australian studies similarly draw on Bourdieu to show how, for middle-class parents, languages, and bilingual education in particular, are desirable as a form of social and cultural capital with exchange value for employment in the global marketplace (Smala, Paz and Lingard, 2013). In the case of our own study of NSW schools, and in relation to independent and academically selective high schools, the choice to study languages involves 'a complex amalgam of elite, cultural identity or trade language discourses' (Wright, Cruickshank and Black, 2018: 108). For middle-class parents (see Chapter 5 in this volume), languages are viewed, somewhat similar to those in Coffey's (2018) study, not only for their instrumental value in terms of overseas travel and employment, but 'as part of being a contemporary citizen of the world' (Wright, Cruickshank and Black, 2018: 109). This incorporates what has been termed 'international mindedness' (e.g. Singh and Qi, 2013), which forms part of being a cosmopolitan/global citizen, and these qualities are reflected through the study of higher-status languages – traditional 'foreign' or 'modern' languages such as French, German and Japanese. In this context, community languages tend to be marginalized.

In the following sections of this chapter, we focus initially on student attitudes in the secondary schools where languages provision is more extensive and where the uptake by students is high, that is, in academically selective high schools and independent schools which comprise students from mainly middle-class families. The students interviewed were studying French, German, Italian and Japanese. Chinese could also be included, although, as we will see, for many students this was also a community language. The younger secondary students interviewed, those in Years 7 and 8, had all experienced languages as a mandatory school subject, and this may have influenced their attitudes to languages study, while those from Year 9 onwards had all elected to study languages. The relative ages/school grades of the students were reflected in their comments cited in this chapter. Students in the junior secondary years (7 and 8) with little experience of languages beyond the mandatory 100 hours often commented more in terms of their overall impressions (e.g. was it fun/ enjoyable). By the time students had reached and completed Years 10–12, their responses to languages provision were more reflective, complex and nuanced. Students from the independent school, Sydney International, were different from those at academically selective high schools insofar as most students at Sydney International had studied one language at the school from the time they were first enrolled, which for many students was pre-school or Kindergarten. In later sections, we consider the views of students from low-SES comprehensive schools where languages have a much reduced profile in the school curriculum.

Secondary student attitudes to languages study in middle-class schools: 'It's fun', 'it's cool'

That many students regarded languages study as 'fun' should hardly be surprising in view of the elevated enjoyment factor for languages students cited in the research literature (e.g. Canning et al., 2010). It does run counter to a commonly expressed view that studying languages at school is 'boring' (Curnow, Liddicoat and Scarino, 2007), but the students we focus on in this section were essentially from middle-class families attending high-status schools where languages were valued. In the following sections we will explore some of the reasons why many of these students found languages enjoyable. We begin by outlining several elements of the languages programs themselves that the students said they enjoyed, and which encouraged them to study languages at school. These elements may comprise attitudes and motivations towards languages study that Dörnyei (2009) identifies as the *L2 learning experience*.

The languages teacher: 'Miss David is really awesome' (Year 9 student, Sherwood High School)

One of, if not the key element of, their learning experience that students attributed to their enjoyment of languages was the teacher – how they taught and their personal characteristics including their fluency in the language being learnt. The quality of the teacher was important regardless of the school grade of students; it determined to a large extent why students wanted to continue with languages:

> The teacher really is important. It can really … it essentially makes or breaks a subject. I have plenty of subjects I don't enjoy because I've got a teacher who I don't really think is that great. (Year 8 Japanese student, Coolamon High School)

> So Year 10, actually I think we had a really good teacher. She was from France and I think that was part of the reason why I decided definitely to continue with it, because she helped us learn a lot more. (Year 11 French student, Forster High School)

Comments such as these provide confirmation from students that 'good teaching is the single most important controllable variable in successful language learning' (Lo Bianco, 2009: 28). By the same token, if for some reason students did not like a teacher, this could well provide a disincentive to study a language. For example, a Year 9 student at Sherwood HS said he was very interested in French history and culture, but instead of electing to study French he chose Japanese instead, and part of his reason for doing so was because the French teacher 'had a scary reputation'.

Mandatory 'taster' courses

For many of the younger students in selective high schools, those in Years 7 and 8, 'fun' was an understandable response to their languages study experiences. After all, these mandatory languages courses, often presented as 'taster' languages, were designed to 'sell' languages to students in order to persuade them to continue to study languages. At Coolamon HS for example, students in Year 7 studied three languages consecutively – French, Japanese and German. It was in the interests of teachers to make their languages classes enjoyable because, one or two years later, the number of students electing languages in Years 9 and 10, and later in senior years, was likely to be influenced by their level of enjoyment studying languages in Year 7. The focus in many lessons in Years 7 and 8 was on cultural aspects of languages study, and games, which students indicated they enjoyed:

> I learn it because I find it easy and I just like the class and I watch *anime* so I guess it's really cool when you can understand what they're saying. (Year 8 Japanese student, Coolamon HS)

> It's just … I find it really interesting to learn a new language and see what the culture is and the people are nice. Just we do fun things like it won't all be just workbooks – we play games. (Year 8 Japanese student, Coolamon HS)

Introductory 'taster' languages courses in Year 7 and/or 8 were more likely to be described as 'fun' by students from academically selective high schools where they may have been introduced to languages for the first time. They did not feature at the independent school (Sydney International) in our study where learning a language in a part-immersion program began from pre-school, and additional languages were studied from Year 7.

Overseas trips and student exchanges

All the high-SES secondary schools and independent schools featured annual or biannual overseas trips for languages students, often starting from Year 9 or 10, and there were also regular student exchanges. Most of these trips/exchanges were to Europe (France, Italy, Germany) and Japan. As Gerhards, Hans and Carlson (2017) indicate, these in-country international experiences can be viewed as a component of what they term transnational human capital which, from a financial perspective alone, is available primarily to students from more affluent families. Inevitably the overseas trip comprised a (but not necessarily *the*) major attraction for students to study languages at school. As one Year 9 languages student at Sherwood HS commented:

> The trip is a really good part of it. I think this may be just a thing with me, but I want to learn Japanese anyway. I think a really good part of it is getting to go overseas and actually being there. I mean, in my opinion I don't think you can really learn a language if you never go to the place it originated really. So that's an important part of it. But I don't think it was the main reason why I wanted to do Japanese in the first place.

Motivations for learning languages linked to overseas school trips need to be seen not just as the effect of the exchange visits themselves, but, in a broader context, as international learning experiences that go beyond the school. For example, many of the students from middle-class backgrounds had enjoyed wide overseas travel as part of family holidays and the cosmopolitan lifestyles of their parents (see later section on the role of parents).

Another factor that may have played a role in students' perceptions of languages study was previous languages learning in primary school, but this was complicated because students may have studied a whole range of different languages at primary school, and not necessarily the ones they were taught in their secondary schools, and many primary schools offered no languages. As indicated in Chapter 4, what was taught and how it was taught could also have been very limited, falling into what one principal referred to as 'your classic primary, half an hour a week of food, fun and festivals' (principal, Sydney International). The limited number of students in selective high schools who did indicate a receptiveness to learning languages as a result of their primary school experiences had received fairly extensive exposure to different languages at private schools.

Instrumental motivations

> I really want to continue with languages after school and probably go and study Japanese in university and see what jobs I can get from there as well because I really love languages. (Year 9/10 Japanese student, Sherwood HS)

Unsurprisingly, instrumental factors such as studying languages for future overseas travel and university study, and obtaining good jobs, featured in student interviews, but not extensively. Moreover, the quote above from a Year 9/10 student at Sherwood HS was an exception insofar as she was one of the few students who indicated she could imagine using languages (Japanese in her case) for travel, study and work. For many students, using languages for overseas travel and for future work was presented instead as a rather vague and somewhat predictable response. Some students expressed a general belief that languages would be 'a good asset to have' (Year 10 Italian student, Sydney International), but without specifying what this might entail. Similarly, a Year 8 Japanese student at Coolamon HS said that he wanted to study Japanese as an elective because 'to be able to break language barriers with a really important country like Japan just seemed so useful and practical'. By the same token, a group of Year 10 Italian students in a focus group interview at Sydney International, even after years of languages study, expressed doubts and provided some qualifications at the practical uses for languages.

Facilitator: How do you think it'll be useful learning these languages in
 your … How will it help you?

Male: I doubt it will.

Female: I think it's not as practical as some people might think, but then it also
 is in that it means you're opening up a whole new level of communication,
 it looks good on your resume, it may be in your area of work or whatever.
 Maybe you could kind of be part of a more …

Female: Maybe learning a language would be an advantage.

Female: Yeah.

Male: Universities seem to like it [unclear].

Female: Yeah.

Female: Yeah, exactly.

Male: It depends on what you want your future to be. If you see yourself in
 business or something and trading …

Male: They say Chinese is quite good for that.

Male: Yeah.

Female: Yeah.

Male: You might be coming into like people who speak that language. Let's say
 if you wanted to do a trade or something. I don't see it being as useful unless
 if you were working for an Italian building company at Five Dock (a Sydney
 suburb with a high Italian population).

As the above extract suggests, the situation may be different for students studying
Chinese (featured later) for whom there appeared to be stronger instrumental
factors at play related to perceived future employment.

Loving languages

> I just find it kind of thrilling because it kind of opens up this whole kind of new
> way of communication which I just think is so cool. (Year 10 Italian student,
> Sydney International School)

For a number of students, and in particular those from the independent school
who had been studying languages in a part-immersion program since their early
primary school years, languages had value as an end in themselves and not so
much for instrumental reasons such as travel, jobs or exam success. One Year 10
Italian student actually stated: 'I have never really seen a lot of practical use. I'm
just enjoying it. It's just so intuitive.' Some students described languages as 'more
a hobby. It's not really something that we'd be basing our lives around' (Year 10
Italian student, Sydney International). These students, in Year 10, after years of

studying Italian, had reached a level of competency in the language where they could use it for their own enjoyment and to a limited degree, they were becoming effective L2 users (i.e. *ideal L2 self*). They spoke for example of texting each other in Italian 'just for fun', and that it was 'really thrilling to be able to do it'. Others spoke of using Italian between themselves as a 'secret code'. Another Year 10 Italian student at Sydney International explained that her enjoyment of languages only developed over time. In the early stages she said that it could be 'a bit brutal ... then as you get better you're like, oh yeah, this is pretty good and then by the end when you can talk and you can understand stuff'. She provided a specific school event to demonstrate how she and her peers enjoyed/loved languages:

> like we had a guest kind of speaker, a friend of our teacher who came in and just talked about school experiences and just ... They were just talking to each other in Italian and we could just understand all of it and it was just so cool. It was just the best experience.

These students at Sydney International contrasted their rich languages learning experiences with those of their friends who went to schools that had limited languages provision ('they do a language for a term for the first two years'), which, according to these Sydney International students, 'just puts them off' studying languages.

The role of parents and the 'ought-to L2 self'

Student attitudes towards languages study were also formed through social pressures from out-of-school contexts, and in particular, from the influence of parents. Most of the students at both academically selective high schools and the independent school enjoyed a home life rich in different languages, although there were differences related to school types. Academically selective high schools had a disproportionate number of students who spoke community languages at home and, in particular, students from Asian-Australian families (e.g. Ho, 2015, 2017a, b). One of the selective high schools in our study, Forster HS, had 81 per cent of students who spoke a community language at home, while at the independent school Sydney International it was 26 per cent (My School website). Many students from both types of schools were immersed in different languages at home and in the research interviews they spoke extensively of their different experiences of using languages. In some cases, it involved community/home languages. For example, a Year 7 Forster HS student stated that because she began to lapse in her use of Marathi, 'my parents enforced a rule in the house that they would ignore English'. In other cases, students played with different languages as part of their regular home interactions. One of the Year 9 Sherwood HS students said that around the house 'we all speak bits and bobs of an array of different languages'.

Middle-class family lifestyles and child-rearing practices were highly conducive to students learning languages. Students were often well travelled through overseas family holidays, and their parents often spoke foreign languages, travelled extensively overseas for their work and had a cosmopolitan outlook (see Chapter 5 on parents, and research on the child-rearing practices of middle-class parents, e.g. Carlson, Gerhards and Hans, 2017; Gerhards, Hans and Carlson, 2017). Some of the students provided examples of their overseas travel with parents. For example, one of the younger students at Sydney International commented that he had travelled to about

> half the world … it's because my dad, … he travels a lot for meetings … The last place I went to was probably Sweden and Scotland. (Year 5 student, Sydney International School)

Learning languages was an important part of this middle-class lifestyle, although it was not always clear from the interviews with students that speaking another language was considered by them to be necessary or useful in a globalized world where English dominates. Parents on the other hand were often very conscious of the importance of learning languages and the need to instil in their children a cosmopolitan orientation and the acquisition of what has been termed 'transnational human capital' (Gerhards, Hans and Carlson 2017). One of the Sydney International parents, for example, travelled to Germany on a school exchange at the age of sixteen and subsequently spent time living and working (as a trainee lawyer) in Prague and Berlin, and she claimed: 'It changed my world'. She was determined that her children learn languages and enjoy similar experiences: 'because I want them to have a broader view of life and the world'. It was less likely that working-class parents would have enjoyed these types of overseas experiences or would have access to the necessary financial resources to enable them to happen.

Students indicated in various ways how their parents may have influenced their attitudes towards languages and their decision to study a particular language. Sometimes the influence was quite direct, as the following extract from an interview with a Year 10 student at Forster HS indicates:

Male 1: Well, I wanted to do German, but my parents wanted me to do French and at the start I wasn't that keen, but I've come to really like it. I wanted to do a language anyway, but my parents wanted me to do French.

Facilitator 1: Why did they want French rather than German?

Male 1: My parents have this kind of romanticised view of French, it's kind of this international official language and I could join the diplomatic corps or something like that … in the United Nations or something.

More often, however, the influence of parents, though apparent, was less direct. For example, a Year 7 student at Coolamon HS stated that he chose French 'because my dad speaks fluent French', and a Year 7 student at Forster HS stated: 'one of my mum's French and she likes me doing it'. It was not just parents, but grandparents also, some of whom spoke several languages and were well travelled. One student in Year 7 at Forster HS said her grandparents 'want me to be more cultured, if that makes sense'. Siblings and other relatives may also have been influential, mainly by providing good role models of language users. A Year 10 student at Forster HS commented that his sister, now twenty-five, had studied Italian for her HSC and at university and she ended up living in Milan. And a Year 9 student at Sherwood HS said he liked the idea of learning another language and drew a comparison with one of his cousins who lived in Indonesia: 'she knows over four languages already. So, you know'?

These quite extensive links with many other languages and cultures through family and the languages they were studying at school may suggest that these students were quite global in their outlook and already possessed a degree of 'international mindedness' (see Wright, Cruickshank and Black, 2018). This was difficult to gauge properly from the student interviews, although it was more apparent with parents (see Chapter 5). At Sydney International, however, the whole ethos of the school was framed around the idea of students acquiring 'a global perspective through diversity and intercultural understanding' (from the school website). A group of Year 10 Italian students at Sydney International demonstrated at the very least their multicultural awareness as it related to the language they were studying and where they lived in Sydney:

Female: If you have Italian down there it's good to see …

Female: Especially because we live in a very multicultural place of the world, so it makes it even more important.

Female: I live in Petersham and my neighbours are Italian, Greek and Spanish and so it is multilingual.

Female: I live in Earlwood but it's primarily Greek.

Female: Yeah.

Female: So Sydney as a whole is very multicultural and multilingual as in the whole area, not just Sydney in the city. You would hear people talking in …

Female: So many different languages, yeah.

Studying Chinese

Chinese parents to a point almost force their children to do Chinese. (Year 10 student, Forster HS)

Attitudes towards studying Chinese at school were different from studying other languages (see also Chapter 9). In this section, we focus on the attitudes of students from just one academically selective high school, Forster. This was the only selective high school in our study that provided Chinese classes, and it was a school where 45 per cent of students were of Chinese background (from the school Annual Report, 2017). The only Chinese course offered at Forster HS was the 'heritage' level course (since renamed 'Chinese in Context' in 2017). The heritage Chinese course was only for students brought up in a home where Chinese was used and where students had a connection with Chinese culture. Student attitudes towards Chinese as a language and their motivation to study it at the school appeared to vary according to the way Chinese was viewed. This included Chinese primarily as, or an amalgam of, an elite academic subject, a community language with strong parental support or a 'trade' language with human capital benefits.

As an academic subject studied for success in Year 12 exams, studying Chinese had some drawbacks. Firstly, unlike the experiences of Chinese-background students studying Chinese in overseas studies (e.g. Francis, Archer and Mau, 2009), studying Chinese at senior school level at Forster HS provided little academic capital for students. This was because the subject was scaled down relative to other academic languages such as French or German in the ATAR scores that determined university entrance (see Chapter 8, and also Cruickshank and Wright, 2016). In other words, in order to maximize ATAR scores, students had a disincentive to study Chinese, and as a consequence, very few students studied the subject in the senior school (Years 11 and 12). One of the Year 10 students commented: 'I just think that if they [other students] had the option of doing something that will get them a 95 rather than a 90 in the HSC, they'll take that any day.' The second drawback was offering only the Chinese heritage level course when some students felt they had insufficient background in Chinese. A Year 10 student said that while she spoke Chinese at home, she (and other

Chinese students) had very little experience reading and writing in Chinese, and the prospect of studying Chinese in senior school was daunting: 'for me whose spoken Chinese is fair enough but not heritage [level] Chinese. I'm going to be forced to do heritage Chinese next year when I pick it because my mother is Chinese'.

Many Chinese-background students chose to study Chinese primarily because it was important for them as a community language, and as part of their cultural heritage, they felt they should study it. This accords strongly with the identity findings in the UK study by Francis, Archer and Mau (2009). One Year 10 Forster HS student stated:

> Oh, I chose Chinese just based on I wanted to learn more about my culture and the language involved. I speak Cantonese back home, but they teach Chinese [Mandarin] at school and it will be more interesting if I learned a different dialect in Chinese, especially now that Chinese is so commonly spoken as well.

Other students experienced various levels of social pressure to study Chinese from within their families. In a group discussion of Year 10 students in the Chinese class one student claimed: 'I think the unique thing about the Chinese class is that Chinese parents to a point almost force their children to do Chinese.' Another student in the same class explained that Chinese 'is a kind of traditional thing, part of your essential learning' and that from their parents' point of view it should be studied 'just so we know that we've given our children a basis of our culture' (Year 10 student). For other students, studying Chinese was an extension of their home lives in which it was essential to know the language in order to communicate well with family members in both China and Australia. One Year 7 student explained:

> Since my grandparents lived in China for most part of their lives, they only come here – well my dad's side only come here – once every few years, but my mum's side are always here. But none of them speak English, so I have to speak Chinese. So speaking is easy for me, but reading and writing is just more complicated.

The instrumentalist view that learning Chinese would have an economic pay-off in terms of later employment and commerce generally was also popular. When students were told by their Chinese parents that 'it will definitely help you in the future', it was likely to relate to the public policy discourse of the 'Asian century' in which Chinese is viewed as a significant 'trade' language (e.g. Australian Government, 2012; Halse, 2015b). As one of the Year 7 students claimed, Chinese would 'definitely' be useful 'because lots of businesses, they always want Chinese speakers, so you can talk to customers who have bad English and stuff like that'.

Student attitudes to languages study in working-class secondary schools

Our analysis of student attitudes to languages study in working-class schools – local comprehensive high schools with a low SES – was limited mainly because languages provision in these schools was limited. At Metro High School only one language, Italian, was taught, and then mainly as the mandatory 100 hours course in Year 8. At Campbell High School, Chinese was taught as the mandatory language in Year 7, and French was an elective subject in Year 9 and there was a small HSC French class. We will consider the two schools separately because, beyond a common low-SES status, there were differences in the school populations and the perceptions by their principals and others of the value of languages for their students (see Chapters 2 and 3). Metro HS was located on the inner-city fringe and had a high percentage of students speaking community languages at home (84 per cent), while Campbell HS was located in a suburb outside a regional city with a low percentage of students speaking community languages at home (14 per cent).

Metro High School students: 'It's just a subject that you have to do at school'

As indicated, the only language taught at Metro HS was Italian, which the students generally seemed ambivalent about. As the mandatory 100-hour Year 8 language, the subject was not taught in any depth and generally failed to motivate students to study Italian as an elective subject the following year. One Year 8 student commented that she liked learning numbers one to ten in Italian, and another commented: 'I don't have anything I really like doing, it's just a subject that you have to do at school.'

The Italian teacher was a young female teacher in only her third year of teaching (see Chapter 3). The students enjoyed being taught by this teacher, but not primarily for reasons related to lesson content or teaching methodology, as a group of Year 10 students who had elected to study Italian beyond the mandatory Year 8 explained:

Interviewee: It's fun because the teacher's really cool.
Interviewee: … to have …
Interviewee: Yeah, the teacher's really cool.
Facilitator 1: We'll talk about this with the teacher first, the teacher's really cool. What's cool about the teacher?

Interviewee: Well, she's nice and funny and she lets us ... Like she doesn't get
   really angry very quickly, she's very nice.
Interviewee: Yes, she never gets angry.
Interviewee: ... and she's very nice. She ... all the time she's smiling ...
   [Over speaking]
Interviewee: ... patient.

These comments confirmed the primacy of the teacher's role as a motivational factor, as was the case with students in middle-class schools outlined earlier, but the difference at Metro was the focus on the teacher's disposition rather than what she taught or how. She was a young, enthusiastic teacher and fun to be with in the classroom.

Other reasons for studying Italian were presented largely in instrumental terms. Students mentioned that Italian 'may be useful in the future', but they could elaborate only in quite vague terms: 'I don't know, like travel or applying for a job or something' (Year 10 student). Not one of the students could imagine learning Italian for their HSC, but this was reinforced by the Italian teacher who actively discouraged them from studying Italian in the senior school. She maintained they would struggle to be competitive in an exam system in which they would be required to study the Italian continuers course (i.e. not beginners), having already studied the language beyond the mandatory 100 hours.

The students at Metro HS were rich in community languages resources, speaking a wide range of languages at home. Some of the main languages spoken included Vietnamese, Greek, Arabic, Portuguese and a range of African languages. Some Year 8 students born in West Africa said they spoke several languages, including Temne, Susu, Mende and Krio, and they also had some knowledge of French learnt when they attended West African schools. Other students spoke a community language which they sometimes also studied in weekend community languages programs (e.g. Vietnamese), and some students said they were studying different languages on the internet simply out of interest (Filipino and Japanese were mentioned). A group of Year 8 students even ridiculed (in a light-hearted manner) the one student in their group who could speak only English. But despite their own rich languages resources, learning Italian did not appear to register as a subject of academic importance at school. Students could not imagine using the language in their everyday lives and using Italian during an overseas trip or for work appeared vague and wishful. When students were asked to elect subjects to study in Years 9 and 10, they focused on more popular vocationally oriented subjects such as woodwork or special interest subjects involving sport. Italian in this 'residual' high school was not always viable as an elective subject because the school lacked the critical mass of students to enable it to function.

Unlike with the middle-class parents outlined earlier, Metro parents did not promote the academic study of languages for their children, at least not Italian. There was also very little support from other teachers in the school (see Chapter 3).

Campbell High School students: 'China's our future, like come on'

A key difference in attitudes towards language study between Campbell and Metro students was that Chinese was seen to be more important to learn than Italian. There seemed to be a belief in the benefits of learning Chinese for future work. One Year 9 student stated explicitly that 'China's our future, like come on', and other comments from the Year 9 students included: 'Asian is more trendy' and 'the Asian languages are the future'. The irony was that these Year 9 students were at the time studying French as an elective and not Chinese (because there had been an insufficient number of students electing to study Chinese), and they did not articulate the same potential benefits for travel and work through learning French.

Another difference in attitude/learning experience was that the Chinese students highlighted they enjoyed not just the teacher, but how Chinese was taught. For example, one student contrasted Chinese lessons to Maths: 'where you just do exercises, exercises, exercises. What we do here, we actually do a bit more hands-on than trying to learn other things'. Another student said he enjoyed: 'just all the fun, like all games and Chopstick Champions' (the Chopsticks game involved picking up jellybeans from a bowl using chopsticks). Students also liked school excursions using local resources ('to Chinatown... we get to eat Chinese food and use chopsticks'), interactive computer activities and practising calligraphy. There was some discussion that in Year 10 it might be possible for students to visit China, but it was yet to happen, and as one student noted: 'Yeah, it just depends how much it costs just to go to China, like flights and everything.' As we outlined in Chapter 3 on secondary teachers, the Chinese teacher at Campbell HS was highly skilled and experienced as a languages teacher.

A key issue for students at both Metro and Campbell that often determined whether they elected to study languages beyond the mandatory language in Year 7 or 8 was competition from other elective subjects. At Campbell students mentioned that in addition to Chinese and French, electives included art, woodwork, metalwork, jewellery, IT, cooking, agriculture and some sports subjects. Some of these electives had more practical appeal to students than languages. It also did not help that students studied Chinese in Year 7 and then had a Year 8 with no languages study before having to decide on their elective subjects for Year 9. The lack of numbers electing to study Chinese could indicate that the enthusiasm students displayed for Chinese in Year 7 had largely dissipated following a year's break from languages study. Most schools deliver the 100 hours in Year 8 in the interests of learning continuity and to increase the uptake of languages as an elective. Those who elected to study French at Year 9 appeared to do so for fairly indeterminate reasons such as: 'I just like the culture and friends and stuff, and I just thought, learn a different language. So yeah, just thought something different'. One student suggested that the French teacher, who was also the Year 9 adviser, had an influence on language electives: 'Miss [name of teacher] was shoving it down our backs.'

While the cultural and linguistic diversity of the student population at Campbell HS was much less than at Metro HS, there was nevertheless a wide range of languages featuring within their immediate or extended families. A group of students mentioned backgrounds in and/or some family members speaking Danish, Serbian, Vietnamese, Indonesian, Malaysian, French and Hungarian. But as with Metro parents, few parents actively promoted languages for their children, despite the hype surrounding the introduction of Chinese (see comments by the principal and Chinese teacher in Chapters 2 and 3). For example, one parent claimed that where they lived, 'foreign languages are foreign to kids. They don't have to learn other languages'. Another commented: 'I tend to prioritise the reading, writing and arithmetic higher than the Chinese.'

A lack of investment in languages study

The students at Metro and Campbell had few incentives to invest in the study of languages at school. There was only the one specialist languages teacher at each school (the French teacher at Campbell was a designated 'generalist' teacher) and languages provision beyond the mandatory Year 7 or 8 was very limited due in part to the lack of a critical mass of students at these 'residual' high schools that enabled languages electives to function. There was also strong competition with other elective subjects with more practical appeal for students. The two languages teachers were well qualified and well liked by students, and in the case of the Chinese teacher, very experienced, but there was little evidence that students could imagine using these languages to their advantage in the future. And this was despite community languages featuring in the home backgrounds of many students, especially students at Metro, who experienced rich languages resources. Parents and other teachers also provided little support for students to study languages, and school exchanges and overseas trips that were a feature of students in middle-class schools were out of the question. As Chapter 3 (on teachers' identities and experiences) indicates, home languages could be seen as a handicap rather than an asset in a school environment in which English skills are privileged.

Secondary students learning community languages

Despite the marginalization of community languages outlined above, there were some secondary school contexts in which students were encouraged to study community languages, and where they were valued and promoted. In this section, we firstly consider the attitudes of students learning Italian at a Catholic secondary school for girls. At this school, Italian could be viewed as both an academic subject and a community language for the many Italian-background students. We then consider student attitudes to community languages in a non-mainstream schooling context, the Heritage Languages School.

A Catholic secondary school for girls: 'At home I only speak Italian because my parents are both Italian'

De Sales Catholic Secondary School for Girls was in an area with slightly above-average SES (ICSEA 1043) in the inner west of Sydney. Its catchment area included a high concentration of Italian-background families, and according to the school principal, a quarter of the students had Italian backgrounds. In Year 7, students were introduced to three languages as 'taster' courses – Italian, French and Japanese – followed by languages electives from Year 8. Italian was by far the most popular language to study, and in Year 9 at the time of the research it was the only language studied. In Year 12 students were studying Italian at continuers and extension (the most advanced) level. The students we interviewed were all in Year 12 and primarily with Italian backgrounds. In a number of ways, they fit the 'typical' Year 12 languages student in Australia – that is, female, high SES, parents born overseas, high achieving and attending an independent school (see Fullarton and Ainley, 2000). For these students, Italian was both an academic subject they studied for university entrance exams, and their community language, and they had a very strong investment in studying the language at school.

Most students studied Italian at the school because they had an affinity with the language and culture, having been brought up speaking Italian at home. For many students, communicating in Italian was integral to their everyday living. Comments included:

> See at home I only speak Italian because my parents are both Italian and they can't string a word of English to save their lives. (Year 12 student)

> I'm part of a big family, right, so all my siblings talk Italian, right, and my brother's kids, he has got six kids and they all speak Italian as well. (Year 12 student)

Even in families where English was widely spoken at home, Italian was often the only language students could use to communicate with their grandparents. For these Year 12 students, motivation to study Italian came largely from within as part of their desire to reinforce their Italian culture and heritage and to identify with other Italian people (*ideal L2 self*). For example, reflecting her affinity with Italian language and culture, one student commented on seeing Italian documentaries on the TV: 'I go, Dad, those are my people.' Their motivation was also inevitably intertwined with informal social pressure (*ought-to L2 self*) from parents and family:

> I want to learn how to speak for my family, I want to learn how to talk with other people. It's not a burden to learn it. It's hard but it overrides the fact that it's a difficult thing to do by how much you actually want to do it. (Year 12 Italian student)

Instrumental motivational factors relating to overseas travel were also important, especially given that some students had extended family living in Italy and they had already travelled there extensively:

> Well I've been to Italy a few times. I just found it really fascinating and I'd like to go when I finish school. It's mainly for that reason that I wanted to learn another language.

Another factor, which we identified earlier with students from middle-class schools, was the enjoyment that came with becoming an effective L2 user (though some of these students were technically L1). Students were able to use Italian amongst themselves as a form of secret communication, a secret code:

> Student 1: … we were at a party once and we wanted to talk about someone that was there. [Laughter] It was the best thing ever because no one knows what we're saying.
> Student 2: I feel that, I feel that! (Year 12 students)

These Year 12 students spoke about the agency they experienced as effective L2 users ('it kind of makes us feel all powerful'), and they provided several anecdotes of informal social encounters that demonstrated this power:

> Me and my sister were at a cafe here and there were these two really gross Italian dudes and they were trying to guess how old we were. Like that's gross dude. We just turned around, oh we know what you're saying. That's terrible. Oh yuk. So gross. But so happy I know this language.

> That happened to me in Italy, right. Last time I went and I was in a store, right, and you know they have [unclear] just have the urge to talk about someone to your sister. We were doing it in English because we were in an Italian place and they started talking about us, and we're just stood there and we're like, hello. Italian, I got you. They were like, look at them. They're from Australia, they probably don't even know what they're doing here. I just looked at them and it was just like, scusa?

The Heritage Languages School: 'I only come in because I get forced to'

The Heritage Languages School provides weekend community languages for students from Years 7 to 12. The school has many centres in and around metropolitan areas using the facilities of mainstream secondary high schools. Students often travel from far beyond the suburbs in which the centres are located. The centres are government-funded and established for secondary school students from all education sectors who do not have access to languages in their mainstream schools. The role of the Heritage Languages School has become increasingly important with the decline of languages in mainstream schools.

Attending a community languages class for two hours every Saturday was a different learning experience to studying languages as part of the regular curriculum at high school, although it was a 'default' languages provision insofar as students could only enrol for a language that their own weekday high school did not provide. Many students, especially younger ones in Years 7 and 8, found it difficult to enthuse about two-hour languages lessons on a Saturday morning, which effectively prevented them from participating in pleasurable social activities, such as sport. Direct familial pressure appeared to play a role in their participation – the idea that students were being forced to attend by their parents. A group of Year 9 students in a Chinese class almost unanimously stated: 'Our parents force us to [attend]', and similar responses were found from younger Polish and Greek students: e.g. 'I only come in because I get forced to. I never really wanted to learn Greek, but I guess I have to. My parents are Greek and stuff' (Year 7 Greek student).

Social pressure (i.e. *ought-to L2 self*) to attend classes was not only applied by parents, and not only to younger students. A Polish teacher provided an anecdote of a Year 12 student who stopped attending Heritage School classes because she already had enough HSC subjects in her regular high school studies. Her parents were disappointed and so was the Polish teacher, who then attempted (successfully) to get the student to change her mind:

> I talked to her. She said I'm sorry, Miss. I am not going to do it. We wrote a letter to her in class. [Sylvia], come back. We love you. We sent the letter. A week later, Sylvia was here. She came second in HSC in Polish [in the State]. She was good.

From this Polish teacher's perspective 'very often … external motivation works better', and while some students might be resentful at the social pressure applied to them, especially at the beginning, 'they are later on very grateful' (Polish teacher, Heritage School).

This view that over time students will come to appreciate their community languages study resonated also with the perspectives of students. Some Year 9/10 Spanish students, for example, explained that while their parents forced them to attend from Year 7 and that they 'didn't want a bar of it', later when their fluency and other language skills improved, they began to understand why they were studying Spanish and compared themselves favourably with friends at school who were not studying languages. They developed a sense of purpose and could identify with and imagine themselves as legitimate members of their own language communities. A large part of this resulted from the enjoyment of mixing with other students 'of the same heritage', and this was a key motivational factor for many students.

Mixing with students 'of the same heritage' served to reinforce linguistic and cultural identity for students across all the languages groups, and it was an additional factor that made languages learning at the Heritage School so different from studying languages in high schools. Identity issues could, however, be quite complex. One Year 7/8 Greek student said that at his regular high school he was fighting to establish his Greek identity (because he had a non-Greek sounding surname, Elliott). He claimed: 'I'm sick and tired of being called the kid who says he's Greek. I want to be the kid who is Greek … people think I'm Anglo.' But when he attended the Heritage School, learning Greek in the company of similar background students, he could more clearly imagine himself as Greek. By way of contrast, one of the Year 7 Polish students provided an example of a trend in the opposite direction, where he felt more distinctly Polish at his regular high school. He explained that at the Heritage School:

> I think the teacher kind of thinks of us as Aussie because a lot of us aren't really up to – you know we're not all perfect in our Polish, so she kind of thinks of us as more these little Aussie kids trying to learn Polish. Whereas at school I kind of like – well for me anyway, I'm like the Polish kid, but I don't say anything.

Most students highlighted and valued the importance of meeting with students of similar linguistic and cultural backgrounds: 'Seeing your friends and, yeah, like communicating with them and knowing that you're all like the same, so you all get each other' (Spanish Year 8 student). For the younger students in particular, this was the counter-argument to the perceived parental coercion to participate.

For students studying their community languages, as students at De Sales and the Heritage School have demonstrated, their attitudes to and motivations for studying languages were a more personal issue than, for example, the highly motivated middle-class students in academically selective high schools featured at the beginning of this chapter. For community languages students, the motivation was not only academic success, but to better understand who they were as a member of their home language community.

Summary

How students perceive languages taught at school and their motivations for studying them are complex. A key element from the literature in recent times is the extent to which students feel they can 'invest' in studying a language at school. Our study has indicated, as with some recent overseas studies (e.g. Board and Tinsley, 2015a), that social class plays a big part in this investment. In the academically selective high schools and in the one private school in our study, students embraced languages as an academic subject. In part, this was because the schools and all the main stakeholders supported languages and provided a strong and varied languages program. Students enjoyed the languages programs, especially as they became more competent speakers of the languages and could use them informally within their peer groups. They were influenced in particular by their parents, for whom languages were often regarded as an integral part of a more affluent, middle-class lifestyle, providing important transnational human capital (see also Gerhards, Hans and Carlson, 2017). Learning Chinese in these schools provided an interesting case insofar as it was learnt primarily by Chinese-background students, but was often dropped as an academic subject in the senior school years due to the vagaries of a university entrance process which saw the language scaled down relative to other languages and subjects. Chinese retained its appeal in the earlier school years for cultural heritage reasons and for its potential in future employment contexts.

Students in low-SES comprehensive schools had few incentives to invest in the study of languages. Languages provision was minimal, and for the most part, support was lacking from other teachers and from parents. Instead, students chose to study elective subjects perceived to be less academically demanding and to have more vocational relevance. The irony was that many students in low-SES comprehensive schools already spoke community languages at home, but these were not valued in a school environment that privileged English skills.

Learning a community language at secondary school level and in weekend community language schools enabled students to identify with and imagine themselves as legitimate members of their own language communities. It also provided enjoyment and a sense of power and agency for students. While younger students were initially reluctant participants in weekend classes, with greater competency in their home language, and through mixing with peers from similar backgrounds, these students came to better appreciate their linguistic and cultural identities.

7

Language Provision in Primary Schools

As indicated in Chapter 1, the uptake of languages studies in Australia is in decline. Differences in access to languages play out the most in primary schools, as studying a language in primary school is not mandated in most Australian states, with the exception of Victoria, where nearly 97 per cent of K-6 (Kindergarten-Year 6) students now study a language. In New South Wales (NSW), however, where only 18 per cent of primary school students study a language other than English, some programs thrive and many struggle to retain students (Chen and Nordstrom, 2018; Cruickshank and Wright, 2016). Many language programs in primary schools are largely delivered as language and cultural awareness classes with exposure only to basic vocabulary and aspects of the target culture (Slaughter and Hajek, 2007). Primary languages programs in our study varied in nature with many focusing on teaching colours, numbers and songs. To a certain extent, the range of programs available in primary schools is opportunistic and they ebb and flow with available (often unpaid) personnel or additional payments from students.

Some schools, however, take a commitment to their students' learning of a language seriously: for some this is about responding to local community needs; for others it is about their understanding of an educated child and global citizenship. In a neoliberal context of school choice this latter is also for some schools a matter of marketing and differentiation. In our study there were schools that followed elements of all of these incentives, and the associated practices. Not surprisingly, how schools made choices around languages was also linked to the social-class demographic of their student population.

In this chapter we examine five examples of primary languages programs in schools where language study was taken relatively seriously and illustrate the relationship between context, including social and cultural demographics of the student population and school leadership, and the way in which the language programs were structured and taught. The case studies presented in this chapter aim to provide a deeper understanding of the aspects of the programs that supported effective languages study across a diverse range of school sectors, that is, public and private school systems, where conditions for the provision of the languages program play out differently.

As was the case with the discussions in previous chapters, data informing this chapter include lesson observation field notes and interviews with principals and teachers drawn from the five primary schools.

Differential access to language study in primary schools

Access to languages varies considerably by sectors and regions. In 2012, only 18 per cent of primary school students in NSW had access to a languages program. Access was differentially distributed across three educational systems (government, Catholic education and private independent schools) and between metropolitan and regional areas. Figure 7.1 provides a summary of the percentages of enrolments in languages programs in primary schools across sectors in the metropolitan Sydney and regional Illawarra area. Overall a larger proportion of primary students in the metropolitan area in NSW had access to a languages program. Of these students, nearly 85 per cent of the students

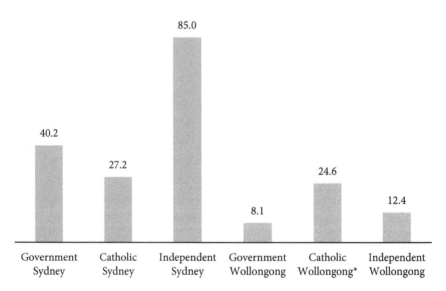

Figure 7.1 Percentage of primary school students studying languages in Sydney and Wollongong.
Source: 2011 cross-sectoral data collected *2013 data (no 2011 data available).

in private independent schools had access to a languages program compared with only 40 per cent of government school students who were able to study a language other than English. These unequal distributions of access suggest that socioeconomic status (SES) is a strong determinant of opportunities to learn a language (Wright, Cruickshank and Black, 2018). The influence of SES played out the most in the regional area, where the students in the government schools had the lowest access to learning a language other than English.

All selected case-study schools are from the metropolitan area of Sydney. The schools represent two of the three main education sectors in Australia, public and independent systems, although neither of these belong to the elite NSW Great Public Schools (GPS) or Associated Schools of NSW (CAS) (Wright et al., 2018). The three public schools draw enrolments from a diverse, multicultural community with a high proportion of LBOTE (Language Background other than English) students. They are referred to as Cheswell Primary School (Cheswell PS), Clarke Primary School (Clarke PS) and Keswick Primary School (Keswick PS) in this book. The demographic of the students in two of the government schools places them around the low and average percentiles on ICSEA (Index of Community Socio-Educational Advantage) measures of SES (Clarke PS and Cheswell PS); the third has a profile more like that of the independent schools (Keswick PS). All of these schools have very few Indigenous students. The independent schools included in this chapter will be referred to as the Sydney International School (SIS) and Dante Bilingual School (DBS). The schools charge fees and draw widely from the Sydney population in the highest economic percentile. As will be discussed below, the schools' decisions about provision of languages programs essentially reflect their responsiveness to the cultural and socioeconomic conditions of the environment within which they are situated (Kramsch, 2002; Pennycook, 2017).

Our analysis has shown that there are apparent regional and sectoral differences in the uptake of language studies (see Chapter 1). Access to languages programs is differently distributed within the same sector and across the same metropolitan area. The analysis of language provision by case-study schools demonstrates that opportunities and choices provided for language learning continue to be distinctly marked by the nature of schools, cultural heritage and SES of the parents (Wright, Cruickshank and Black, 2018). Language choices in low-SES government schools are generally limited to community language offerings because of support provided by the State Community Language Program funding. Even though the same languages may be offered across different schools, the meanings and value of learning those languages are often conceived and enacted differently. For example, while Chinese is offered as a community language at low-SES government schools, it is offered as a prestige language of trade that offers 'a marker of distinction' at the middle-class private schools (Black, Wright and Cruickshank, 2018; Wright et al., 2018).

The case-study schools

Cheswell PS is a medium-large school in the inner west of Sydney. The school draws on a multicultural community with nearly 97 per cent of the students coming from a LBOTE background (myschool.edu.au). The school has an ICSEA value of 1014, which is just above the national average (1000) with over half of the students (56 per cent) in the lowest and low medium quartiles for socio-educational advantage. There is a variety of choice of Asian and European languages offered to cater for the diversity of the local community. All students from Kindergarten to Year 6 can choose to study one of the eight languages: Chinese, Korean, Vietnamese, Arabic, Hindi, Indonesian, Greek and Spanish. Chinese, Vietnamese and Arabic are offered as a community language, providing opportunities for language maintenance and development for students with heritage family backgrounds. Chinese is offered as a LOTE (Language other than English) subject along with Hindi, Indonesian, Greek and Spanish. The school offers a Korean bilingual program where students learn curriculum topics in Korean for five hours per week. This is one of the four bilingual programs offered in NSW under the funding support provided by the National Asian Languages and Studies in Schools Program NSW (Fielding and Harbon, 2014). The principal strongly promotes an Asian perspective, including adopting 'Asian' methods in teaching Mathematics. Eleven of the teachers have undertaken professional training and gained a Graduate Certificate in Teaching Asia (from the Australian National University).

Clarke PS is a multicultural school in a low socioeconomic setting (ICSEA=941), located in the south of the Sydney metropolitan area with approximately 57 per cent of students in the lowest quartile for socio-educational advantage. According to myschool.com.au, 93 per cent of students have a language background other than English. The school offers an extensive community languages (CL) program in Chinese, Arabic, Macedonian, Greek and Maori, while Indonesian is offered to the children who do not have a heritage language offered at school. All students study a language, either their community language[1] or Indonesian. At the time of the study there were ten language teachers, some of whom were teaching part time. Two of language teachers had primary training and three were secondary language teachers who had shifted to primary. All the community language teachers were native speakers and qualified to teach languages.

Keswick PS is in a high socioeconomic setting (ICSEA=1127) south-east of the Sydney metropolitan area, with over half of the students (57 per cent) in the top quartile for socio-educational advantage (myschool.edu.au). Like the other two public schools profiled in this chapter, Keswick PS draws on a diverse student population with 66 per cent LBOTE students from forty-five nationalities, according to the school website. There are two languages offered from Kindergarten to Year 6, Chinese and Greek, both supported by the CL programs. The Greek program has been taught in the school for over twenty years. With changing population demographics, Chinese now dominates due to the high proportion of Chinese-background students in the school and funding from the China's Confucius classroom program. Non-background students can choose between Greek or Chinese. There are two Chinese teachers and one Greek teacher. The school's vision is for the Confucius classroom to become 'a hub within our local area, region and state in providing exemplary teaching and learning programs of Chinese language and culture' (myschool.edu.au).

The SIS located in central Sydney is an independent, secular, co-educational school for pre-school to Year 12. The school draws on a highly socioeconomic advantaged community (ICSEA=1148) with 75 per cent of students in the top quartile and only 31 per cent of students from language backgrounds other than English (myschool.edu.au). The school prides itself in its languages program as part of its aspiration to provide 'a globally-focused bilingual education' (myschool. edu.au). Languages studies are compulsory for all students from pre-school to Year 10 and can be chosen from a range of choices, including Chinese, Japanese, French, German, Italian and Spanish. Not surprisingly, languages chosen are of trade and cultural appeals and are promoted as 'a marker of distinction' to aspiring students, parents and the broader community (Teese, 2013; Wright et al., 2018). In addition to a rich provision of language choices, language provision in SIS is substantial, with all students across pre-school and primary years having access to a partial bilingual immersion program and a further opportunity to take up a third language in Year 7. Languages are taught by some thirty dedicated languages teachers in the Languages faculty.

---

[1] For some, such as the Chinese students, their community language is not spoken at home.

The DBS is an independent, co-educational primary school for Preparatory to Year 6 with the smallest proportion of LBOTE students (25 per cent, the ICSEA score was not available). It was the first school in Australia to provide a bilingual and bicultural education in English and Italian (myschool.edu.au). Although Italian provides a pathway for 60 per cent of students with Italian backgrounds[2] to develop their heritage language, the school promotes its language provision for its contribution to 'a global existence' (myschool.edu.au), describing language learning as a form of social capital in the global job market (Wright et al., 2018). Italian is offered as a distinct key learning area (KLA) and is studied for two and a half hours per day. In addition, it is integrated into other learning areas such as Science and Technology, and Human Society and Its Environment (HSIE) and Personal Development, Health and Physical Education (PDHPE). Each class has two teachers: an English and an Italian teacher. The English teacher has the responsibility for teaching English and Maths while the Italian teacher takes charge of all the other areas such as Science and Technology, HSIE, PDHPE and Creative Arts.

In the sections below, we discuss contextual factors that have contributed to the nature of language provision across the different schools.

Contextual factors affecting language provision

Policy initiatives

In Australia, each state or territory determines whether and how languages should be mandated. Victoria, for example, provides the most comprehensive and well-resourced education policy (Kohler, 2017). Its recently developed policy, *Languages – expanding your world: A plan to implement the Victorian Government's vision for languages education 2013–2025*, requires for the first time that all government schools provide a Foundation (Pre) level languages program as one of the eight key learning areas by 2015 (Department of Education and Early Childhood Development, 2013). It further sets the target for all government schools to provide a languages program and award the new Certificate of Language Proficiency at Year 10 by 2025. Such a supportive policy environment has seen a rapid increase in the percentage of primary school students studying a language from 62.6 per cent in 2013 to 83.4 per cent in 2017 (Department of Education and Training, 2017).

---

[2]　Some students have Italian family members of the third or fourth generation.

In NSW, however, the policy context is generally not one that specifically favours language study in the primary school. This is largely a consequence of a policy environment which does not mandate or prioritize languages study as a KLA (Board of Studies NSW, 2013). Decisions about whether or what languages to teach remain within 'Local Schools, Local Decisions' (see Chapter 1 for detailed discussion). Despite this unfavourable policy context, our analysis has found for the schools in our study, their schools' initiation, expansion and maintenance of languages programs have been in part a result of their principals' eagerness to respond to the ideals promoted by policy and curriculum initiatives at the time. For some schools this was particularly important as the survival and the quality of their programs was dependent on government funding, following policy commitments in relation to the maintenance of community languages and bilingual education. For others, recent policy priorities such as *Australia in the Asian Century* (Australian Government, 2012) presented an opportunity to promote Asian languages such as Chinese and Korean. For example, in the following quote, the principal of Cheswell PS makes reference to the place of Chinese and Korean in the school curriculum in relation to the opportunities promoted in 'the Asian Century' policy.

> We're trying to be an early adopter of Asian perspectives and we think that we can serve both of those things by the sort of examples I've just given you because you're getting the Asian perspective.

Keswick's provision of a language program was strongly associated with the value of intercultural understanding – learning a language, and through it, to develop cultural understanding (Black et al., 2018). The national curriculum highlights the importance and value of intercultural understanding as a cross-curriculum priority: *Asia and Australia's engagement with Asia* (Australian Curriculum, Assessment and Reporting Authority, 2013). Asian perspectives are regarded as a priority and a gateway for intercultural understanding. Keswick PS embraced this new requirement enthusiastically by integrating the work of language teachers with that of the generalist primary teachers: 'bring in the language teachers who are involved in that at every step of the way, and particularly those into cultural understandings' (Interview with the principal, Keswick PS). At this school the national curriculum policy provided the leverage to elevate the status of the languages program and particular (Asian) languages. In both schools, however, principals were the key drivers, who had considerable influence in the uptake of language provisions (see Chapter 2 for more detailed discussion).

The influence of the global environment around languages was particularly pronounced in the precedence given to languages study in the private schools in the study (Singh and Qi, 2013). Wright et al. (2018) point out that 'international mindedness' or what Resnik (2009) calls 'civic multiculturalism' – 'the capacity to see the world from the point of view of the other' (Wright et al., 2018: 110) – reflects the aspirations of middle-class parents. This latter position was more evident in the ways in which languages were promoted by the independent schools in our study. For example, on the SIS school's website,

> we believe that students acquire a global perspective through diversity and intercultural understanding. Our languages-learning program is a key plank in this process. Children develop an understanding of themselves and others through languages, music and art.

The attachment of language study to membership of a global culture is largely influenced by the demographic of the school (Wright et al., 2018). As with the programs at SIS and DBS, the school accords the learning of languages a central place in its educational program with a strong focus on the development of students' awareness and knowledge of other cultures. Its bilingual and bicultural education served as an important means to 'empower students for a global existence' (from DBS website).

The school community

Across all case-study schools, the language programs enjoyed strong support from the school leadership and had the acceptance and support of all staff and influential members of the school community (e.g. parents). The principals' supportive attitudes were a key influence in determining the provision of the languages programs (see Chapter 2 for detailed analysis of the principals' attitudes) and how they were resourced and enacted. In the case of the two government schools, Cheswell PS and Clarke PS, the choices of languages were the result of the schools' deliberate decisions to respond to the multicultural community within which the schools were situated. The principal from Cheswell PS, for example, was strongly supportive of the community languages program, in part because of his desire to cater for 'a 95 per cent Asian-Australian community': 'What I've taken the opportunity of doing is I invest into the community language program, by that I'd say it's meant for background kids only.'

It was evident that some principals' positive attitudes were closely associated with their strong beliefs in the value of studying languages in producing a particular kind of an educated child. For example, the principal at Cheswell PS commented:

> You're not really educated if you don't have a language. It doesn't matter even how well you do with a language, but you're a different human being because you studied the language.

The parents' attitude towards language learning also played another influential role in sustaining the growth of a languages program. In all of the schools discussed in this chapter, parent support was central to the survival of the program. For the two private schools, the DBS and SIS, parents chose the schools because of their particular programs, both of which were committed to languages and the integration of languages into other subject areas. In the three government primary schools, the languages chosen made sense for their local context (Pufahl and Rhodes, 2011; Rhodes, 2014). Where the languages taught reflect those in the community, parental support was strong, as in the case of Keswick, where the school draws from a high percentage of LBOTE student population: 'and then the ones that don't speak anything other than English at home, I think they think that it's a great opportunity to learn another language.' (Principal, Keswick PS). See Chapter 4 for more on parents' liking of language programs at schools.

Funding and resources

Adequate funding of resources was a primary factor contributing to the schools' ability to provide and grow languages programs. For most of the government primary schools in the study, provision of languages programs was supported by different funding sources. They included federal government funding, state government funding and programs and overseas government funding. For example, the federal government's commitment to the National Asian Language and Studies in Schools Program (NALSSP) (2008–9 to 2011–12) gave rise to a significant increase in the number of government schools providing languages programs in the four targeted Asian languages: Chinese, Indonesian, Japanese and Korean. The majority of the languages programs taught in our selected government primary schools were funded by the state government's community languages programs. The NSW Bilingual Schools Program provided further funding for four schools in NSW to develop bilingual programs in early primary years. The Bilingual Korean Program at Cheswell PS emerged as a result of the state government's initiative to promote priority Asian languages. With the support of the state government's funding, the school was provided with one full-time bilingual teacher and one volunteer/part-time language assistant (Fielding and Harbon, 2014).

Both European and Asian countries have also had a history of providing funding and other forms of support for the teaching of their national language in schools. More recently, for example, the Chinese government-sponsored Confucius Institute has provided money and personnel to support the teaching of Chinese in Australian schools under the Expanding Horizons Asian Program (Board of Studies NSW, 2013). This program substantially supported Keswick PS's provision of its Chinese program. Being one of the only two sponsored primary Confucius classrooms in NSW, the school was able to elevate its Chinese provision to be one of the largest in the region.

> Last year in June the Confucius Classroom was introduced in the Keswick PS. It is a collaboration/joint venture between the NSW DEC and the Office of Chinese Language Council International (Hanban). Through this program all students at Keswick PS have the opportunity to learn about the Chinese language and culture. The plan is that Keswick PS to become a hub within the local area. Goals are to establish sister school relationships, promote Chinese language and culture and to provide opportunities for those students who don't have access to instruction in the Chinese language via video conferencing facilities. The school also received 30 iPads and a big TV as well (not used yet). (Lesson observation field notes)

While regular languages classes received about $280 per year, the Confucius classroom was provided with more than $9,000 of resources from the Confucius Institute (Principal, Keswick PS). The substantial financial support has provided the school with additional technology, teaching materials and professional development opportunities.

The vulnerability of languages provision in government schools as a result of its dependence on external funding has been discussed by a number of studies (e.g. Liddicoat et al., 2007; Pufahl and Rhodes, 2011). This means that the status and existence of the language programs described above could be threatened if funding were to be withdrawn. Recently the arrangement of the Confucius Classroom is being reviewed by the NSW DEC (see Gil, 2018). The outcome of this review could place considerable limitations on the continued growth of the Confucius Classroom at Keswick PS.

Support for language provision was also evident in the availability of dedicated teaching spaces. Having access to dedicated space means that teachers can decorate their rooms with language-specific wall prints, which are crucial for the creation of a language-rich environment for language learning (Asia Education

Foundation, 2012; EREBUS Consulting Partners, 2002). Description of such a designated space for languages can be found in our field notes: 'We saw the lesson taking place in the "Greek Room," a designated room for Greek language classes. The classroom was well decorated with posters featuring various Greek language forms (alphabet, colours etc.)' (Keswick, Year 6 field notes). At Clarke each language also had its own dedicated room. This provided the students with the opportunity to display students' work: 'The [Indonesian] room at Clarke is set up with posters, artwork, books and things the kids have made. There is also a computer' (Field notes, Clarke PS).

Having dedicated teaching space also meant that the teachers had good and consistent access to reliable Information and Communication Technology (ICT) infrastructure – interactive whiteboards – which would not have otherwise been possible. The use of smartboard, tablets and Internet was strongly promoted in all the case-study schools. These technologies provide access to free language resources such as videos and online language programs, connecting learners to interactive learning resources and opportunities. Teachers valued the easy access to technology as it made it possible to 'look at clips or … virtual tours' (Italian teacher, DBS).

The resources and infrastructure in the government primary schools we have described above were far in advance of those available in most primary schools, where dedicated language rooms and technology resources would be very much the exception. The resources available in the two independent case-study schools were even more impressive and afforded a richer array of learning opportunities. For example, the digital technologies available at SIS included a video resources subscription with the Yabla computer-assisted language-learning program, and at DBS, class blogs and iPads for all students enabled exposure to rich and authentic input necessary for languages studies. The available rich array of resources in the private schools was evident in the field notes of the Year 1 French class at SIS: 'When we arrive there are children outside the room waiting to go in. Just across the hallway is a window into a little room which has a 3D printer and some 3D printed figurines on display!' (Field notes, SIS).

Enactment of language provision

In this section, we discuss ways in which language provision was enacted across different case studies. As noted by Norris (1999), the quality of the languages program is recognized as the most important element underpinning the success of the languages program. Successful language programs are substantial and build upon 'gradual, carefully planned, and well-articulated curriculum development' (Donato and Tucker, 2010: 127). The programs are integrated into other discipline areas and are taught by well-qualified teachers who apply effective pedagogical practices appropriate to their learners. Below we discuss these factors that contribute towards how the languages programs are enacted.

Provision of hours

According to a number of sources, where language programs are timetabled with ample instruction time, students are provided with regular exposure to the language in use (Asia Education Foundation, 2012; Rhodes, 2014). The Center for Applied Second Language Studies (2007), for example, recommends provision of a minimum of 83 hours over one year, equating to a total of nearly 5,000 minutes of instruction time.

Finding time for languages programs presents a significant challenge in primary schools: the 'overcrowded curriculum' is a common theme in the literature on teacher perceptions of their work (Fielding and Harbon, 2014), and schools are facing increasing pressure to perform in high stakes testing in the areas of literacy and numeracy (Paolino, 2012; Scarino, Scrimgeour and Kohler, 2012; de Silva, 2005). While these were reasons espoused in many of our schools for the limited time allocated to languages study, all of the programs in our case-study government schools provided language instruction for a minimum of two to five hours per week per language. At Clarke PS, for example, languages were taught to all Years (K-6) for two hours per week, usually in two separate one-hour classes. At Cheswell PS, the Korean bilingual program was delivered through a Content Language Integrated Learning (CLIL) approach where students studied mainstream content in Korean for five hours per week. At Keswick PS, students received two hours of languages per week, except Kindergarten students who receive thirty minutes. There was also one hour per week for each student to be exposed to Chinese and Chinese culture in the Confucius classroom.

However, the way time is organized has a significant impact on the status and consequently the vitality of a languages program. As languages are yet to gain their status as a KLA in the primary curriculum, languages are often taught during the period when classroom teachers are released from face to face time (RFF) for marking, team planning and professional learning (at Clarke PS, for example). This timetabling practice continues to marginalize the provision of languages programs in government schools.

Language provision at SIS was substantial, increasing from forty minutes per day in Kindergarten to eighty minutes per day as part of the partial immersion program in Years 1–6: 'so effectively a quarter of the curriculum is spent in the language' (principal). The students had two teachers (broadly, three home classes of twenty-five students which break into four language groupings). With the languages taught exclusively in the target language, students received a total of about 1,000 hours of exposure to languages by the end of Year 6 (Principal, SIS). Students at the bilingual DBS were addressed in languages at all times in the classroom or the playground throughout the day. Such provision of hours reflects the schools' strong commitment to languages, in contrast to the practice in most NSW primary schools where students are taught for only thirty to forty minutes in a typical language program (Board of Studies, 2013).

Coordination, integration and planning

As Norris (1999) points out, language proficiency does not simply come about through quantity of time spent on instruction, but the type and quality of the program. There were a range of programs provided across the case-study schools, most of which had involved an integrated language program. However, the degree of integration varied from full immersion programs at DBS and the K-2 Korean program at Cheswell PS, to partial immersion programs at SIS. At other schools, some languages (e.g. Indonesian and Greek) were linked with topics taught within another key learning area, that is, HSIE (Human Society and Its Environment).

Provision of immersion programs is rare in NSW and Australia, with only fifty schools across Australia offering languages in an immersive style (Moloney, 2008). Nevertheless, Norris (1999) argues that it is only immersion style programs in primary schools that enable students to develop the most sustained and extensive progress towards proficiency. The bilingual program offered at DBS provides an example of an intensive, immersion program where both languages are developed simultaneously (Fielding and Harbon, 2014). Fielding and Harbon (2014) argue that this dual language program or CLIL program is the most successful for LOTE teaching and learning. The following interview extract is an illustration of how the dual language program was utilized at DBS:

> So the way the school works is that every class has got an Italian and an English teacher. The English teacher teaches Maths and English, and the Italian teacher teaches all the other areas, like Science and Technology, HSIE, PHPD (physical education, health and personal development), Creative Arts, all in Italian. (Kindergarten teacher, DBS)

At Cheswell PS generalist class teachers and the Korean language teachers collaboratively planned to teach Korean as an immersion program, beginning by using the interdisciplinary affordances of the NSW Department of Education's Connected Outcomes Groups (COGs) and then of the new Australian curriculum. As the principal points out in the following quote, this has not been a seamless process but the supportive environment has meant that issues of ownership have been negotiated and, as discussed in Chapter 4, the generalist teachers have embraced learning Korean as part of their role in the process.

> Well, we teach it [Korean] through the curriculum. We teach a content-based one. It's usually out of the social sciences. Of course for the first few years, we were using the COGs units, the connected outcomes groups, which are in the social sciences, a bit of science in there. But we've decided to be early adopters of the national curriculum … So … it's a normal Australian curriculum that the children will be getting and we negotiate and determine which outcomes are taught in the language classes and which outcomes are taught by the home base teacher. Sometimes there are ownership issues there when – you know, primary teachers are quite fanatical about reporting and accuracy and sometimes they're a little bit they lack confidence in giving an area to another person. But we had to overcome it and are overcoming those things. (Principal, Cheswell PS)

Where the curriculum integration was partial, the teaching of languages was taught following the curriculum topics of other subjects, usually HSIE. At Clarke PS, for example, language teaching was embedded within social science curriculum topics such as natural disasters: 'We learn about the continent, that some major countries Japan, China, Philippines, Indonesia, India, Pakistan and all these countries, and the last one is, the last passage is about damage (i.e. earthquakes).' Languages were seen to support mainstream learning in the school.

At SIS, there was a concerted effort to develop a sustained integrated program where the units of the core curriculum were carefully selected for integration, so that language learning occurred in the context of History, Geography, Science and Creative Art. What this program looked like in practice is explained by the SIS principal:

We take on the HSIE. So, for instance, we look at – we take bits of science. We do a little bit of maths, a bit of numeracy as well embedded in that. We do history and we do the – we do a lot of environment. So we do natural disasters in Year 6. We'll do ancient people in Year 6. So the Italians do the Romans, the Japanese will look at theirs and the French et cetera. In Year 2 we do a lot of science, we do the water cycle, the body, things like that. (Interview with the principal, SIS)

According to Fielding and Harbon (2014), integration is in its strongest form where the languages curriculum is negotiated to incorporate learning outcomes from other subject learning areas. In a strongly integrated curriculum, languages are not a standalone curriculum. Outcomes are negotiated and determined by language and mainstream teachers collaboratively. In the Korean bilingual program at Cheswell PS, the syllabus was taught by the generalist classroom teachers and others by the language teachers: 'It's a normal Australian curriculum that the children will be getting and we negotiate and determine which outcomes are taught in the language classes and which outcomes are taught by the home base teacher' (Principal, Cheswell PS).

Fielding and Harbon (2014) point out that such an integrated program often addresses the timetabling challenges discussed previously. However, the integrated delivery mode requires extensive collaborative planning and creation of additional resources. The principal at Cheswell PS commented on the challenges of creating bilingual materials and resources for integrated units: 'and the biggest problem for us is actually developing material and resources and whatever it is'. The technicality of specific curriculum topics also posed some additional challenges. At Clarke PS, for example, Indonesian teachers found the imbalance between the student's language proficiency and demands required to learn about topics that contain 'really technical scientific stuff'. The teachers adapted the unit by shortening the period of CLIL instruction and focused instead on the conversational language: 'We deliberately do a small unit so in terms of a ten-week term, with Antarctica; it might only last six weeks so that the last three weeks we can just do more conversational stuff' (Indonesian teacher, Clarke PS).

Curriculum articulation and continuity

The first K-6 languages syllabuses were not developed in NSW until 2003 and so primary schools had to develop their own programs (NSW Education Standards Authority, 2019). As indicated in a report for the Australian Council of State

School Organisations, primary languages programs are often fragmented and lacked continuity (Australian Council of State School Organisations, 2007). There has also been a concern about the lack of curricular alignment between languages programs through the years of schooling and the cumulative development of the target languages (Board of Studies NSW, 2013).

The lack of articulation between different levels of schooling and continuity into secondary schools has been considered a significant factor that impedes the sustainability of programs in Australia and elsewhere (Hunt et al., 2008, and see Chapter 8). Our case-study schools had overcome articulation difficulties to a certain extent within the school. At Cheswell PS, for example, there was a continuation of languages – Chinese is offered as a LOTE subject in Years 2, 3 and 5. At Keswick PS, there was a coordinated effort to consider what to cover across different years, as is reflected in the interview extract below:

> A lot of the time it's a similar or a two-year cycle. They always start with the little ones and they do numbers and colours and things like that but they do look at the ... there are some guidelines and then when the new Australian curriculum comes out, hopefully there'll be more but it's very much at a school level. I haven't seen their programs yet for this term but that's what they've done in the past and they'll pick on greetings and they'll work on those and families and then clothes and seasons and all that sort of thing. (Principal, Keswick PS)

This interview extract, however, exemplifies a limited conception of language learning as constituted of some commonly used vocabulary for basic conversations. The commitment to curricular continuity was most evident in the private schools. At SIS the school was strongly committed to progression in languages learning across different years of primary schooling. This was ensured through the creation of a carefully mapped and well-articulated Scope and Sequence plan. This curriculum design specified what was to be taught and the order in which it was taught within and across year levels in keeping with 'what we believe kids of each age need to know' (SIS languages coordinator) and from the SIS Italian head teacher: 'We've also got a grammar scope and sequence that everything is embedded through unit of work and through content.' As the head teacher pointed out, the 'connected' curriculum helped ensure the overall coherence of the language programs.

> What I expect from the staff is, whatever they do, then at the end of the term, we have the program with the activities and they tick what they've done in that programme, annotate it and then, for example, they would highlight

which … what the topic is and see which grammar bits fit into that particular topic. So, it's all connected. (Head of Department Early Learning and Primary Languages, SIS)

The disconnect between primary and secondary school languages programs has been highlighted as a significant barrier to the continuity of language study (Australian Council of State School Organisations, 2007). This is largely due to the fact that primary and secondary schools in Australia operate independently even in schools which offer K-12 education on the same campus. At DBS there was some concern about suitable high schools where students could go to sustain their development in Italian after a significant period of bilingual study in Italian and English. In our case-study schools some deliberate efforts had been made to ensure continuity to language study into secondary schools. At Cheswell PS, for example, two memorandums of understanding were signed with local high schools to facilitate continuation of language study in Korean and Chinese.

Language pedagogies

There was a large variation in the quality of languages provision across all of the primary schools in the study. Primary languages programs in our study varied in nature ranging from tokenistic provision of commonly used vocabulary (e.g. colours, numbers, etc.) and basic conversation skills, to substantial provision of partial immersion and full immersion programs as described above. There was further difference in the opportunities and kind of learning experience provided in the government schools and well-resourced private schools.

Pedagogy has been a subject of a sociological analysis in education. Within the sociology of education, Bernstein (2003), for example, points out that any pedagogic practice can be considered as 'a relay of culture' – 'a uniquely human device for both the reproduction and the production of culture' (p. 196). In the field of language provision, Black et al. (2018) make reference to 'classed pedagogies', arguing that there is classed difference in pedagogic orientations to the teaching of languages.

Bernstein (2003) describes two types of pedagogic practice: traditional, knowledge-oriented and progressive, child-centred, with each orienting to different ways of making meaning. We found many examples of more traditional, knowledge-oriented pedagogic practice in teachers' reflections of their pedagogic approach and the lesson observation notes in the low-SES schools (i.e. Cheswell PS and Clarke PS). For example, the Chinese teacher in Cheswell PS described a route to languages acquisition as one that began with 'building up their vocabulary first and then gradually introduc(ing) some sentences or grammar thing into it'. The Macedonian teacher at Clarke PS, while electing to engaging students in learning the language through poems, had based her pedagogy on rote-learnt activities. As the extract below suggests, the teacher strongly believed that memorization – 'learning off by heart' – was an effective way to acquire a second language.

> If they start from Kindergarten we have very strong program, very strong oral program with the children. I do lots of drama, poems, so lots of learning off by heart things like little poems. In Kindergarten in my class they are supposed to know 100 poems until the end of the year. They are short ones, one stanza or something, but they do know them, both poems and songs which they have to learn off by heart. So by Year 1 when they start to do really a bit harder work, a bit harder means more copying and things like that, they will then see the difference and they will see the difference between the letters in the English alphabet and Macedonian azbuka or the same letters, different sounds, things like that. (Macedonian teacher, Clarke PS)

The words 'learning off by heart' and 'copying' undoubtedly encode a particular form of language-learning experience that was teacher-dominant with a strong orientation to rote learnt and memorized materials. What was relayed in this form of pedagogic practice was knowledge to be transmitted, and the hierarchical pedagogic relation between the teacher and students. In the private schools, on the other hand, we found a different kind of pedagogic orientation, one that centred around more meaningful learning outcomes, opportunities for target language use and supportive learning environments. This is evident from the extract below:

> My Year 6s were doing the Roman Empire and they have written a ... they had to pretend whether they were a slave or a gladiator or a pleb or a [pagizio] and they had to, over the term, write about them. My name is, they had to be a [unclear] Roman name, I live in a domus. You should see it. Then they had to pretend they were a soldier in the Roman army. They had to write a letter to their mum and dad saying ... here I ... I said 'do you guys realise what you've just done'? Then they're going to present it again tomorrow. They're going to come dressed up and present 'I am this person'. It's crazy. It's amazing. Even I don't realise it sometimes what we've got until I see it again when I film them. (Head of Department, Early Learning and Primary Languages, SIS)

This illustrates a different form of learning experience and a different way of making meaning, which was absent in the data collected from the low-SES schools. Core to this pedagogic practice are students who are placed at the centre of the learning process. Language learning was supported through role play and authentic learning activity (i.e. writing to your parent). There was a strong element of intellectual engagement and creativity, which resembles the kind of pedagogic orientation often found in socioeconomically advantaged schools (Black et al., 2018). This form of learning experience was supplemented by a rich provision of extra-curriculum activities such as assemblies and performances, providing additional opportunities for meaningful engagement with the target language. Cultural engagement contributed positively towards the languages being seen as a core part of the school's curriculum, thus creating an effective learning environment that supports and fosters the interest in learning the languages. This is illustrated in the following extract:

> We have assemblies; we have performance assemblies every Wednesday for home class and languages and we all have to do a performance during the year. The kids get on stage. No English is spoken and yet everyone else is just listening to Japanese, but they've got no idea what it's meaning. But somehow, the culture of the school is that you're respectful and somehow they understand it. (Head of Department, Early Learning and Primary Languages, SIS)

As argued by Opie (2006), languages can be learnt more effectively when learners are able to see the meaningful connection of the target language to their lives and have opportunities to experience it outside of the classroom. As well as classroom interactions, the private schools in our study promoted the use of languages outside the classroom through a range of language-learning opportunities, including language camps, excursions and exchange programs. Annual language camps at SIS offered an immersive experience for students to interact in, and connect with, the languages:

> So, Years 4, 5 and 6 we take them away for three days at different sites. All the Italians are together, all the Germans, the Japanese. So, a home-class teacher comes with us to help us, to be our assistants, but the camp is all done in that language. They come and they help us. There's bonding. So, yeah, it's pretty unique I think. Pretty unique place. (Head of Department, Early Learning and Primary Languages, SIS)

When students are provided with opportunities to interact with target language speakers in the form of language camps, the desire for learning languages can be generated and programs are enhanced (Asia Education Foundation, 2012; EREBUS Consulting Partners, 2002; Norris, 1999). Other opportunities such as overseas exchange trips offered at DBS provided enriching experience that was of significant benefits to students' development of language fluency:

> The fact that they have the experience in the land where Italian is spoken just makes magic things happen because it just means so much to them. Once they realise, now I know how much I know, people there can understand, I can communicate, I can make myself understood. How lovely is this? (Italian teacher, DBS)

As remarked by the teacher at DBS, immersion activities such as these encouraged and stimulated motivation to study a language and were an effective means of promoting continuation of languages study.

> When they came back they were like different children. Their Italian just blossomed because I think, even though they practise, practise, practise in here, when they go there and really feel the communicative need of using it, it comes out, all the Italian which was kind of hidden inside them because they don't make the effort 100 per cent every day, obviously. (Italian teacher, DBS)

It is evident that social class features strongly in the enactments of language pedagogy between the schools in ways that language provision is enacted pedagogically. Both private schools, SIS and DBS, had extensive overseas exchange visits, none of which were available in the government case-study schools, nor could be afforded by most of the parents. The variety of enriching learning opportunities available in private schools confirms Wright et al.'s (2018) claim that language provision continues to widen the gap brought about by social class.

Outcomes and continual progress/assessment in languages

A key driver of well-articulated and sequenced language programs is the development of students' communicative proficiency (Norris, 1999; Pufahl and Rhodes, 2011). The success of languages programs therefore entails the embedding of assessment that reflects language progression from the curriculum: 'I'm saying, well if they're getting three hours or more then you really should be assessing this the same as we assess everything else we do in this school' (Principal, Cheswell PS).

In Australia there is an established assessment for languages at Senior Secondary Level through the Collaborative Curriculum and Assessment Framework for Languages (CCAFL) (Australian Curriculum, Assessment and

Reporting Authority, 2011). There was some interest in evidencing and profiling the achievements of students studying Asian priority languages supported by the NALSSP (e.g. Hill et al., 2004; Scarino et al., 1998). Much of the focus, however, was on the nature of student achievement in each of the NALSSP targeted languages at Years 6/7, 10 and 12 (Kohler and Mahnken, 2010). Our analysis suggests that some case-study schools had clear expectations of what students should accomplish in the language at different year levels. However, there did not seem to be consistent assessment practices that measured what students were capable of achieving at each stage. As is evident in the interview extract below, the Greek teacher at Keswick PS spoke of indicators of students' language achievements using general terms such as 'half a page', 'a full-scale page' and 'to write and to say it as well':

> By stage 3, to be able at least to ... I'd be very happy if they're able to write and say at least half a page, but independently without me helping them. To be able at least to write something about themselves. You know half a full scale page by the end of Year 6, and to actually speak it as well. So by stage 3 they should be able to have the basics at least and talk about themselves at least, without any help from me though, independently. To write and to say it as well. (Greek teacher, Keswick PS)

Our case-study schools in the private sector were again the exception. At SIS and DBS, where languages study was mandated, there were well-established assessment procedures in place to monitor students' progress towards the indicators specified in the school's languages program.

> We'll expose them to a lot but there's what we call core, is what we expect them to be able to produce. We have indicators that we assess these kids on. So at the beginning of every term we know that somewhere in that term we are going to assess the kids by looking how they cope with the particular task in class ... That assessment informs us on how we should be continuing to teach but also what level that kid is able to reach or has been reaching and, therefore we can give them a grade and a report on that. We keep samples and we often meet as a group to monitor those samples as well so that we're on about the same page. (Languages coordinator, SIS)

It is apparent from the quote above that the schools have established a systematic benchmarking system to describe, report and monitor students' language achievements. DBS adopted a comprehensive benchmarking framework based on the Common European Framework of Reference for Languages: 'We are the only case in, not just in Australia, probably around the world, where we have devised a benchmark system for a bilingual student in this' (Italian teacher, DBS).

Now what we have done from this year onwards, we are at the bottom of our program, we put the European Framework, the level of the European Framework and we achieved it, we give them feedback according to that and not according to [unclear]. It's the only way to go. (Italian teacher, DBS)

Summary

This chapter has discussed social, cultural and economic factors that influence the access to, and enactment and assessment of, language provision. All our case-study schools have achieved some success in sustaining languages provision. As indicated in other chapters, this chapter demonstrates that the socioeconomic and cultural nature of the context is a strong determinant influencing the status of the program, the support and quality of the program, and the students' continual progress. Significantly our analysis shows that access to language provision differs between the sectors and schools in the ways languages programs are provided and enacted pedagogically. Our study demonstrates that social class strongly influences provision of hours, resources, the quality of learning opportunities and language-learning experiences. Our examination of programs in practice also points to the issues and challenges even the best school-based language programs face and from our analysis how programs in government/ state schools are much more vulnerable to the vagaries of policy, funding and staff changes.

The findings of the study have several implications for pedagogic practice. Given that a language program has both a concrete tangible existence and intangible existence, the design and management of language programs should reflect not only what it is but what it symbolizes and is evolving towards (Pennington and Hoekje, 2010). A vision of where the program is headed, what its potential is, projections and strategies for achieving this may help us redress the disturbing decline of the languages program in primary schools in Australia.

8

Secondary School Languages

Background

The issues confronting secondary school languages education are depressingly similar across English-speaking countries despite the vast differences in educational systems, syllabus and organizational structures (Christian, Pufahl and Rhodes, 2005). All share a decline in numbers of students taking languages for their final years of schooling and an absence of ways to reverse this decline. There is also growing social inequality in access to language learning, which is often related to the perceived devaluing of languages study in the wider community. Languages are being squeezed out of the school curriculum by other subjects, and the questions of which languages, how many languages and the status or value attached to these languages haunt most conversations about languages policy and practice. In addition to these shared issues, there is also the retreat in Australia from the 1980s policies of multiculturalism and the parallel failure to take into account the growth of community languages in the broader community. In this chapter, the narrative threads of languages study in secondary schools, described in Chapter 1, are developed. We present an alternative account of the decline of secondary school languages to that commonly taken in the media of blaming student and community attitudes or teacher shortages (Stein-Smith, 2019). We examine instead the failure of educational systems to address SES factors in the shift to comprehensive schooling in the 1970s and the failure of educational systems to account for language fluency gained outside the classroom with community languages. This chapter compares how these issues have been addressed through case studies of individual schools.

The chapter raises several questions. What percentage of students can realistically be expected to continue languages study to Year 12? How can uptake increase and what outcomes should be achieved? How can social inequality of access to languages study be addressed? How can continuity be achieved in languages study from primary to secondary school and then through secondary schooling? To what extent can different levels of fluency and entry points be catered for in the stages of schooling?

For many students, secondary school is the first time they get to learn languages in depth; a phenomenon which has historically been the situation in many countries (Tinsley and Board, 2017). On the other hand, secondary school is also a contested place where languages continue to struggle for recognition and survival in competition with higher-status STEM subjects or less 'difficult' and more 'relevant' subjects (Rhodes and Pufahl, 2010; Tinsley and Board, 2017). This has particularly been the case in Australia in mid- to low-SES government comprehensive and non-government schools.

Although most Australian students attend government schools, attendance at non-government schools has increased from 22 per cent in 1980 to 25 per cent in 2013 (Ho, 2015). NSW government secondary schools have become differentiated, with forty-seven selective academic or semi-selective schools, and there is now consequently more segmentation in terms of class and ethnicity (Ho, 2015). These changes coincided with the devolution of some administrative responsibility and decision-making to local schools, dezoning and competition for enrolments, but greater central control of curriculum and external testing.

The structure of comprehensive schooling in Australia is that the first two years, usually Years 7 and 8, serve as a general introduction to curriculum areas with little choice of subjects. In NSW during these years, students must complete 100 hours of languages study. In Years 9 and 10 languages study may be offered as an elective. However, languages compete with more 'practical' electives such as Drama, Art and Photography and with text-based electives such as Commerce. In the senior years, Years 11 and 12, students specialize in five or six subjects for their Year 12 examination and tertiary entry. Within the comprehensive system, the NSW government encouraged the establishment of specialist schools such as technology, performing arts and sports high schools. This has enshrined parental 'choice' in the education of their children, embracing a neoliberal market orientation and competition between schools. Between 1998 and 2002, the NSW government established eighteen languages specialist high schools in an attempt to halt the decline in languages study (Vinson, Esson and Johnston, 2002).

Other attempts to reverse the decline in languages (see Chapter 1) included the broadening of curriculum options in Years 11 and 12 by introducing 'beginner' courses for students who had only done the mandatory 100 hours in junior secondary school. The Australian government, in addition, launched two major programs to increase uptake of Asian languages: the National Asian

Languages and Studies Strategy in Australia Schools (NALSAS, 1994–2002) and the National Asian Languages and Studies in Schools Program (NALSSP, 2009). Like other governments across Australia, NSW expanded the number of languages that students could take in Years 11 and 12 in response to the impact of Australia's post-war immigration program: first Italian and Modern Greek and then another twenty-two 'community' languages. These subjects provided a key pathway for students whose parents often had limited access to education to access tertiary study: around 80 per cent of students from community language backgrounds in low-SES secondary schools were studying 'heritage' rather than traditional and modern languages in the 1980s (Teese and Polesel, 2003).

Having learners with language proficiency gained outside the curriculum mixed with students whose only access to the language is in the classroom is an issue now confronting languages teachers in North America and the UK. The most recent Language Trends report found that the increase in the first group of learners is masking the crisis of decline in 'traditional' languages (Tinsley and Dolezal, 2018). The issue of how to credit language proficiency gained outside the school without disadvantaging other students is a key issue. A policy shift which was intended to increase the uptake of languages by students from English-speaking backgrounds in NSW in Year 12 has had the opposite effect of further diminishing all languages programs in low-SES secondary schools. Concerns were raised in a major review of Years 11 and 12 that this gave students with a community language an 'unfair advantage' as they had gained their fluency outside the classroom and that having 'background' students in languages classes deterred English-speaking-background students enrolling (Department of Training and Education Coordination, 1997). It was determined that individual languages would all be scaled separately. This negative reaction to community languages also led to the establishment of separate curriculum and syllabus for 'background' speakers. In NSW, for example, students in four key Asian languages were allocated to 'background', 'heritage', 'beginner' or 'continuer' courses, depending on their home background and amount of exposure to the language.

What's happening with languages in the contemporary landscape?

Government support for multiculturalism, community languages and 'language for all' was encapsulated in the National Languages Policy (Lo Bianco, 1987). Since then, neoliberal policies of choice and marketplace competition in education have increased social inequalities in access to languages study. At the time of this study, only three of the eighteen languages specialist secondary schools established in the 1990s remain, all in higher-SES areas. In 2000, there were sixteen languages faculties with head teachers in the Sydney and Wollongong government and Catholic secondary schools in the ninety-nine schools in our study. By 2018, our data show this had shrunk to one in Catholic schools, four in government schools, three of which were selective and two were high-SES girls' schools. This compared with eighteen languages head teachers and languages departments in the thirty-six Sydney independent schools. The low access to languages is most evident in the regional city, Wollongong, where SES is lowest: mandatory languages study in Year 7 and/or 8 plummeted to 7 per cent of students taking elective languages in Year 9. Enrolments in Asian languages in NSW plummeted after NALSAS in 2002 because funding was used for employing teachers on short-term programs with little structural or financial support from the state government: an example of top-down policy gone wrong (Slaughter, 2009). The curriculum differentiation of subjects into beginner, background and heritage has also not led to increases in overall enrolments, with only one subject gaining above 1 per cent of enrolments and the majority (nine out of fifteen) with enrolments below one hundred (Universities Admissions Centre, 2018). In terms of aggregated data, Year 12 study has continued a gradual decline, from 15 per cent in 1994 to 12.8 per cent in 2014 and to under 8 per cent in NSW in 2017 (Liddicoat et al., 2007). Underlying the aggregated data, the real narrative of languages is more complex. Exploring the interweaving of social differences in access to languages study with the overlay of community languages in secondary schools provides a clearer account.

Only 35 per cent of Year 12 students taking languages are in the lower-SES schools in our study; 65 per cent are in high-SES schools. Only 20 per cent of lower-SES secondary schools compared with 65 per cent of higher-SES secondary schools offer Year 12 languages courses. Differences between education systems are marked. Independent schools with only 16 per cent of Year 12 students make up a third of Year 12 language enrolments. The majority of students taking continuer courses (i.e. language studied in junior high school and receiving highest tertiary ranking) are in independent schools. Students in Catholic and comprehensive government schools had the least access to languages. Only 8 per cent of Catholic secondary schools offered languages in Year 12. Students in Catholic schools constituted 20 per cent of enrolments but only 4 per cent of Year 12 languages students. Only 0.3 per cent of Catholic school students in Wollongong and 3.1 per cent in Sydney studied a language for

Year 12. Differences between and within education jurisdictions boil down to the social inequality in access to and provision of languages study.

How successful is the compulsory 100 hours of languages study in Years 7 and/ or 8? The findings of our study show that, by itself, this mandation of languages study is insufficient to have positive outcomes and has created problems for languages continuity. Teaching 100 hours of languages to large classes means that teachers need to devise programs that are 'stand alone'. Offering a 'taste' of languages means that teachers are in the position of privileging enjoyment through games and cultural activities over noticeable gains in language proficiency. The pressure on teachers to 'sell' their subject has also led to schools often repeating what students had learnt in primary school. The main problem has been that languages offered in the 100 hours in secondary schools rarely match those that students learnt in primary schools: for example, in government schools the main languages taught in primary school are Italian and Chinese, but in secondary school, they are French and Japanese (Centre for Educational Statistics and Evaluation, 2018). Most government and Catholic secondary schools also have no way to take into account learning continuity in learning different levels of proficiency. Students, for example, may come from a primary school with strong languages programs while others may never have had access to languages study; all start 'beginner' programs.

Schools have the flexibility to run their 100 hours in Year 7 or 8 or both. Our analysis of data collected from over 400 schools in Sydney and Wollongong indicated that mid- to low-SES government schools in Sydney and Catholic schools in both sites ran the compulsory languages 100 hours in Year 8 (see Figure 8.1). The reason reported for this was that having the 100 hours in Year 8 could increase student uptake in Year 9, where languages have to compete with more 'practical' choices such as Photography, Commerce, Music and Art. The downside of this arrangement is that students may not get to study languages in Year 7; however, this does mitigate against absence of language study between Year 7 and the choice of an elective in Year 9. The selective schools often ran the 100 hours or more across Years 7 and 8.

There is a dramatic fall in elective language uptake in Year 9 when languages compete with a range of more practical (e.g. Dance, Photography, Graphics Technology, Sports Studies) or other text-based subjects (e.g. Commerce). Across all systems in both research sites there was a dramatic drop in Year 9 languages study down to 24 per cent in Sydney and to 7 per cent in Wollongong schools. Uptake of elective languages in Year 9 was lowest in Catholic and government schools. The main difference in provision is in school SES: only 34 per cent of

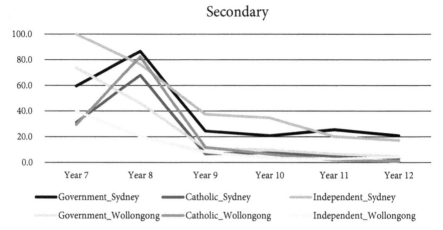

Figure 8.1 Percentage of secondary school students studying language in Sydney and Wollongong.
Source: 2011 cross-sectoral data collected.

lower-SES schools have elective language programs compared with 79 per cent of higher-SES schools.

The typical profile of languages in the low- and mid-SES comprehensive high schools is of a lone language teacher spending most time on the 100 hours in Years 7 and 8, with little or no chance or time for elective languages in later years. The lowest access to and uptake of languages is thus in lower-SES schools with large numbers of students from English-speaking backgrounds. The picture is one predicted by Teese and Polesel (2003) of languages shrinking 'into the enclaves represented by the most highly educated Australian-born families' (p. 84).

The narrative of community languages

The story of second- and third-generation students of migrant background has been ostensibly one of social mobility. Australia is one of the few countries where first- and second-generation students of migrant background score above the average on international tests (Culley, 2015). There has been upward mobility in Greek and Italian communities in terms of education, home ownership and income: the students who were studying their languages in the 1980s (Khoo, McDonald and Giorgas, 2002). Neoliberal reforms in the past decades, however, have had a dramatic impact on community languages and the cultural and linguistic diversity in schools (Butler, Ho and Vincent, 2017). Anglo-Australian parents shifting children to private schools have led to patterns of ethnic segmentation. The majority of students in government schools (52 per cent) now have a language background other than English; the figures for independent and Catholic schools are much lower (22 and 37 per cent) (Ho, 2017b). Within the government school sector, there is also segmentation: the majority of families in academic selective schools in our study are from the highest-SES quartile (73 per cent) and also from language backgrounds other than English (74 per cent). The majority of these students speak Chinese, Korean or Indian languages at home (Ho, 2017b). Students of Arabic, Vietnamese, Filipino and Pasifika language backgrounds attend mainly mid- to low-SES non-selective government schools (Ho, 2017b). Thus, the segmentation in terms of advantage between and within education sectors is mirrored in the segmentation between and within ethnic community groups. As in other countries where 'choice' has become government policy, the segregation of schools is now more pronounced than levels of segregation in local neighbourhoods (Keels, Burdick-Will and Keene, 2013).

The story of community languages, however, has been one of decline and marginalization from secondary schools. In 1992, for example, there were Modern Greek programs in twenty-seven government secondary schools; 2,850 students in government schools were studying the language. Forty per cent of students of Greek background studied their language for Year 12 (Tamis and Gauntlett, 1993). By 2011 enrolments had dropped by 60 per cent and only 7 per cent of Greek-background students were studying Greek. One reason could be the demographic dispersal of the community from traditional suburbs of settlement to middle-class areas. However, Greek enrolments also collapsed in the Saturday School of Community Languages which was established for students who could not access classes in their day schools.

This pattern of decline in the established community languages has been replicated in languages such as Chinese and Arabic with more recent settlement patterns. Arabic is now the third language, after English and Chinese, spoken by school-aged students in NSW (Centre for Educational Statistics and Evaluation, 2018). Our data analysis indicated that government school enrolments of Arabic-background students increased by 63 per cent from 1992 to 2011, but in the same period Year 12 enrolments for these students in Arabic language study dropped from 21.7 per cent (1992) to 9 per cent (2011). Patterns are more complex for languages such as Italian and Chinese, which are both 'community' and 'trade/prestige', but our data show that under 10 per cent of Chinese-background students were studying Chinese in Year 12. In fact, sixteen of the twenty-four 'community' language courses now have enrolments of less than fifty Year 12 students (Universities Admissions Centre, 2018).

Community languages have disappeared in junior secondary with most schools offering the 100 mandatory hours in French or Japanese. This creates continuity problems in the transition from primary school. The main languages taught in government primary schools are Chinese, Arabic, Vietnamese and Italian, but in secondary schools it is French and Japanese (Centre for Educational Statistics and Evaluation, 2018). There is thus little chance for students to continue learning the same language. The disappearance of languages in mid- to low-SES schools has thus resulted in the marginalization of community languages to the complementary sector, the out-of-hours voluntary community languages schools.

We argue that the decline in community languages study is very largely due to the change in 1999 in the way tertiary ranking scaled languages according to how students performed in other subjects (Department of Training and Education Coordination, 1997). The argument behind the 'McGaw report' (Department of Training and Education Coordination, 1997) was that because proficiency in community languages was gained outside the school curriculum in the community, it presented a disincentive for other (i.e. non-background) students to take languages. Examinations were 'too easy' for community languages. In general, the algorithm for student ranking means that students from lower-SES backgrounds do not perform well: several studies have found that low-SES students achieving similar grades to high-SES students in secondary school and later in university achieve around ten points lower ATAR scores (Cardak and Ryan, 2006; Messinis and Sheehan, 2015). The ranking for students taking community languages was perhaps compounded by the decision to include two units of English in the tertiary entry score (Universities Admissions Centre, 2015). One of our teacher interviewees, a head teacher, stated:

> We saw the writing on the wall after 2000. Up until then we had strong programs in schools like ours (i.e. lower-SES) but after that it was only a matter of time before they disappeared. I got out in 2004. (Head teacher, School of Languages)

The most common response from the sixty-two senior students in our case-study interviews as to why they took languages in senior secondary school related to the tertiary entry scores, as indicated by a male Year 10 student when asked, 'Why do your friends not take languages'?

> I think it's because they see themselves as able to do other subjects with greater ease and now it's just massive focus on the final ATAR of the HSC. I think that the main thing that kills any desire to do French … sorry, just languages

is something that … they are difficult. I think if they had the option of doing something that they will get a 95 rather than a 90 in the HSC they'll take that any day. (Student focus group, Forster HS)

In the same focus group interview another female Year 10 student talked about parental influences on not continuing with community languages because of perceived (and real) low tertiary entry ranking.

They [the parents] just want their children to have a basic knowledge of Chinese. Then when it comes to HSC (i.e. Year 12) learning they think okay now it's Physics, Chemistry, Chinese isn't important, it's not going to rank very well. So, the Chinese classes go from being full classes in Year 10 to about four in Year 11. (Student focus group, Forster HS)

The differences in language subject ranking are large. All prestige languages studied in higher-SES and independent schools such as Latin, Classical Greek, German, Chinese, Hebrew and French continuers are in the top quartile of scaled mark means. The main languages studied as community languages – Arabic, Vietnamese, Chinese and Japanese background, Persian, Filipino – are all in the bottom quartile of mean scaled scores. Over 40 per cent of community languages students have their language in the lowest quartile. The ranking thus replicates SES differences rather than differences in language proficiency in different languages. The difficulty in applying this algorithm is compounded in NSW where thirty-five of the sixty-two language courses had enrolments of less than seventy (Universities Admissions Centre, 2018). This individual ranking of languages leads to anomalous results. Students who take 'beginner' Chinese, Korean or Japanese (i.e. starting their languages study in Year 11) score higher tertiary entry ranking than 'background' learners of Chinese, Korean or Japanese (who bring proficiency from home). The attempt to address this issue through differentiated curriculum has not led to any appreciable increase in 'non-background speakers' taking the subjects. None of the courses have more than 1 per cent of student enrolments (Universities Admissions Centre, 2018).

The second government response has been to introduce differentiated curriculum for students. Many states introduced 'first' and 'second' language learner syllabuses. The challenge is how to define such learners. With such a diversity of family backgrounds and language learning experiences, how can this be done? Students may have parents with different language/cultural backgrounds; they have a range of experiences of travel and living overseas; they have varied access to languages in their families and communities. Despite this, eligibility for different courses has been defined by student background.

For example, in NSW students who have three years of study overseas have to enrol in 'first' or 'background' courses; students who have parent/s from that background must enrol in 'heritage' courses. In NSW the government also introduced 'beginner' courses for students who have less than 100 hours study of the language in an attempt to pick up learners who have not taken elective languages; students who have only learnt the language beyond the 100 hours through the school curriculum then take a 'continuer' course. The attempt to address the challenge of community languages through curriculum has been inadequate.

School-level responses

The following section explores how individual schools have managed to continue with strong languages programs despite the problems besetting languages. We also look at the situation of Victoria, a state with similar student profiles but with a Year 12 uptake of languages three times that of NSW: 21 per cent compared with under 8 per cent. The school accounts are not comprehensive but highlight specific aspects of school programs that address issues identified in the first section of this chapter.

Barnsley Girls High School

Barnsley Girls High School is a low-SES school in the south-western suburbs of Sydney. Fifty per cent of the 1,100 students come from out of area and 96 per cent of students speak languages in addition to English at home, the main ones being Arabic and Chinese. The school has a strong languages department and offers five languages: Arabic, Modern Greek, French, Chinese and Italian. The school was the only lower-SES secondary school in our study with a languages department and head teacher. All Year 7 students study each of the languages and then choose one or more of the languages in Years 8–10. In Years 11 and 12, the school offers all curriculum levels: beginner, continuer, heritage and background courses. The principal, Cal, is strongly in favour of languages because they have given the school a strong academic and social equity reputation. Barnsley acts as a 'lighthouse' in languages, attracting students from thirty-five different primary schools.

The two key features of the program at Barnsley are: firstly, the way that 'community' and 'modern' languages work together and the flexibility of the curriculum and, secondly, the experienced teaching staff, their pedagogy and the value-added nature of languages in the school. The head teacher, Mark, argued that the choice of Italian and French together with the community languages was strategic. This combination saved the languages faculty at his school when the other eighteen programs in government secondary schools collapsed after the change in tertiary scaling.

> All of them collapsed. Mine's the only one that hasn't. It's been through not introducing Japanese but introducing community languages, fighting with the principal, doing things like dangling overseas trips... to attract the kids, employing... hand-picking staff by employing native speakers. (Head teacher, Languages)

Languages specialists also teach other subjects such as History. Smaller languages electives survive because of the principal's support, but also because the languages teachers combined classes and differentiate in their teaching, with sometimes different year levels combined and different level groups in the same class.

> In the one classroom you might have beginners Italian and continuers Italian. Now that is not ideal but we can't run a separate class of three kids doing beginner Italian and a group of six kids doing continuers, so we put them together and the teacher's meant to differentiate the curriculum ... This also includes different age groups together, for example, Year 9 and 10 combined. We're creative, creative I think is the word to say, and flexible in getting some groupings together. (Head teacher, Languages)

The school is also flexible and strong on student access to languages. For example, there are no 'exemptions' from languages for students studying English as an Additional Language (EAL) or for special education students.

> The other, if I can tell you about it, the other wonderful thing is I'm teaching them Italian. There are Chinese girls in the class who can't speak English. We were doing a word the other day and it was – oh the Italian word is *maledizione* and it means curse because they haven't got an idea. So there's two girls that are Chinese. They typed the word. I wrote the word on the board for them. They typed it into their Apple iPhones, they see the word in Chinese and they said to each other, *zǔzhòu,* the word curse. So they're learning English through Italian. So I said, look, this is your English class because we're going to learn the value of English because that's what it is. Because at the end of the day... in fact I don't see myself as an Italian teacher ... I see myself as a teacher of English, teacher of language. (Head teacher, Languages)

Students are encouraged to choose languages as electives. Those from community languages backgrounds are not forced to take their community language and non-background speakers are encouraged to take community languages.

> What about the kids? Let them choose. How dare you say, oh you're Chinese you have to do Chinese. Or you're not Chinese, you can't do Chinese. You have to do French. What if I want to do Chinese? In my school I've got Arabic kids who want to do Chinese because they want to do Chinese. Good luck to them. And vice versa. There should be choice. (Head teacher, Languages)

This flexibility extends to working closely with the communities to keep the languages viable. The Greek program was in decline because families had shifted out of the area and students were often third generation with little Greek spoken at home. The teachers lobbied successfully in the community, attended the church and community events to build up the numbers of students.

The quality of the teachers and their pedagogy were common explanations from the students as to why they studied languages. Constant themes in the student interviews were enjoyment, fun and interest and also the engagement and caring of the teachers. Barnsley had a sister school in Italy (and was developing one in China) and there were annual visits, something which also figured in student interviews. Students mentioned also cultural, identity, travel and career reasons like responses in other schools, but the element of enjoyment was key in their responses. Teachers and students also mentioned the use of IT. All students had laptops and iPhone apps, and smartboards were used in most lessons. The interaction and engagement were evident in the lessons we observed. The striking feature of the school was the ways in which languages were promoted.

> They [the students] just see the value of the other subjects. What I do is I just – if they're in Year 10 and I can get to them – I sit them in front of the Board of Studies website and pull up the Year 12 exam paper. I'll say, well, look, you can already half answer this paper now. Then I pull up the Biology and the Chemistry and the Economics questions and the History questions and say, can you answer these and they can't. Then I say, well, why are you throwing this away? You've got to be proactive and do it in a nice way. You can't, you don't want to coerce them. (Head teacher, Languages)

The position of Barnsley as a lighthouse school is partly due to the increase in school autonomy and school choice. There is flexibility in employing teachers and also for the school to badge itself on the basis of its languages and Year 12 results. The strength and also fragility of the languages department lie in the principal's support and the agency and dynamism of the head teacher and languages staff.

De Sales College

De Sales College is a mid-SES Catholic secondary girls' school in the inner west of Sydney; 64 per cent of its students are from language backgrounds other than English and a large proportion are from Italian background (14.5 per cent). The school is more diverse than the surrounding area because it continues to attract students of Italian and other language backgrounds. The languages program is strong. All Year 7 students take three languages, Italian, French and Japanese, as 'tasters' (twenty to twenty-two lessons, thirteen weeks of each language) and then choose a language for the mandatory 100 hours in Year 8. There are three Italian classes in Year 8 and one each of French and Japanese. There is Italian elective class in Years 7–12 and a Japanese class in Year 10.

The principal, Stella, is very supportive of the languages program. A Science teacher, she is of Lebanese heritage and studied French through secondary school. Stella would like all students to take languages to Year 12 and supports Year 12 classes with small numbers, but admits that it is difficult maintaining languages.

> I bend the rules with languages, the same as Physics and Chemistry. I keep small classes going by being very creative in timetabling.

A key feature of De Sales is how languages are embedded across the school: there are teachers in Science and other subjects who teach languages and there is a diversity of languages in the teachers' own backgrounds. Typical is John, a History teacher. Both his parents are multilingual, speaking German, Russian, English, French and Polish. John is fluent in Polish and attended Polish school when he was young. The impact of this critical mass of teachers with languages skills across the school is evident in the positive attitudes towards languages. Teachers report valuing the languages study in the school for a range of reasons: cognitive, cultural, community links and communication. Peter, a Maths teacher of English-speaking background, is married to a Polish speaker. He has travelled widely in Europe and argues for the benefits of languages for brain function, even though he himself is monolingual:

> It makes your brain work. I watch my wife. That's the closest thing I've seen. Her work, her mind works on a different level because she can go back to Poland and she will drop into Polish. She actually thinks in Polish. So she is multilingual so she drops between the two languages.

Not all teachers are so positive. Shelly, an English teacher, commented:

> I've been to Indonesia eight times and I know this is so ignorant of me but I don't
> need to know the language because they want to speak to me in English. It's very
> rare you come across a – I've only been to Bali – a Balinese person who can't
> speak really good English.

She also sees students' language background as a problem: 'Many of them go home to Italian-speaking families and it's such a disadvantage.'

This link between teachers' own family and study backgrounds in languages confirms our survey results across schools: the three factors impacting on positive attitudes towards languages in schools are having teachers who had a community language at home; who had studied languages; or travelled widely or who taught in a school with a strong language program.

The Languages head teacher, Ben, has been at the school for many years and is key to the growth of languages in the school:

> Look, there are a lot of battles we fight. We fight against the growing number of
> other subjects offered going into Year 9. There's a perception that languages are
> difficult. Sometimes there's the fight we fight on the home front, like oh, I want
> to do Italian but mum says I should do Commerce. Or I want to do language but
> dad says it's no good.
>
> So there is a sell and we try to make it as interesting as we can in Year 8. We'll
> take them on excursions; we'll show them the odd DVD; we try to just keep
> that Year 7 enthusiasm rolling. Not always easy but, as I mentioned before,
> we're doing okay.

This commitment to selling the program flows through to apparently minor actions that work to counter perceived bias and negative attitudes.

> I said it to the girls, I said, okay, such and such a day once a week I'll sit down
> with you guys. Because what I noticed in this particular school because of the
> fact that we're speaking and trying to get them to speak in Italian, so I said, okay
> fine, I'm going to be sitting down, having my lunch in the courtyard on such a
> day. Whoever wants to come in and have a chat, it doesn't have to be something
> structured or I'm teaching you any; come down and have a chat. What you did
> on the weekend, we were having it in Italian, and we've been doing that … They
> come for the whole of lunch, half a lunch, it's just to come by and say hi. As long
> as they're doing Italian they're listening to it, and they're doing really well. (Head
> teacher, Languages)

The head teacher advised his staff to see their role as active and noticeable citizens of the school, to use any opportunity to market language.

[I say to the other languages teachers] Put your hand up to be a year adviser, make yourself in charge of the social club. All of that, because ... ask the principal to come to your lessons and hand out prizes for whatever, origami or whatever the kids had been doing. Yeah, marketing.

The teachers were very aware of the student needs and background: for example, that they were second, third of fourth-generation Italian background, often having a dialect or English only in the home or were English-speaking background. Teachers built on these backgrounds:

> With the Italian language they have dialect, they're ashamed of using the dialect. I'm saying why are you ashamed of it? It's Italian, it's another beautiful language. It's a part of Italian, you should be using it, and it's trying to get them out of their shell. (Italian teacher)

Students, parents and teachers also reported on the disincentives for languages study, including the competition with more practical electives in Year 9. Steve, a Physics teacher, parallels the situation of languages and Science subjects.

> I know they should choose subjects they like but there's been an explosion of vocational education subjects. They're obviously hands-on and, I guess, more fun and not as rigorous when it comes to learning content. But, yeah, I wish our kids extended themselves a bit more.

Tertiary ranking was reported by the students constantly as the main reason for not taking languages for Year 12 and this also had a washback effect on languages uptake in Years 9 and 10. As one Year 9 student said, 'Year 10 marks don't count towards your HSC.'

Students who continued to Year 12 reported doing so despite concerns about ATAR; their love for the language and sense of identity and power from being a languages learner motivated them to continue with their study, as evident in the following two quotes:

> Me and my sister were at a cafe here and there were these two really gross Italian dudes and they were trying to guess how old we were. Like that's gross dude. We just turned around, oh we know what you're saying. That's terrible. Oh yuk. So gross. But so happy I know this language. (Year 12 student interview)

> Sally: I think we feel kind of it's a good thing.
> Susana: I know another language you don't.
> [Laughter]
> Sally: It kind of makes us feel all powerful. (Year 12 student focus group)

The dominance of talk around marks and tertiary entry was tempered by the range of discourses around languages used by teachers, parents and students at De Sales. The key aspects for teachers were the cognitive and learning benefits, something confirmed as common understandings in the findings in our system-wide surveys. Teachers from all subject areas, parents and students commonly referred to a mix of social and cognitive reasons.

> It [language learning] opens up a whole new world for you, travel, reading and socially. I think it's very good for your brain as well, for learning. It can be any language. (Year 9 student parent)

Parents and students also mentioned the prestige values of Italian in the same breath as heritage and cultural values. Discourses which are discrete in government policy documents coexisted in our interview data. This mixing of discourses is discussed in Chapters 4 and 5 in this volume. The positive comments from teachers, students and parents were balanced also with a perception of the low status of language learning in the broader school and community. Despite the support and active marketing of languages in the school, one of the language teachers could still provide the following disheartening example of parent attitudes and her student's acceptance of these:

> Oh look, [I said to my student], you haven't made an appointment to see me. 'Oh no, mum only wants to see the important subjects.' (Languages teacher)

Languages study at De Sales was clearly still fragile, but the way in which the teachers promoted the prestige, cultural and heritage values of Italian and the ways languages are embedded across the school both augur well for its survival.

Forster High School

Forster High School is a high-SES selective government school, drawing students from across metropolitan Sydney and its outskirts (see as also Chapter 1). The majority of its 940 students come from language backgrounds other than English, with the highest proportion from Chinese and Indian language backgrounds. Languages have always had a strong presence in the school, particularly the classical prestige languages of French and German, with Latin also on offer. A languages tradition remains strong with a head teacher and nine full- and part-time, experienced and highly qualified languages teachers, teaching across French, German, Japanese and Chinese. The school addressed the issue of continuity of language study in interesting ways. There is a continuing emphasis on French, but with options for other languages. In Year 7 students take the mandatory 100 hours in French, Latin, Japanese, German or Chinese. In Year 8 students who studied Japanese, German and Chinese in Year 7 must take another language but students who took French may take French 'continuers'. The term continuers, which usually refers to the Year 11/12 course, is used for students who choose to keep studying their language in junior secondary. In this way continued study in French is encouraged. In Year 9 there are strong elective classes, with both 'beginner' and 'continuer' classes in French. Only continuer classes are offered in French, Japanese and German for Years 11 and 12. This is another way to ensure continued language study. It is also because 'beginner' courses scale lower on tertiary entry ranking. The school is proud of its outcomes in languages. Generally, all students get in the top Bands 5 or 6 for their Year 12. The school average is above 80 per cent in French and German and 90 per cent in Japanese. The languages department is thus built around French with Japanese, German, Latin and Chinese for smaller groups.

The issue of 'background' and second-language learners is seen as problematic by the school: Japanese-background students are not allowed to take Japanese. In Chinese classes there is a mix of complete beginners, dialect speakers of Cantonese and fairly proficient speakers of Mandarin Chinese. The Chinese teacher commented that he differentiates by teaching students in two or three groups within the class. The school could not offer Chinese in Years 11 and 12 because of the high dropout. This confirms studies which find an attrition rate in Chinese of 94 per cent by Year 12 (Orton, 2008). The head teacher commented that they were thinking of dropping Chinese from the languages offered in the school. This conflicted attitude to community languages and Chinese in particular is explored further in Chapter 9.

A key feature of Forster is the pedagogy. Teachers are all experienced and were clear about their approaches and the strategies they use and why. Students and parents alike commented on the value of the teaching, more so than for other subjects. Our observations indicate interactive teaching with a reliance on communicative activities, but also a clear progression in the development of the languages. Teachers used technology judiciously. As Sabine, one of the French teachers, reported, 'I don't embrace it; I shake hands with it.' We observed her lessons, on a Friday afternoon after sport, where she managed an interactive lesson with thirty Year 8 students using iPads. When we interviewed students in her class they were unanimous in their praise for their language learning in secondary school, especially when compared with their experiences of languages in primary school.

For me I honestly think that any language I learned in primary school was just negligible. I've got no memories except for Italian colours. Well, in kindy, Year 1 and 2, I did Spanish, but we didn't really learn it. We got a worksheet. So we didn't actually really learn it. It was just … words. (Year 7 student)

At the time of our study, Sabine was teaching Years 7, 8 and 9 French. She trained in France as an English teacher and undertook postgraduate study in Australia because she 'needed to study learning and teaching French grammar'. She likes the multicultural nature of the school and commented that students from diverse backgrounds pick up the notions of formal and informal language more easily. Although her students are interested in languages in their junior years, she sees a big dropout after Year 10 because of 'the difficult and cumulative nature of languages'. She describes her classes as 'activity-based'. She uses 'interaction point boards' in her class but she tends to avoid the smartboard as she says students are bored with them. She prefers to cut up and do activities with hard copies. She regularly gives students websites to research and has her own Facebook page where she posts articles and items of interest.

The other feature of the languages program at Forster is the 'value-added' components. The school has regular exchange programs to France, Japan, Germany and China. Students attend classes for two weeks and travel for the third week. Students from Japan, France and Germany make exchange visits in alternate years. The opportunity for the exchange was mentioned by many students as the reason for taking languages to Year 10. Hosting exchange students was also mentioned by many of the parents. In our study, it was the only school with established languages programs that has the resources to have exchanges. Forster also hosts assistant teachers from Germany, France and China. It is part of a Confucius classroom with six other schools and has a dedicated room with Chinese government funding. The school also has around 150 students sitting for national competency tests in the four languages and they have achieved way above the state average.

The broader role of languages in the school is reflected in the students' families and life experiences. The school data of 80 per cent from language backgrounds other than English actually under-represent the diversity. In one focus group of six students of 'English-speaking' background, three spent extended time living and travelling overseas; three have languages in their background through relatives and parents (Hebrew, Gaelic, Chinese); all have parents who are fluent in languages in addition to English. This diversity is rarely evident in aggregated school data.

At the time of our study, Forster had a 'critical mass' of experienced languages teachers who have managed to establish continuity in language learning from Year 7 to Year 12. The program was supported by a strong raft of exchange programs, visits, excursions and participation in out-of-school programs. The long tradition of languages in the school has been built around French, Latin and German. In recent years Japanese and Chinese have been added, but it is the traditional languages which still attract most students, as in many selective schools. This is despite the change in school enrolment, with 75 per cent of the students having a home language in addition to English.

Sydney International School

Sydney International School is an independent, secular, co-educational school in central Sydney which aims to provide its 1,200 students (K-12) with 'a globally focused bilingual education, rich in the study of music and the arts' (myschool. edu.au). It draws on a high-SES population, with three-quarters of parents in the top SES quartile. Parents are predominantly professional and well-travelled. Most students live within five kilometres of the school and reflect the mixed, multicultural nature of the population. Few are 'background' speakers of the language/s they study. However, according to the principal, that does not accurately reflect the range of languages in the students' backgrounds: 'What we do have is mum's French, dad's Canadian, mum's Chinese, dad's German, we've got scores and scores of those.'

The school offers French, Italian, Japanese, Chinese, German and Spanish. Students learn in one of four languages through immersion from age six (40–80 minutes per day) and then take a second language in upper primary through to Year 10 (5 × 40 minutes per week). Students have 1,000 hours in their main language by Year 6 (school website). They then start a third language in Year 7 (4 × 40 minutes per week) which can be continued as an elective from Year 9. According to the principal, programming is the key to having the range of languages, and the languages and other subject teachers plan their programs collaboratively; the school timetable is planned around languages, with a strong emphasis on the role of languages across the school curriculum. All languages have exchange programs.

The key feature in the school is the way students construct their identities as bilingual or multilingual. Their fluency in languages means that using that language is fun: they are able to play with the language outside the classroom and use their languages locally and when travelling. They talk of accessing films, music and friends in the language they are learning. For students, the motivations centre around their languages and what they can do with them. They talk of the cognitive and cultural benefits of learning and knowing languages. There is also talk of future career opportunities.

> Facilitator 1: How do you feel about learning Italian, German, French?
> Female: I find it fun.
> Female: Yeah, I find it fun.
> Facilitator 2: Do you use Italian or Spanish outside of school?
> Female: Sometimes …
> Female: Sometimes when we're talking about anything we just text each other in Italian just to …
> Facilitator 2: Really?
> Female: Just for the fun.
> Female: Just for fun.
> Female: It's really thrilling to be able to do it because …
> Female: Yeah. So then sometimes we'll just be texting or we'll be talking about Italian and then jokingly I'll say something in Italian and then by the end we're just in a full conversation with a dictionary on hand. (Student focus group)

Student responses mirror those of the parents we interviewed. Nearly all parents have experiences of learning languages through travel, school and university or from family. Parent comments were often on their pride at the children's fluency.

> Misha [the daughter] recently met friends of ours who travelled to Japan for their business, had a young Japanese woman visiting. We went over and met her. She was with a friend and what was really lovely, because I don't have any background in Japanese, they were talking to Misha. She was doing some writing for them and things and they were just blown away that this girl of 10 and they said her accent is beautiful. That's what I think is really amazing. (Parent interview)

The parents talk drew on what has been referred to in the literature as a 'cosmopolitan discourse' (Wright et al., 2018; see also Chapter 5), that is, one that sees an amalgam of benefits from fluency in another language that are global, societal and individual. As indicated in the following quote, this was also combined with perceptions of other benefits, such as cognitive training and improved learning capacity.

> For me it was very much just, I want them to learn a language because I want them to have a broader view of life and the world. But it's really interesting that you have this idea that the more that your brain works, the more that it can

think in different ways, that it actually increases the learning capability in other ways. It's very much there with the whole kind of play Mozart to your babies, that whole idea of... because music stimulates the brain. It makes sense that languages will do the same. (Parent interview)

The second feature of Sydney International School is the focus on assessment; the continuity of languages from primary to secondary and the expectation of fluency provided a context in which indicators available in the government system (only available for Year 12) were completely inadequate. As a way of providing a framework for languages learning from the early years, the teachers developed indicators based on the Common European Framework of Reference (CEFR). These were used more as formative and summative assessment tools and as a support in programming. This school was one of the few where teachers mentioned assessment as a key factor in the curriculum. At the same time, they perceived a tension between the achievement of fluency and student enjoyment and learning and final Year 12 exam results. Several teachers expressed concern that the final Year 12 results were not as good as had been expected because there was less emphasis on formal study.

In NSW there are currently no government secondary schools with this commitment to languages and to a bilingual program. Such schools are therefore generally not accessible to low-SES students. What they do offer is a model of what is possible, where there is a serious commitment to languages learning. As was indicated in Chapter 1, this is not an impossible goal for government schools (see Cheswell PS), and in a context with such language diversity and an increased emphasis on Australia's position in the global world.

School of Languages and Saturday Heritage Languages School

All Australian states have secondary schools where students who cannot get access to languages in their own school can study languages up to Year 12 by distance, online or outside the school day. At the time of our study, the NSW School of Languages (SoL) was offering classes in twelve modern languages by distance materials, email, telephone lessons, video conferencing, online activities and forums, school visits and study days. The Saturday Heritage Languages School was offering 'community' languages up to Year 12 on Saturdays in fifteen sites across the state, again for students who do not have access to the language in their home school. Both schools act as 'safety' nets for secondary-aged students from government, Catholic and independent schools who do not have access to languages study in their day school. The deputy principal of the School of Languages was clear about the purpose of the school in providing access to languages study as an equity issue.

> My concern is those lower-economic areas, where the non-English-speaking background students who should really … I think the non-English-speaking background students have a talent because they already speak one language fluently, learning the second language, which is English. The fact that they – if they are literate in their first language, they'll get very literate – they'll become literate very quickly in their second and third languages.

Leo, head teacher at the Saturday School in an inner Sydney suburb, was also aware of the role of community languages in providing access to further education:

> The Saturday School is obviously a brilliant structure because in a nutshell, it allows students who don't have an opportunity to learn their language to do so formally across fifteen centres … It provides an opportunity for members of that community through education to raise themselves personally, but then the perception of the whole community eventually to something appropriate and into good roles for society.

Our case studies of these two schools confirmed a key finding emerging from our other data. In schools with three or more languages the teachers formed a 'critical mass'. Teachers reported learning from each other; they were more likely to belong to professional networks; they were generally happier in their teaching. Sole languages teachers in primary and secondary schools complained of isolation and the lack of professional conversations. As a German teacher at the Languages High School commented:

> I don't know how many German teachers we've got here, six or seven or something. You're totally immersed in German all the time. We're talking in German all the time. Yeah, the professional development, bouncing ideas off one another and – you know, I don't think that will work. Yeah, that will work. How about you use this. Whereas, you never had that at your face to face.

This sense of solidarity and identity in relation to languages mirrors student responses. Many of the students we interviewed from regional and rural secondary schools were the only ones in their schools studying languages. The response below was a common one:

> I just love languages. Honestly, I'd do my whole HSC, just all languages, but I couldn't. My school didn't offer it and I couldn't really do more than two with

open high school, because then I'm always on my own sort of thing. So it was only do those two. But when I'm older I just want to know every language. (Year 11 student)

The sense of agency and responsibility was also commented on: students involved in learning online and by distance, by necessity, are more self-directed. Both teachers and students commented on the value of one-to-one teaching in developing this agency.

For students with a community language background, the links between their language and their cultural and linguistic identities were more complex. Several students reported being characterized as 'ethnic' in their mainstream school but 'Aussie' in the Heritage Languages School.

> I think the teacher kind of thinks of us as Aussie. Aussie, because a lot of us aren't really up to … you know we're not all perfect in our Polish, so she kind of thinks of us as more these little Aussie kids trying to learn Polish. Whereas at school I kind of like, well for me anyway, I'm like the Polish kid but I don't say anything [in Polish]. (Year 8 student focus group)

Other students reported that the experience of learning their community language had developed a position of strength and choice, what Clare Kramsch refers to as the 'third position' (Kramsch and Uryu, 2012). One Year 11 student described the solidarity he gained from his attendance and learning.

> Yeah, for me it's the same ['my parents forced me']. I've been doing Spanish for nine years maybe. For the first seven of them I didn't have a bar of it, but something that I really enjoy now is knowing that there are people like me in my class and people of the same heritage. That connects us. (Year 11 focus group)

Paul, a Year 8 student at Saturday School, has a mother of Greek and Italian background but a father of Anglo-Australian background. For him, speaking Greek is the only apparent marker of his Greek identity, even though he is involved in family and Greek community networks and events.

> At school people don't know that I'm Greek unless I speak Greek. But with a name like Paul Ellis no one would think 'is that kid Greek?' But that's why I want to … I want to change my name to what my papa's last name was … It's Veronese, or my *yiayia*'s last name, which is Papademus, because then people would say, Paul Papademus, he's Greek. I'm sick and tired of being called the kid who says he's Greek. I want to be the kid who is Greek … people think I'm Anglo. (Year 8 focus group)

The role of these schools as a 'safety net' for students in government, Catholic and independent schools to access languages study not available in their mainstream schools is important. Many of the students in the Languages High School were in rural or regional high schools with no elective languages; others were in schools which only allowed one language to study. The Saturday Heritage Languages School provided the opportunity for students from all sectors to study their community language from Year 7. In both schools, the students were able to develop and negotiate their identities as languages learners and users. Their agency (and sometimes lack of agency) in doing this figured much in our interview data. The second feature was the benefits for the languages teachers. Many compared their experiences in the Languages High School and the Heritage Languages School with experiences in other high schools. They identified the professional conversations, the professional learning and the sense of achievement they gained in their present teaching.

The six high schools in this chapter should not be taken as representative. Barnsley Girls High School is a lighthouse lower-SES government school, the only one with a languages department; Forster is a high-SES government selective school; De Sales is a high-SES Catholic girls school; Sydney International School is a high-SES private school; the Saturday Heritages Languages High School and Heritage Languages School are specialist alternative languages providers. The schools were selected on the basis of aspects in their organization and teaching which could inform the provision of languages in other schools. The final section explores the implications of findings from these schools.

Summary

Findings from school program data, lesson observations and interviews with teachers, young people and parents in our study point to factors that support secondary school languages provision and uptake. In terms of programs and organisation it is being able to continue language learning from primary to secondary and then through each year from 7 to 12. For teaching staff it is the existence of a 'critical mass'; having a group of experienced and highly qualified teachers acting as sources of professional learning for each other; it is also having languages embedded in the overall school with teachers in different subjects and positions having languages skills and expertise. It is also the opportunities beyond the classroom: exchange programs, trips, events and accreditation and community support. Finally, it is the quality of the pedagogy;

the sense of approach/es to teaching based on realistic assessment of learner strengths and needs; teaching which is challenging, engaging and interactive. What accompanies this is the agency and identities of students: how they see themselves as learners of languages and cultures and the affordances of these understandings. The structural impediments to languages in low-SES government and Catholic high schools still loom large in constraining their growth. Government initiatives often take the approach that building languages in the primary schools will increase secondary uptake (Lo Bianco, 2009), but the findings from our study indicate that the low provision and uptake of languages in senior secondary school is more to do with specific factors relating to tertiary entry.

Victoria, the state to the south of NSW, has a similar profile in terms of its student population. Government school population includes 27 per cent of students from language backgrounds other than English. However, the provision of languages could not be more different. In Victoria 21 per cent of students take a language for their final year of schooling, three times the number in NSW. Part of the reason for this is the greater flexibility of provision in Victoria; many students do accelerated programs and complete their languages examination in Year 11 (about 8 per cent); there is much more provision of languages outside the regular schools on weekends and weeknights through the Victorian School of Languages.

The main difference, however, seems to lie in the tertiary ranking. In Victoria, 78 subjects count for tertiary entry. When comparing the scaled means of all these subjects, 85 per cent of languages are in the top half and 50 per cent are in the top quartile. In NSW the three key community languages Arabic, Chinese and Vietnamese are in the bottom quartile; 36 per cent of languages (nearly all community languages) are in the bottom half. German, French, Latin and Classical Greek are ranked highest. We have not been able to ascertain the reasons for the different rankings, but the impact of the differences in tertiary entry scores must be a key factor in the differences in uptake. The key challenges for languages in secondary school are threefold: firstly, how to credit and not problematize the language resources in the community and proficiency gained outside the school curriculum; secondly, how to address the inequity of access to languages in lower-SES, rural and regional schools; and finally, how to credit achievement in tertiary ranking and provide incentives for senior secondary uptake in languages. The achievement of schools in addressing these issues becomes all the more remarkable considering the systemic barriers.

9

Teaching Chinese in Australia: A Case Study

Since the 1980s, Australian government policy and funding have focused on the promotion of Asian languages. In the first comprehensive language policy report in Australia, 'the National Language Policy' in 1987, Chinese was identified as one of the nine priority languages. In the 1994 Council of Australian Governments (COAG) report, Chinese was one of the four Asian languages 'made the exclusive priority of language policy funding' (Lo Bianco, 2009: 20). Despite this policy support for teaching and learning Chinese in Australia, the evidence is that 94 per cent of students studying Chinese in the junior years of school drop out by Year 12 and there are now more students studying Latin than Beginner Chinese for the NSW final matriculation exam, the High School Certificate (HSC) (Board of Studies NSW, 2014; Orton, 2008). This raises the following questions: Why has the policy support and funding not resulted in positive outcomes in the teaching and learning of Chinese in schools? What are the reasons for students dropping out of Chinese learning in the senior levels? Why is the uptake so low considering the fact that Chinese is the main language, after English, spoken in NSW?

The teachers, parents and students in our study were asked for their views on: why students chose to (or not to) study languages; the value of learning languages; and the influences on students' uptake of languages. The interviews were conducted in schools and questions were in English or Chinese, where appropriate. The data were analysed using QSR Nvivo after the identification of key content themes. The resulting node reports were then interpreted and theorized to describe how the two constructs of Chinese as a 'community' language and a 'global' language have played out in NSW and what this means for the cultural capital associated with specific languages and groups of language learners.

History of Chinese language and community in Australia

Chinese is one of the oldest community languages in Australia, with Chinese immigration to Australia dating back to the earliest days of British colonization in 1788. In the 1850s, attracted by the discovery of gold in New South Wales and Victoria, Chinese immigrants, mainly from Guangdong, arrived and the period witnessed serious anti-Chinese prejudice among other European immigrants. In 1888, a shipload of Chinese, many of whom were residents or born in Australia, was turned back from Melbourne and refused permission to disembark in Sydney. Crowds marched on the NSW State Parliament House and demanded the premier 'stop the invasion'. In response the NSW government enacted anti-Chinese legislation which was subsequently adopted as the Immigration Restriction Act by the federal government and became known as the 'White Australia Policy'. This act stood in place until its final elimination in 1973 (Zhang, 2009). Following the elimination of the White Australia Policy, Chinese immigration increased, with Chinese being the largest group of immigrants from non-English-speaking backgrounds in Australia (Australian Bureau of Statistics, 2016). For the early generations of Chinese immigrants, Cantonese was their home language and the first community schools established in the 1880s were for the children of Cantonese-speaking restaurant workers and market gardeners in Sydney. Cantonese was still one of the main languages taught in community language schools in the 1970s (Lo Bianco, 2009).

Although the original migrants (1840s–1970s) were Cantonese speakers from southern China and Hong Kong, Mandarin speakers from China PRC and Taiwan have constituted more recent immigration. Chinese (Mandarin) is now the main language, after English, spoken by school-aged students in NSW and in Australia (ABC census, 2). Table 9.1 is a summary of Census data from 2016.

Table 9.1 Speakers of Chinese in Australia, language spoken at home

Year	2011		2016	
	NSW	**Australia**	**NSW**	**Australia**
Mandarin	139,822	336,410	239,947	596,713
Cantonese	136,373	263,673	143,338	280,947
Other Chinese	19,272	51,245	18,164	50,285
Total	**295,479**	**651,327**	**401,448**	**927,944**

Source: ABS 2016 census data.

Chinese has also suffered the prejudice traditionally attached to all community languages in Australia (Clyne, 2008; Clyne and Kipp, 2011). Attitudes to community languages and background learners reflect societal prejudices. Slaughter (2007) argues that many school communities and students view students with a Chinese heritage that are born in Australia as the 'problem'. In our survey of school staff, attitudes to the study of community languages were much more negative than to modern languages: only 40 per cent of staff thought that these languages should be taught in primary school. This compared with 94 per cent supporting the study of 'languages' in general.

The terms in official use for students speaking Chinese, 'background' and 'native' speaker, cover a wide range of circumstances, including, for example: students who have recently arrived from China and speak a number of dialects fluently; those from second- to fourth-generation Chinese background who speak Chinese to grandparents but not in any day-to-day communications; and those who may come from mixed marriages where no Chinese is spoken at home. As Pachler (2007) points out, traditional distinctions between 'owners' and 'users' of languages as well as of ethno-national identities being associated with speakers of a particular language are becoming increasingly blurred. For example, distinctions between 'native' and 'non-native' speakers of a language are becoming progressively understood in terms of differentials in functional proficiency in a language (Pachler, 2007), although government policy still often uses simplistic divisions. The use of these blanket terms is discussed in Chapter 1.

According to a 2017 report of the NSW Department of Education, 15.9 per cent of students are identified as Chinese-background speakers (See Table 9.2).

Table 9.2 NSW school students of Chinese-speaking backgrounds

Language	2016		2017	
	Students	**% out of total LBOTE**	**Students**	**% out of LBOTE**
Mandarin	25,140	9.2	26,569	9.4
Cantonese	15,392	5.7	15.031	5.3
Other Chinese	2,891	1.1	3,141	1.1
Total	**43,423**	**16.0**	**44,741**	**15.8**

Source: Centre for Education Statistics and Evaluation (CESE), 2018.

Chinese as a modern language

Chinese (Mandarin), although first introduced as a community language, has gained considerable status in elite private and academically selective government schools (Clyne, 2005). In recent years Chinese has been promoted as a trade language/global language for future economic development by both Australian federal and state governments and the People's Republic of China through its Confucius institutes. For non-Chinese-background speakers the acquisition of Chinese has become associated with opportunities in the future. For example, unlike most other CLS, Chinese community language schools now include substantial numbers of non-Chinese-background students in their student enrolment. A teacher interviewed in a Chinese community school indicated 70 per cent of the students were Chinese students who were born in Australia, 10 per cent non-background students, the remaining students were born overseas. As the quote below suggests, the idea that speaking Chinese opens up employment opportunities has become a common discursive trope:

> I think the media plays a big part in promoting Chinese learning. There is a lot of media write-up about China in terms of economy, in terms of trading partners, employment, things like recently when they were talking about the James Packer casino and he was asking for bilingual employees. In recent articles it is reported many Chinese tourists are coming to Australia and people who speak Chinese will have advantage gaining work in the tourist industry etc. (Languages teacher, Campbell HS)

The same teacher articulated a commonly held position that Chinese is the language of the future:

> If you look at the statistics, I think it's a 56 per cent increase in Mandarin. Now, outside of English, it's the number one language spoken. It's surpassed Italian and it's only going to grow exponentially. The numbers speak for themselves. If you were going to go on that trend and work for the future, you can pretend that things don't happen or you can open your eyes and understand them. The world's changing and Australia's changing. Even the fact that our Prime Minister [Kevin Rudd at the time of the interview], little things like this, just little moments where people can see oh, he speaks some Mandarin. (Languages teacher, Campbell HS)

These comments were typical of the ways non-Chinese-background parents and teachers constructed learning a Chinese language as having social and cultural values. Indeed, some non-Chinese-background parents felt this so strongly that they sent their children to Chinese community language schools to learn Chinese because they wanted their children to be in an immersion context where most children speak Chinese. The same sets of values were mentioned by Chinese-background learners. A number of Chinese-background students from Forster HS, for example, told researchers that their parents wanted them to refresh their Chinese language so they could conduct business in China.

The following quote from a Chinese primary school teacher in our study is indicative of explanations as to why many non-Chinese-heritage parents want their children to learn Chinese. While this quote is specific to Chinese, it points to typical reasons espoused by many of the middle-class parents in the study, who were themselves used to living, working or holidaying in different countries and wanted their children to learn another language as a form of cultural capital or 'international mindedness' (see Chapter 5).

> I have to say, parents in this school, they're very well-educated and they travel a lot too. They take the kids on holiday to different countries, so they do recognise the importance of having a second language and being fluent in it. An example is an Australian family whose two girls are my students. They [parents] were taking the girls to Beijing and they came and spoke to me and said is there anything they can do to learn [Chinese] because they want to use this trip and let the kid have more motivation in learning. I said okay, that's different and that's very supportive. (Australian Chinese languages teacher, Keswick PS)

In this context Chinese could be seen as adding value to a profile of the school, to differentiating the school in a very competitive marketplace (see Smala, Paz and Lingard, 2013 and Chapters 2 and 8). Again, as the languages teacher at Campbell HS said:

> I think it's looking for a distinction; it's looking for something to sell. I think when you're looking at different products the different schools are selling, some schools are looking down the line of sports high schools, there are IT schools, performing arts schools. So I think it's looking for a niche.

Chinese as a community language

The teaching of Chinese as a community language has burgeoned in both community languages schools and government primary schools under the government-funded community languages program. Data from the Board of Studies NSW (2013) show more than 28,000 students in NSW study Chinese in

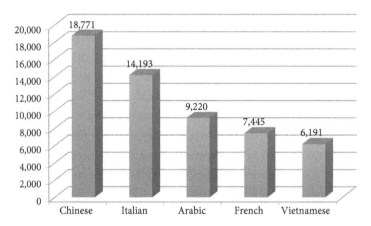

Figure 9.1 Numbers in government primary schools learning languages.
Source: 2013 data collected from Department of Education.

primary and secondary schools in 212 government, independent and Catholic schools. Chinese is now taught to primary-aged children in NSW schools. Some children learn Chinese as a 'modern' language in school- or parent-funded programs. These are generally in mid- to high-SES government and independent schools where students are not from Chinese backgrounds. In government primary schools, Chinese was the most commonly taught language (see Figure 9.1).

In our study twenty-four government schools had introduced Chinese language study in the last five years and many high-SES independent schools also offered Chinese to non-Chinese-background students.

Chinese as a community language, however, becomes problematized in the secondary school, where the presence of 'background' speakers has often been seen as discouraging second language learners from taking Chinese. Many of the secondary schools in our study, for example, especially the selective and private schools, were less likely to encourage students from Chinese-background families to enrol in Chinese classes. Some teachers we interviewed suggested that students, particularly those in senior classes without an experience of speaking Chinese in their homes, were intimidated by those from Chinese backgrounds because they felt they could not compete with background students, a finding confirmed in other studies (Orton, 2008). Many students in the Chinese weekend community schools reported that their teachers at mainstream day schools asked them to do French rather than Chinese for the final Year 12 Higher School Certificate. Some schools in our study refused to accept learners from Chinese families or from mixed marriages into Chinese language classes, even when their parents didn't speak Chinese, or students from mixed-marriage parents, in when the home language was English not Chinese.

The NSW government, to address the issue of proficiency gained outside the curriculum, developed four different Chinese language syllabuses for the last two years of secondary school. These syllabuses identify students not by language proficiency but by cultural/educational background: beginners Chinese, continuers Chinese, Chinese for heritage learners and Chinese for background learners. The beginning Chinese syllabus is for students of non-Chinese background who study Chinese only for the final two years. The continuers syllabus is regarded as second language learning and caters for non-Chinese-background students who have been studying Chinese since primary school. The heritage syllabus is for students who were born in Australia or came to Australia as babies from Chinese families. The background syllabus is for students who received Chinese education for more than five years in China. Teachers in our study reported that the eligibility rules for HSC language examinations are a key factor in deterring Chinese language (and other heritage languages) study in the senior years of high school.

The ostensible aim of this range of syllabuses is to encourage more non-Chinese Australian learners to learn Chinese. Our evidence for the past decade is that the Chinese-background speakers course deters students while there has been no increase in enrolments for the non-background continuer course (Universities Admissions Centre, 2007, 2017). As one head teacher in a government high school explained:

> Chinese is certainly the flavour of the month, most definitely the flavour of the month, however, there are so many pathways for Chinese speakers. There are the students who have just recently emigrated, so they have to be background speakers. There are students who are background speakers, and they might not want to study Chinese at a background-speaker level. There are the kids who came at the end of primary school. They are heritage speakers, but the heritage course is hard, so they might not want to do it. They might want to do the continuers course, but they are ineligible. (Head teacher languages, Sherwood HS)

The small numbers of students taking languages study means in reality that all Chinese classes are generally combined and so the purpose of different syllabuses is negated. In the following quote a principal from a selective government school committed to language provision explains why Chinese is not offered at the school. In this case, students are able to take up language study at the local Saturday Community Language School and/or the Chinese Community School, but unlike the students studying other languages in the school they have to do this in their own time without the support of school resources.

They [referring to other schools like her own] can't have … they might have 30 kids wanting to study Chinese, but they all have 10, 10 and 10, neither of which is viable as a class. Yes, so there's certainly no … their parents, from time to time, say that they'd like their kids to study Chinese, but since we've got Saturday school here that has the heritage and beginners' school here, there is an actual option. There's also a Chinese school that meets here on Friday afternoon. (Principal, Sherwood HS)

Although in this quote the principal suggests that students could study Chinese for the HSC in their community language schools, our data suggest that students in CLS schools also dropped their Chinese language study in senior years. Figure 9.2 shows a decline of Chinese-background learners in the last ten years taking the HSC.

Most students in the community language schools in our study were enrolled in primary and junior secondary levels, but there were few enrolments of Year 11 and Year 12 students. The teachers in these schools, like the teachers in the mainstream schools, explained that many students drop Chinese after Year 10, because they want to concentrate on other HSC subjects. The teachers explained that the students would be disadvantaged by taking Chinese for the HSC because the Chinese paper was very difficult to pass or to gain good grades. The quotes below, from three different Chinese CLS teachers, speak to their

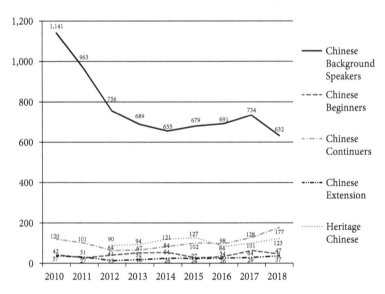

Figure 9.2 Trends in Year 12 student enrolments in Chinese (2010–18).
Source: Universities Admission Centre 2011–19.

direct experience of the difficulty of the papers through their involvement with the HSC exams in Chinese.

> No, I don't encourage them to continue with HSC learning. I went through, I taught Year 11, Year 12 at [name] High for HSC in our course, it's not worth it [for them to do Chinese as HSC subjects].

> Because the Chinese teachers in the … who set the exam paper for HSC, they don't have the student's ability or levels in mind, they set it very high and very hard to achieve. Then when I taught them, most children from China, where Chinese is very strong, then if they got 85 it is considered a good mark.

> The Board of Studies asked me to try to do a listening paper for that year, they asked me to go and try it. It was so difficult. As a language teacher, as a Chinese teacher, as a teacher who had done most of my study in China, I found it very difficult to write in detail and say in full detail. I cannot believe my students can pass it.

In 2018, only 214 non-Chinese-background students took Chinese at HSC level. Based on Table 9.2 there are 43,424 Chinese-background students in NSW schools, but only 755 students took Chinese-background and heritage HSC examinations. Figure 9.2 indicates that despite strong government policy and the push for learning Chinese, only a very small percentage of students chose Chinese for the HSC. The few Chinese-background students who do opt to study Chinese do so outside the day school system. The government-differentiated curriculum, therefore, has had the effect of marginalizing students of Chinese background while having no impact on increasing enrolments from other students. Curriculum by itself is not enough to address the underlying issues but entrenches, in fact, existing discrimination. The findings show a rapid decline in uptake of Chinese in upper secondary schools. Students of non-Chinese background reported dropping Chinese because of the 'difficulty' or because of competition from 'background' speakers. Students of Chinese background reported dropping Chinese because of the low ranking of Chinese for tertiary entry and that they could get higher tertiary entry scores in other subjects. These trends then influence schools in their choice of languages to offer.

One key factor for both non-Chinese-background and background students dropping Chinese in Year 10 is the scaling of marks for tertiary entry in NSW. Up until 2000, marks for all languages were scaled the same as French for the University Admissions Centre. After 2000, each language was scaled separately under new ATAR rankings (see also Chapter 8). This ranking system has been perceived to discriminate against both non-Chinese background and background learners. When the scaled mean ranking of all subjects is compared,

Chinese background (now called 'Chinese and literature') is in the lowest quartile, whereas French, German and all traditional/modern languages are in the top quartile (Universities Admissions Centre, 2018).

The teaching of Chinese in mainstream schools has been conflicted. For students of Chinese background the access to studying Chinese in government primary schools is good because of the government-funded community languages program. At secondary school level, this is not the case as their language proficiency or 'background' becomes problematized, especially in the competition for marks in the tertiary entrance scores. The construction of 'unfair advantage' has led to separate syllabuses and exams which are ranked lower than other languages. On the other hand, Chinese for non-background speakers has grown in strength, particularly in government primary and secondary schools where there are few 'background' speakers. This does not lead to uptake in senior secondary school. It is as if Chinese as a language of trade and diplomacy has become a prestige language, but attitudes to it as a community language continue the history in Australia of traditional attitudes to Chinese immigrants.

Chinese community schools

Community languages schools, which constitute a key complementary system of language provision outside the day schools in North America and the UK, have been operating in Australia for over 160 years and now have enrolments of over 100,000 students in over 64 languages. These schools have often been seen as bastions of conservatism where community groups struggle to maintain 'traditional' cultures into future generations. There is now a substantial body of research into these community-run schools (Blackledge and Creese, 2008; Garcia, Zakharia and Otcu, 2012; Lytra and Martin, 2010). This section examines findings on the impact on the community school sector of government policy of Mandarin as a prestige language in the context of the other policies which marginalize Chinese-background speakers.

The past decade has seen an unprecedented growth in the teaching of Chinese in the out-of-hours complementary school system. Traditionally Chinese migration to Australia was from Guangzhou in China and the majority of the community were speakers of Cantonese dialect (Mu, 2014). More recent immigration has been Mandarin speakers from other parts of China, a large number of whom have the Shanghai dialect as their home language. Recent data indicate an even split between Cantonese and Mandarin as home language.

Recent government policy, however, has led to the privileging of Mandarin Chinese over all other dialects and varieties of Chinese.

In the community schools we studied, most students were second-generation Chinese with parents from Malaysia, Indonesia, Hong Kong and places in China such as Shanghai, Guangzhou and Fuzhou. One of the Chinese community languages schools in our study was established in the 1970s as a Cantonese school and now offers both Putonghua (Mandarin) and Cantonese; another was established in the 1990s and, based on a strong Shanghainese community, offers only Putonghua. Many students have attended these schools for five to ten years. Their language repertoire varied: some spoke their home Cantonese, Hokkien, Chouzhou, Shanghainese and some spoke Mandarin. Most students were dominant in English. The teachers (and students) reported that it was primarily the parents who were instrumental in sending their children to the community school to learn Chinese. As indicated above, the value of learning Chinese (and specifically Putonghua) for future career opportunities was reported as one of the main reasons for learning the language, a finding confirmed in other studies (see, for example, Francis, Archer and Mau, 2009).

> Because most Chinese parents know the value of learning Chinese, it is something very practical in the future, you know, for their children to get jobs in China. (Teacher, Chinese community school)

When the students talked about their parents, employability again came up as a central theme:

> My parents said China will overpass US in the future and become No 1 economic superpower; there will be a lot of jobs for us if we know Chinese. (Student, Fort Street HS, focus group interview)

> My parent said I already know English very well, if we know Chinese, they are the two most useful jobs for our future careers. (Student focus group interview, Chinese CLS)

Maintaining a Chinese identity

Our study also shows the desire to maintain Chinese identity as a key reason for students learning Chinese in community schools. Like Francis, Archer and Mau's (2010) study of students in Chinese complementary schools in the UK, our study also found that the desire to maintain their Chinese identity was a key reason for students learning Chinese in community schools. The finding is useful in understanding broader notions of cultural and social capital and relations with identity. Many students we interviewed also believed that, as Chinese, it was expected that they would know Chinese. Learning Chinese was for family connection and for high education attainment. Many Chinese students interviewed said that even though they were born in Australia they still felt Chinese first and Australian second. They reported mixing primarily with Chinese-background students.

S6: 'I am a Chinese although I was born here. I must learn Chinese, so when I go to China I can talk to my relatives.'

S7: 'My parents sent me to this school and said if I don't know Chinese people will think I am not schooled, not educated.'

S8: 'My parents said I can only speak Putonghua, but I don't know Chinese characters. In China I will be regarded as illiterate.'

S10: 'Oh I chose Chinese just based on I wanted to learn more about my culture and the language involved. I speak Cantonese back home but they teach Mandarin at school and it will be more interesting if I learned a different dialect in Chinese, especially now that Chinese is so commonly spoken as well.'

As students S7 and S8 indicate, Chinese language is traditionally regarded as the most important element in education. An educated Chinese is expected to read and write Chinese characters. This belief of full 'Chineseness' is closely linked with the mastery of the Chinese language.

Some parents also indicated that the purpose of learning Chinese is to maintain their cultural values. They felt integration in Australia is still a problem for them and they were worried they cannot communicate with their children if their children don't know Chinese.

I have been teaching Chinese in this school for over ten years. The most profound feeling for me is that our thoughts are still influenced by the Chinese education although we are in Australia. Even though we can speak English very well, we don't have an educational and cultural background in this country. Therefore, there are also some differences between locals and us; we find it difficult to integrate into the local community. We sometimes are unable to communicate with our children in English, so our thoughts also can't transfer to them. After you let children here learn Chinese language and culture, you enable children to understand how you consider the problem. Then, you can more easily communicate with them. (Parent teacher, Chinese CLS)

The parent speaking above indicates a cultural gap between first and second Chinese generations and suggests that Chinese language as a form of important social capital can bridge these gaps. Other studies have also found that community schools are providing Chinese children with 'better communication with family members' (Francis et al., 2009; Lao, 2004; Mu, 2014). As a teacher explained:

Many students made friends in the school and this is also a key reason they continue to come to the school to learn Chinese. Students normally stay here until they started their high school, especially, the 8th and 9th grade students that are willing to study Chinese at day school. They have been studying Chinese here since they were children … Also, they have made more friends in this school, and they can study together, so their Chinese progress could be improved faster. (Teacher, Chinese community school)

Our study also shows that, because their receptivity is so strong, students in the community schools were able to reach levels of competence that would mean learning Chinese was unlikely to be difficult for them in the future. However, our findings indicate that most of these same students will give up learning Chinese in their senior years of schooling.

Chinese language hierarchy among other Chinese varieties

Mandarin or Putonghua has replaced Cantonese and other dialects and varieties as the preferred language in many of the community language schools in the study. For example, the oldest Chinese CLS, which started teaching Cantonese to five students in the 1970s and gradually built numbers up to 900 students in the 1980s, is now struggling, with student numbers reduced by half. In order to compete with other community schools, School A started teaching Putonghua, while maintaining their Cantonese classes. Some parents wanted their children to learn both, but the Cantonese classes are getting smaller and more students enrol in the Putonghua classes. The deputy principal explained the decline in Cantonese classes.

In the past, the numbers of students who learned Cantonese was more than those learning Putonghua, but more students have been studying Putonghua recently. After Australia opened to China, everyone studying Chinese, I feel Putonghua is very important. Students of Cantonese class are less and less [enrolment], so we changed to teach Cantonese and Putonghua together. (Teacher, Chinese CLS)

Another teacher in the same school explained that lack of recognition for Cantonese language is the reason why Cantonese has been replaced by Putonghua (Mandarin) teaching.

Initially, we set up two and half hours for Cantonese, and a half hour for Putonghua. Then, we realized that Putonghua is more and more important, and the NSW School Certificate accepts Putonghua rather than Cantonese. Thus, we require that our graduating class must learn Putonghua. At that time, the Day

School required students for 28 hours Chinese learning to get School Certificate. So, the Cantonese class is required students to begin Putonghua learning since the 9th grade, and they have to take Putonghua learning for three hours. (Teacher, Chinese CLS)

The dominance/dominating effect of Putonghua has acted as a 'dividing practice' (Foucault, 1982: 208) in the Chinese community, where those who can speak Putonghua are regarded as more 'cultured' and 'better educated'. Teachers now expect parents to speak Putonghua to their children at home so that the children can learn Putonghua more quickly, even where the home/heritage language is Cantonese or Shanghainese. Children who come to school unable to speak Putonghua are likely to be embarrassed (like all non-standard language students). At the same time, many teachers, such as those quoted below, reported that they had the support of parents to teach Putonghua, not Cantonese, because of the status and values of Putonghua.

> The Cantonese parents they all agree that Putonghua is very important, because Putonghua is the official language in China, so if you think of it in a practical way, it's no harm to learn how to speak Putonghua. (Teacher, Chinese CLS School)

> A lot of parents want their children to learn Putonghua, so they can get ahead in jobs and things like that. (Teacher, Chinese CLS School)

However, parent interviews revealed several parents who wanted to maintain Cantonese as their heritage language. They maintained the Cantonese language at home, for family values, especially for communication with grandparents. Other languages such as Shanghainese and Chouzhou were retained for the same reasons. With Putonghua replacing other Chinese languages in most CLS, however, they no longer had a school that suited this purpose.

> I speak Cantonese at home. I want my child to learn more Cantonese at this school. He was studying Cantonese at the beginning but he was transferred to Putonghua class three years ago, because the Cantonese class doesn't have enough students. (Parent, Chinese CLS)

For some students this now meant learning two languages, one in the afternoon and one in the morning. In some classes designated as 'Cantonese' classes, teachers also taught Putonghua. The following exchange from one of our field notes of class observations in the older of the two Chinese CLS in our study demonstrates how, where this was the case, Putonghua was privileged as the language the students needed to learn for examination purposes. The class consisted of eight students (five boys and three girls). At the beginning of the class the teacher asked students to read a poem in Cantonese; then she asked students to read in Putonghua.

> T: *ngo5 dei6 seung5 go3 lai5 baai3 hok6 jo2 si1，nei5 dei6 duk6 yat1 chi3 la1。* [we learnt a poem last week, can you read it once more]
>
> Ss: (Reading a Poem in Cantonese)
>
> S: 《*ngo5 giu1 ngou6 ngo5 si6 jung1 gwok3 yan4*》。*duk6 yat1 sau2 si1，yung6 gwong2 dung1 wa2 duk6.* [I am proud I am Chinese].
>
> T: *ho2 yi5 yung6 pou2 tung1 wa2 duk6 yat1 chi3 ma1?* [Can you read it in Putonghua]?
>
> Ss: *m4 dak1，ngo5 dei6 m4 sik1 duk6。* [No, no, we cannot].
>
> T: *nei5 dei6 ying1 goi1 hok6 sik1 yung6 pou2 tung1 wa2 duk6，yan1 wai4 nei5 dei6 yiu3 yung6 pou2 tung1 wa2 haau2 HSK。* [You need to read in Putonghua because you have to do the HSC test in Putonghua]
>
> Ss: *hou2 la1. yung6 pou2 tung1 wa2 long5 duk6* (Reading it in Putonghua) …

As we can see from the above lesson notes, the teacher has tried to encourage students to use more Putonghua in a Cantonese lesson. The discourse of this persuasion is 'Putonghua is useful for your future career and you need to do HSK [Hanyu Shuipin Kaoshi, a Chinese proficiency test] in Putonghua'. The students were reluctant to speak Putonghua, because their Putonghua proficiency was poor and they were embarrassed or resistant to learning a new second language. After the class, the teacher explained to the researcher that she used to have a big Cantonese class of more than twenty students. Now the class sizes are becoming smaller as many parents send their children to Putonghua classes.

> They [her students] prefer learning Cantonese because they speak it at home but they need to do the HSC and therefore need Putonghua, so they are not against learning it. They speak to me in Cantonese and also to each other in Cantonese. There is no Cantonese Pinyin, so we learn Cantonese by hearing other people speak. It is good to learn Putonghua. I teach them Pinyin as part of teaching Putonghua. Some students are good but some students are far behind the rest of the class.

Summary

The findings present a complex picture. The goals of learning Chinese expressed by the parents and students in our study often conflicted with one another: languages for career; exam success; academic interest; family background and cultural identity. We argue, as do other researchers (e.g. Francis et al., 2009;

Lao, 2004; Mu, 2014), that learning the Chinese language is seen as a means to gain social, cultural and economic capital. However, the high status of Chinese language within the broader community and in mid- to high-SES schools has not translated to HSC study, despite policy and funding. The decline in the study of Chinese at the senior level could be seen as the result of lack of coordination and cooperation between Chinese community schools and mainstream schools, between federal and state governments, and between different states. These factors, among others, have made teaching Chinese to young Australians an unsuccessful endeavour.

A key reason for the low uptake of Chinese in secondary schools has been characterized as being due to the high numbers of 'background speakers' that second language learners ('Australian' students) have to compete with. The teaching of Chinese has thus been complicated by the perceived conflict between Chinese community schools and day schools, between Chinese as a 'background' and as a 'second' language, particularly in NSW where Chinese is the main language after English spoken by school-aged students (Orton, 2008). On the basis of our study, we argue that the perceived dichotomy between 'background' and second language learners has not been productive and that a focus on equality of access to languages and language competence and proficiency is needed. In other words, there needs to be a system which does not reconstruct the traditional discrimination against the Chinese community in Australian society, but which credits language proficiency – one which enables equal access to language learning without marginalizing background speakers.

The picture in the community is also complex. The Chinese community language schools played a role in a shift to the standard Mandarin at the expense of Cantonese and Shanghainese, spoken in the home, despite the home language potentially carrying more social capital in the family home and Chinese communities. The economic effect of globalization on languages can be seen through the increased awareness that language has value as social and cultural capital and different languages have different values and symbolic power on the global market (Li and Zhu, 2012). Students choose to learn Chinese as a second language because they and their parents have seen the economic value of Chinese language in the job market. However, for Chinese-background students, Chinese in the NSW examination context seems to have little value as academic capital – other subjects which offer better chances for university entry into highly competitive courses have more value in the senior years. In some schools, students from Chinese-speaking backgrounds were also deterred from studying Chinese because they were perceived to make non-Chinese-background speakers feel inadequate. The differentiated eligibility of students for the HSC – background speakers, continuers, beginners and heritage learners – has served to discourage schools from offering Chinese particularly to background speakers – and has deterred Chinese-background students in particular from studying Chinese in the senior years. Background speakers have had to look to the community language schools for courses that enable them to learn Chinese as both a heritage language and a language of academic and cultural capital for future employment. The latter purpose increasing privileges Mandarin/Putonghua as the preferred Chinese language taught in these schools, marginalizing heritage languages such as Cantonese.

10

Languages Curriculum and Change

The study that provided the data and discussions presented in this book was motivated by our strong interest in understanding why the provision and uptake of languages have remained so low despite the long history of government languages reports, initiatives and support for multiculturalism. In this book we have explored how limited access to and uptake of languages study have persisted as effects of educational policy, social and cultural forces, school practices and attitudes, and institutional practices such as tertiary selection. Our aim has been not simply to identify structural inequality but to show how individual schools, teachers and communities have actively responded to social and educational changes. In this chapter we look at languages curriculum in the context of neoliberal education and the shift away from multiculturalism. While our focus has been on languages in Australia, the trends and influences on languages study and access clearly have relevance to North American and UK contexts, where contemporary studies point to widening inequalities in access to languages (e.g. Rhodes and Pufahl, 2010; Tinsley and Dolezal, 2018). Nonetheless, we do not venture into the debates around global English. In the final section of this chapter, we explore possible structural and policy changes to enhance access to quality languages study in schools.

Inequality, school curriculum and languages

There is a long tradition of research into the role of curriculum, subject provision and choice in the reproduction of social class and educational (in)equality (Ayalon, 2006; Ianelli, 2013; Teese, Lamb and Duru-Bellat, 2017). Studies often explore the different roles of 'vocational' and traditional 'academic' curricula of which languages are a part. Several studies also explore the changes in the 'academic' curriculum with the shift to comprehensive schooling in the 1960s and 1970s. Teese (2013), for example, traces the history of curriculum reform and counter-reform in English, Mathematics and Languages, showing little discernible impact on social inequality in the patterns of results. He finds the same patterns across school subjects and argues that inequality relates to the ways individuals are brought together in different sites within school systems (2013: 230). Despite the wealth of research into Science, Mathematics, English and other curriculum areas, there is still little on the ways in which they reflect and reproduce social inequality in the segmented school systems of this decade; there is even less study of the role of languages in these contexts.

Our review of the over eighty policy-related reports, investigations and substantial enquiries since 1972 (Lo Bianco and Gvozdenko, 2006) on languages in Australian schools indicates that despite addressing issues of teacher supply and training, gender differences in uptake, classroom pedagogy and curriculum, not one has addressed issues of social inequality to languages. These issues have begun to receive attention, however, especially in systems where there has been consistent and coherent data collection on the provision and uptake of languages. The *Language Trends* reports in the UK, for example, have been central to the analysis of social inequality and access to languages (Board and Tinsley, 2014, 2015a, b, 2016, 2017; Tinsley and Board, 2013, 2017; Tinsley and Dolezal, 2018). The most recent report (Tinsley and Dolezal, 2018) looks particularly at socioeconomic and educational variables. It finds a widening gap between schools moving towards the government target of 90 per cent of students taking a language and schools where languages are not a priority. Schools where students had least access to languages in Year 9 were those with a higher proportion of students eligible for free school meals, urban or northern regional schools, academies and schools with lower educational achievement. There were great regional differences between London and the South East and the North East. National surveys in the United States have also identified lower-SES urban, regional and rural elementary schools as least likely to be offering languages and as having the greatest difficulty in attracting trained languages teachers (Pufahl and Rhodes, 2011; Pufahl, Rhodes and Christian, 2000; Rhodes, 2014; Rhodes and Pufahl, 2010). Only one Australian study has relevant data and these data indicate that disadvantaged schools are least likely to provide languages study (Coghlan and Holcz, 2014). The findings of these studies and reports are still to be reflected in government policy, programs and initiatives. In this book we have attempted to explore social inequalities in languages study further through an investigation of the wider social and cultural factors influencing schools' language policy and practice. We also consider local factors, such as the perceptions of school executives, teachers, parents and students of the value of languages study, the value of specific languages and the relevance of languages study to particular groups of students. The next section retraces how broader changes in education in the past three decades have impacted on the provision and uptake of languages.

Sites of inequality

In the 1980s, Australia began introducing market-based changes in education. In NSW, for example, government schools were dezoned to allow parents to enrol children outside local catchment areas; the number of academically selective government schools was increased to forty seven and other specialist schools were established to increase parental 'choice' (Marginson, 2006). Increased federal government funding to non-government schools accompanied increased enrolments to the extent where 41 per cent of secondary students now attend private schools, one of the highest of any Organisation for Economic Co-operation and Development (OECD) countries (OECD, 2011). There is growing international evidence that the marketplace in education actually increases inequality in schools and students (OECD, 2012). This approach represents a shift from addressing the needs of students to testing their performance; it also increases government control by promoting competition between students, between school subjects and between schools and types of school (Marginson, 2006). The term 'provision' is replaced with 'choice', as individual families are encouraged to negotiate school 'markets' (Campbell and Proctor, 2014: 259–260). Choice is very directly and powerfully related to social-class differences and it is a key factor in reinforcing social inequality. As Ball and his colleagues point out, 'the exercise of choice as a process of maintaining social distinction and educational differentiations ... is likely to exaggerate social segregation' (Ball, Bowe and Gewirtz, 1996: 91).

The impact of this segregation on schools in our study was marked: Metro HS, a local comprehensive with under 400 students, had one languages teacher and limited subject choice; Forster HS, five kilometres away, a selective secondary school with over 900 students, had eight languages teachers and a range of language and other elective offerings. Eighty per cent of Forster parents were in the top ICSEA quartile compared with 18 per cent of Metro parents. A 'residualization' of comprehensive schools into places of 'last resort' (Campbell, 2005: 21) was also clear in terms of cultural diversity. Metro HS has 75 per cent of its students from non-English-speaking backgrounds while its feeder primary school, Metro

PS, has 35 per cent (myschool.edu.au, 2019), confirming what has been called a 'white flight' in secondary schools (Ho, 2011). Forster HS also had 76 per cent from non-English-speaking backgrounds, exemplifying the growth of the new 'ethnic middle class' (Ho, 2011). This gentrification of inner cities leads, in fact, to greater segregation because of middle-class parents opting for private schooling for their children (Keels, Burdick-Will and Keene, 2013). 'Choice' is accompanied by a growth of external testing examinations, school ranking and the rise of private tutoring (Watkins and Noble, 2013). At the individual school level, the range of subject offerings becomes more limited in lower-SES schools and the choices available continue to entrench social reproduction directing post-school opportunities along class lines (Tranter, 2012). The OECD report *Equity and Quality in Education* (2012: 92) states that 'providing full parental school choice can result in segregating students by ability, socio economic background and generate greater inequities across education systems'.

Languages education is implicated in and affected by this growing divide. Lower-SES primary schools have limited funding and it has been more difficult to find and employ suitably qualified languages teachers. The focus on competition between schools, based on high stakes testing, means that languages are often dropped to allow greater focus on English language literacy and numeracy. The constraining effect of *No Child Left Behind* in the United States and of nationwide NAPLAN testing in Australia on languages provision has been well documented (Thompson and Harbaugh, 2013). 'Choice' at secondary school level also impacts on languages: they are perceived as more difficult subjects and so not suitable for the 'less able' students or students who have English as a second (or third) language in comprehensive government schools. The notion that languages were 'difficult' subjects emerged in parent comments in our study. In addition, lower-SES students tend to be offered and hence to take 'easier' and more vocationally oriented options in secondary school when compared to middle-SES students of similar ability (Gayton, 2010). The socioeconomic circumstances of families mean that parents in lower-SES schools have fewer opportunities for travel and fewer experiences of languages and languages learning, two key motivating factors in children choosing to study languages (Carr and Pauwels, 2006; Gayton, 2010). Excursions for languages students in lower-SES Campbell HS in Wollongong were only to Sydney. In contrast, students at higher-SES Forster HS went on exchanges to France, Germany China and Japan. There were few examples in our study of any lower-SES school offering overseas trips, exchanges, excursions and languages events; it was only the higher-SES schools which offered 'value-added' languages study.

The divide between higher- and lower-SES schools emerged in other ways in our study. For example, devolution of responsibility to schools and greater local autonomy was a double-edged sword for the principals (see Chapter 2). The pressure to compete for enrolments led principals in higher-SES primary schools such as St Catherine's and St Francis and Keswick PS to choose languages as a marker of distinction in response to real or perceived parent demand. There was also a pattern of 'lighthouse' primary schools offering languages (e.g. Clarke PS, Cheswell PS); in the same way others, such as Pennington PS, chose to specialize in Music and Art. This competition and reliance on the initiative of the principal also meant that languages programs remained fragile. At Cheswell PS, Barnsley Girls HS and Sherwood HS, when the supportive principals retired, the languages programs went into decline under new principals. Our study also showed that the choice of subjects of 'distinction' such as Languages, Drama and Art was more a feature of mid- to high-SES primary schools.

School segmentation impacted on languages teachers. Mid- to high-SES secondary schools tended to have a 'critical mass' of experienced languages teachers; low-SES secondary schools such as Metro HS had single, often early-career languages teachers. Being a sole languages teacher linked to lower teacher morale, less ability to promote languages and offer extra-curricular activities (see Chapter 3). Whole-school approaches to languages teaching were most evident in higher-SES schools with a large number of languages teachers. At De Sales HS and Cheswell PS, there had been specific drives to get subject and classroom teachers with expertise in languages teaching. Finally, school segmentation was reflected in teacher segmentation: in our survey, 42 per cent of teachers (excluding languages teachers) reported some ability to speak languages in addition to English. The majority, who had skills in traditional languages such as French, were in high-SES independent or selective government schools; those with community languages skills were mainly in lower-SES government and Catholic schools. Schools with majority English-speaking-background students had few, if any, teachers who could speak a language in addition to English.

In summary, the divide in access to languages emerged as strongest in senior secondary school with the competition for tertiary places impacting on teacher, parent and student attitudes. Parents, who were happy with their children to study languages in primary and junior secondary schools, pushed for more 'important' subjects to be chosen in senior secondary (see Chapters 5 and 9). The uptake of languages for tertiary entry was lowest in government comprehensive and Catholic secondary schools and highest in independent and government selective secondary schools. The key finding of our study is that for students in the lower-SES secondary schools, especially those from English-speaking backgrounds, there was little or no access to languages beyond the mandatory 100 hours. The next section considers the overlay of cultural/ linguistic diversity in this segmented school system.

The retreat from multiculturalism?

Much has been written about the 'retreat from multiculturalism' in the Netherlands (Entzinger, 2003; Koopmans, 2006; Prins and Slijper, 2002), the UK (Back et al., 2002; Hansen, 2007; Vertovec, 2005), Australia (Ang and Stratton, 2001) and Canada (Wong et al., 2005). The picture emerging from our study, however, is more complex. Evidence of cultural and linguistic diversity was present in all the schools we studied. Our parent interviews suggested much greater diversity in parents and families than captured in school statistics. Parents we interviewed at Campbell HS, where 20 per cent from language backgrounds other than English were reported, generally reported cultural and linguistic diversity in their family and extended family. In selective schools, traditionally the pathway for lower-SES English-speaking-background students, we found over 80 per cent of the students now from language backgrounds other than English: the new 'ethnic middle class' (Colic-Peisker, 2011; Ho, 2011). The reality of growing demographic diversity was not reflected in schools, where we found a progressive marginalization of community languages. It was almost as if social mobility and a stronger voice for ethnic communities had come at the price of marginalizing languages: multiculturalism but not multilingualism.

   In the 1980s, the narrative of community languages had been one of young people, mainly in lower-SES schools, being able to maintain and extend their home language in primary and secondary schools. Modern Greek and Italian provided pathways to tertiary study for many students whose parents had not been able to complete schooling (Teese and Polesel, 2003). We reported in earlier chapters how Australia is one of the few OECD countries where first- and second-generation migrants scored at or above national averages on standardized testing. Neoliberal reforms, however, have seen a segmentation of schooling along ethnicity as well as class lines. The shift of parents in Sydney to private schooling has led to 78 per cent of students in private schools being of English-speaking backgrounds (Ho, 2011). The majority of students speaking languages other than English are in government schools where they constitute 52 per cent of enrolments. Within the government school system there is also marked segregation as Australia's immigration policy, favouring middle-class migrants, has led to a change in the nation's socioeconomic landscape. Asian residents from various source countries comprise the largest group of migrants to Australia from language backgrounds other than English (Australian Bureau of Statistics, 2016). In these communities there has been rapid growth of commercial tutoring colleges and paid private tutors as parents compete to gain entry for their children to selective schools (Sriprakash, Proctor and Hu, 2016). This industry is on the rise, as is families' expenditure on private tutoring (Watson, 2008). A disproportionate number of Asian-Australians are enrolled in the state's, selective high schools and prestigious university courses (Watkins and Noble, 2013; Watkins, Ho and Butler, 2017). Eighty-five per cent of students in the four Sydney selective schools in our study were from non-English-speaking backgrounds (myschool.edu.au, 2019). Watkins, Ho and Butler (2017) report that these schools are viewed as being taken over by 'Asian' students, who are seen as taking places once held by (middle-class) Anglo-Australian students. The corollary is the higher than average enrolment of students from non-English-speaking backgrounds in lower-SES government schools. It is against this backdrop that the issues of access to and uptake of languages are being played out.

Our account of the study of Chinese (see Chapter 9) illustrates the contradiction. In primary schools with large numbers of students of Chinese backgrounds, Chinese was taught to both beginners and 'background' students with reported good levels of success; in secondary schools with students of Chinese backgrounds there were often problems. Chinese parents and teachers in our study counselled children against studying Chinese in senior secondary school; non-background learners of Chinese dropped the language because of concerns about 'difficulty' and lower exam scores. In the current assessment system, the problem of how to encourage uptake of Chinese and other community languages by non-background students without disadvantaging 'background' learners was insurmountable. From our study, it seemed that, in school terms, multiculturalism was thus more acceptable than multilingualism. In the late 1990s, Teese and Polesel predicted this situation that without community languages, languages would return to their traditional position:

> It was the rise of ethnic languages in the upper secondary curriculum and the strong academic motivation of many immigrant communities that saved languages from retiring into the enclaves represented by the most highly educated Australian-born families. No doubt the salvaging operation performed by universities in offering bonus marks greatly encouraged the academic exploitation of ethnic languages. But without the widening of the curriculum to

include non-traditional languages and without the drive of ethnic communities themselves, this mechanism alone would have done little but reinforce the advantages of already advantaged families and their traditional academic culture. (Teese and Polesel, 2003: 84)

Recognizing inequality

Languages educators and researchers are used to hearing media and governments bemoaning the decline of languages and announcing grand plans to address this.

> Every preschool child would have to study a foreign language if the Coalition wins the next election, as part of Tony Abbott's vision to help prepare Australia for the Asian boom. And within a decade, 40 per cent of Year 12 students would be studying a second language under a target set by Mr Abbott in his Budget reply speech last night. (Scott, 2012)

Seven years in Coalition government and the Year 12 uptake nationally is still around 10 per cent! Similar statements are made by many politicians in many Anglophone countries. In a study of the failure of the NALSAS program (1994–99) to reach any of its targets in increasing Asian language study, Slaughter (2009) argues that planning needs to take into account 'the complex and varying local linguistic ecologies of each State and Territory in Australia'. It is precisely this information on local schools, teachers, parents and young people studying/not studying languages that we need to inform policy and planning. Although the structural inequality we have tracked in this book limits the development of languages and constrains schools and teachers, it also makes local responses to this inequality more important. Solutions are thus not simplistic recipes abstracted from the schools, teachers, young people and their families involved in the teaching and learning of languages. The final section of this chapter explores possibilities that arise from linking specific contextual responses to broader policy development. We thus bring our findings back into a policy agenda.

What if languages were part of core curriculum?

In many English-speaking countries, learning a second or third language is a normal curriculum requirement. In England, language learning is compulsory between the ages of seven and fourteen. Scotland requires language study from

Grades 4 to 10 with an expectation of six years of study of the same language. Some forty states in the United States mandate at least two years of languages study and all Canadian provinces have levels of mandation, with Ontario requiring second language study from Grades 4 to 10 (Liddicoat et al., 2007). In Australia, only Victoria has compulsory languages in primary schools. The last available figures show that Victoria had 71 per cent of K-12 students taking languages compared with 23 per cent in NSW (Liddicoat et al., 2007). Making languages part of the school curriculum means that provision becomes a systemic not an individual school responsibility and thus addresses problems of the lack of access to languages in mid- to low-SES, regional and rural schools.

In NSW the only systemic requirement or support is the government-funded Community Languages Program running in 143 government primary schools and the compulsory 100 hours languages study in Years 7 and 8 secondary school. We found that it was mostly in the K-6 Program that children received two or more hours of languages teaching per week. However, the majority of primary school, usually parent funded programs, were around thirty minutes: more language 'awareness' than language learning. The provision of 100 hours in secondary school also emerged in our study as important for both parents' and their children's positive attitudes to language learning (if not actual gains in proficiency).

The problem in having languages as curriculum options or electives is that there can be no continuity of language learning. Young people in our study reported being taught several languages by the time they reached Year 10 in secondary school. They reported this as superficial and repetitive, learning to count one to ten, sing songs and colour in worksheets. We found that languages in primary schools generally relied on the chance of having a teacher or parent who could teach a language – any language. We found few instances of students being able to continue languages study in the same language from primary to secondary school. Within secondary schools there was also lack of continuity: there was often a break before elective languages in Year 9. Then in Year 11 students were able to start 'beginner' languages for the Year 12 exam but they would usually be mixed in with other students who were continuing students from Year 7. It was only at Forster HS, the Dante Bilingual School and the Sydney International School that we found any semblance of continuity of languages study. At Forster HS, Year 8 students could take 'continuer' French and were encouraged to undertake continuous study to Year 12. At Sydney International School and the Dante Bilingual School, there was coherent languages planning K-12. There is thus a need for languages to be a core part of primary curriculum and for all schools to be required to offer languages. In secondary schools the increase of mandatory hours from 100 to 300 would also ensure continuity. In the context of NSW it is crucial for mandation to begin at Kindergarten (and even better in pre-school) because of the numbers of children entering school with languages in addition to English. With government schools in Sydney having 52 per cent of students speaking languages in addition to English, there is no alternative but to extend and develop these skills from the beginning of schooling. The recent introduction of mandatory languages in Victoria has seen the numbers of students learning languages jump to 79 per cent (DET, 2017). This has enabled the introduction of pedagogical approaches such as Content and Language Integrated Learning (CLIL) (Cross and Gearon, 2013). Issues of teacher supply also become less of an issue as tertiary institutions respond by including language teaching method in primary pre-service teacher education.

Simple mandation of languages provision, however, may not be sufficient by itself to address the issues of educational inequality. Recent evidence from England identifies several issues in compulsory languages study, all of which are similar to those identified in chapters in this book: the lack of time given to languages, difficulties in provision in lower-SES; rural and regional schools and withdrawal of EAL and special needs students from classes in primary schools (Tinsley and Dolezal, 2018). It is important to recognize that lower-SES schools lack resources to support languages and moves to make them part of the core curriculum need to include additional government support.

How can the uptake of languages in senior secondary school be increased?

Languages have suffered in policy changes in the senior secondary schools in Australia and other countries. When the Higher School Certificate in NSW began in 1967, 30 per cent of Year 12 students studied one of twelve languages, mainly French (NESA, 2019). A series of policy changes around 1999, some specifically targeted at community languages, led to a consequent decline which has never been addressed. Languages were no longer specifically included in the calculation of the tertiary entrance score; the requirement for 'breadth' of studies, including languages, was changed to only the study of English; the number of units required for a tertiary score dropped from twelve to ten, and languages were the 'first to go' (BOS, 2000, 2001). After 1999 all languages were scaled separately instead of being linked to French and German (DTEC, 1997). The change in tertiary ranking in NSW seems particularly harsh on community languages, with the mean scaled score of all major community languages being in the lowest quartile of subjects (Universities Admissions Centre, 2018).

In our study we found that the Australian Tertiary Admission Ranking (ATAR) and the perceived 'difficulty' of languages were the main reasons for students not taking languages. The marketization of education across Anglophone countries seems to have had the similar results: parents and students are forced to 'game' the tertiary entry system, choosing subjects on the basis of possible marks rather than student interests, ability and utility. The series of policy changes seems to explain the disappearance of Year 12 languages in mid- to low-SES secondary schools.

How can this decline be reversed? Again, we would argue that the lack of uptake is not an issue of simply developing languages in primary or junior secondary school, but a problem specific to senior secondary school that would require a range of policy shifts. In NSW the most immediate need is to address the issue of the ATAR and its impact on languages. There needs to be an examination of ATAR leading either to a change in ranking or to the exception of languages from the ATAR ranking system. The question of how to compare student performance in different subjects is a difficult one. It could be argued that student performance in languages should not be compared with performance in mass candidature subjects such as English and that there are better ways to assess subject difficulty. There is also a case for arguing that if there is scaling, then all languages should be scaled the same as they are set at comparable levels of difficulty by boards of studies. Whatever the solution, this discrimination in the algorithm against languages must be addressed if languages study at the senior level of schooling in NSW is to increase.

Tertiary ranking by itself does not explain the low uptake. Both NSW and Victoria apply the ATAR to languages, albeit with significantly differing algorithms. Victoria, with the same student profile, has three times the number of students taking languages in senior secondary. Key factors emerge explaining the difference: incentives and flexibility. In Victoria, universities offer bonus points for languages; students can take languages in Year 11; there is more flexibility in studying outside the school and outside the school week. In the United States the requirement by almost 25 per cent of tertiary institutions for languages study in Year 12 is reported as ensuring higher uptake; in England the E-Bacc (English Baccalaureate) also has similar impact on languages uptake (Tinsley and Dolezal, 2018). There is clearly a need for the government to work with tertiary institutions in providing flexibility and incentives for languages provision and uptake in Year 12.

Languages: Assessing proficiency or curriculum outcomes

Studying languages in school involves a tension: languages are school curriculum subjects which require the meeting of curriculum outcomes but they also involve the gaining of proficiency; these are overlapping but different goals – Music, Art, and Health and Physical Education have similar tensions. In Australia state governments are mainly responsible for education: developing and implementing curriculum, employing and monitoring teachers. Their concern is primarily that languages curriculum outcomes are reached. The federal government, on the other hand, is responsible for educational programs which aim to expand languages uptake and increasing proficiency. The problem for the federal government in Australia is that it has very limited control over curriculum implementation or teacher employment. It also does not have consistent and coherent data on which to base policy and programs as this is not collected by states.

The burden on state governments and curriculum authorities has thus been to address the problems of languages through curriculum. Languages curricula in primary and junior secondary school have designated different entry points and different curriculum pathways where possible. At the senior secondary level (see Chapter 8) up to four different syllabuses have been developed for beginner, continuer, 'background' and 'heritage' learners. Unfortunately, with the low numbers of languages learners, all levels are generally placed in the same class. The problem has been that at federal level the reliance has been on funded programs to halt the decline of languages and at state level the reliance has been on curriculum changes. Neither have been successful.

The missing link is assessment. At present, there is no way of knowing which students at any stage of learning in any school gain any level of proficiency in any language. Christian, Pufahl and Rhodes (2005), in their review of language teaching internationally, argue that curriculum must involve assessment which is of course outcomes-based but also, more broadly, proficiency-oriented. They argue for 'a framework [which] indicates when students should start a foreign language, how much instruction they will receive, and what levels of proficiency they should attain. The framework should also be transparent, in the sense that both educators and students should clearly understand what the levels of proficiency mean' (2005: 25).

Proficiency testing in school-level languages study is not new: so much research and development in Europe has stemmed from the CEFR (Common European Framework of References) for languages, and there is a strong body of research into the Canadian immersion programs (Swain and Lapkin, 2005, 2013). There is also Asset Languages (AL), proficiency rating scales and tests, which came from the National Languages Strategy in England (2002) drawing on the CEFR (Jones, Ashton and Walker, 2010). The language proficiency scale, called the Languages Ladder, has materials and tests in twenty-five languages bringing together modern and community languages in primary, secondary and adult learning contexts.

Many institutions have also developed proficiency testing in different languages. In our study we found students at Forster HS sat for Assessment of Language Competence (ALC) in one of eight languages; many also sat for the Chinese proficiency test *Hanyu Shuiping Kaoshi* (HSK). We also found students who had sat for external second language tests in Japanese and Korean. None of these students were in lower-SES schools, perhaps because of the costs involved in sitting for such tests.

On the one hand, we have syllabus outcomes which do not assess language proficiency and, on the other, we have language proficiency tests which do not align with syllabus. How can proficiency assessment be integrated into education systems and aligned with curriculum? In Australia an instrument for EAL student language development based on classroom-based assessment has been found to meet standards for validity and reliability (Centre for Educational Statistics and Evaluation, 2013). This shows one pathway may be to develop proficiency rating scales, resources and professional learning which could be implemented at classroom level by trained teachers. This would provide low cost access to proficiency rating by all students and would ensure greater alignment of curriculum and assessment.

There are many possible benefits of integrating and aligning learning progressions or frameworks with curriculum. Such an alignment would have a greater washback effect on pedagogy. Achieving real-life competences, for example, would increase learner motivation and sense of achievement. Aggregated data compiled from the results of classroom-based assessments would also be crucial in policy and program development, providing information on strengths and needs. Proficiency gains could be credited no matter how and where they were gained. For students in mid- to low-SES schools the crediting of proficiency could provide the motivation to achieve in a 'difficult' subject.

The implications of such proficiency rating scales for continuity are interesting. Secondary schools would have a clearer idea of the proficiency students were bringing from their primary school languages study and differentiation in learning could be better managed. Students who were not able to maintain continuity in learning within schools could also be catered for. Where students with backgrounds in a community language entered senior secondary school, their levels of proficiency on entry to the curriculum study could be assessed. In Australia this could lead to streamlining of curriculum from five or four syllabuses (beginner, continuer, heritage, extension and background) to one syllabus with possibly two exams – one rating proficiency improvement and the other assessing analysis of understanding of literature, history and cultural issues. Students, for example, could be awarded a score on proficiency in speaking, listening, reading and writing that might be some combination of the level gained and improvement made during the course of study; their second examination could be in cultural aspects, history, literacy and other areas, which could be answered in their target language or English. In such a way, proficiency would be credited without disadvantaging students who are non-background learners. The 'passport to languages' is widely used in Europe as a way for learners to assess their own progress and achievement in languages. Self-assessment could be combined with teacher assessment to provide a more valid and reliable document.

Perhaps the most important impact would be at school level with the status and role of languages. At present there is a strong perception of languages, particularly in the primary school, as contributing to a 'crowded' curriculum. Languages teachers have little to show in terms of student achievement in a context of high stakes testing and school competitive marketing. This was not the case in four of our case study schools: Clarke PS, Cheswell PS, Sydney International School and Dante Bilingual School. In these schools, students learnt languages through different curriculum areas, through integration. At Dante, students learnt History, Geography, Science and Italian every morning in Italian. At Cheswell PS, Korean and other languages teachers planned on an equal basis with classroom grade teachers, apportioning outcomes from the range of curriculum areas that each teacher would work towards. Languages teachers taught through Art, Music, History and Maths. Classroom grade teachers did not talk about a 'crowded curriculum' but about how they appreciated getting support in achieving outcomes. These schools would normally be labelled as bilingual, and not every school can achieve this organization. The movement towards CLIL that grew in Europe and now especially in Spain and England from the 1990s has shown how learning language through curriculum areas can be implemented in classrooms where students have smaller amounts of time (Coyle, Hood and Marsh, 2010). As stated above, these programs have been implemented in the UK and other European countries, and in

Australia – Victoria and Queensland – with great success (Cross, 2010, 2012; Cross and Gearon, 2013). With an assessment framework aligned with languages and other subject curriculum, outcomes in languages study would be transparent and respected. Government support for such an approach is vital if languages are to succeed in competition with other demands in mid- to low-SES primary schools.

Retreat from policy

One of our researchers was sitting on a government advisory group involved in the development of a languages policy. In response to a suggestion that the proposed policy and initiatives would benefit from being based on research and a knowledge of what was happening in schools, the chair of the committee replied: 'It's our job to come up with this policy and the ideas and programs; it's your job to tell us how they have worked.' Sadly, the draft policy went the same way as many initiatives lost in the files of someone's office.

In our review of the literature we found two or three Anglophone jurisdictions where there has been strong development of languages: England, Scotland and Victoria. The commonality in these jurisdictions is the collection of consistent and coherent data on the provision and uptake of languages.

The answers to the questions we raise in this book may not be as simple as we hope. It is obvious that a range of strategies and initiatives must be employed. The potholed road of languages reports, review and programs is littered with failed targets, political backflips and glossy publications. What we can add to this track is perhaps a recommendation for using research into the issues of SES and community languages for the development of strategies to increase the study of languages. Such a development, we argue, would challenge much of the thinking behind school-based management and the devolution of responsibility for curriculum and staffing. However, without such an approach we will continue to have regular media dramas on the decline of languages, impossible policy targets and great-sounding initiatives for change based on very limited research.

References

Ang, I. and Stratton, J. (2001). 'Multiculturalism in crisis: The new politics of race and national identity in Australia'. In I. Ang (ed), *On Not Speaking Chinese: Living between Asia and the West*, 95–111. London: Routledge.

Ardzejewska, K., McMaugh, A. and Coutts, P. (2010). 'Delivering the primary curriculum: The use of subject specialist and generalist teachers in NSW'. *Issues in Educational Research*, 20 (3): 203–219.

Asia Education Foundation. (2012). 'Building demand for Asia literacy: What works'. Melbourne: University of Melbourne. Available online: http://www.asiaeducation. edu.au/docs/default-source/what-works-pdf/building_demand_report.pdf?sfvrsn=6 (accessed 9 August 2019).

Asia Education Foundation. (2015). *What Works 10: Teacher Education and Languages*. Melbourne: Asia Education Foundation.

Australian Bureau of Statistics (ABS). (2016). '2016 Census: Multicultural'. Available online: https://www.abs.gov.au/ausstats/abs@.nsf/lookup/Media%20Release3 (accessed 6 August 2019).

Australian Council of State School Organisations (ACSSO). (2007). 'Attitudes towards the study of languages in Australian schools: The National statement and plan – Making a difference or another decade of indifference?'. Available online: http://www.aftv.vic.edu.au/resources/whylearnfrench/ attitudestowardsthestudyoflanginausschools.pdf (accessed 24 June 2019).

Australian Curriculum, Assessment and Reporting Authority (ACARA). (2011). 'The shape of Australian Curriculum: Languages'. Available online: http://docs.acara. edu.au/resources/Languages_-_Shape_of_the_Australian_Curriculum_new.pdf (accessed 6 August 2019).

Australian Curriculum, Assessment and Reporting Authority (ACARA). (2013). 'Asia and Australia's Engagement with Asia'. Available online: https://www. australiancurriculum.edu.au/f-10-curriculum/cross-curriculum-priorities/asia-and-australia-s-engagement-with-asia/ (accessed 6 August 2019).

Australian Curriculum, Assessment and Reporting Authority. (2019). *My School*. Available online: https://www.myschool.edu.au/ (accessed 13 August 2019).

Australian Government. (2012). 'Australia in the Asian Century: White Paper'. Available online: http://www.defence.gov.au/whitepaper/2013/docs/australia_in_the_asian_century_white_paper.pdf (accessed 6 August 2019).

Ayalon, H. (2006). 'Non-hierarchical curriculum differentiation and inequality in achievement: A different story or more of the same?' *Teachers College Record*, 108 (6): 1186–1213.

Back, L., Keith, M., Khan, A., Shukra, K. and Solomos, J. (2002). 'New Labour's white heart: Politics, multiculturalism and the return of assimilation'. *Political Quarterly*, 73 (4): 445–454.

Baggett, H. (2016). 'Student enrollment in world languages: L'égalité des chances?' *Foreign Language Annals*, 49 (1): 162–179.

Baker, C. (2006). *Foundations of Bilingual Education and Bilingualism*. Clevedon: Multilingual Matters.

Baker, J. (2018). 'High school principals call for religious education to be scrapped'. *Sydney Morning Herald*, 1 December. Available online: https://www.smh.com.au/national/nsw/high-school-principals-call-for-religious-education-to-be-scrapped-20181130-p50jeo.html (accessed 20 June 2019).

Bakhtin, M. (1984). *Problems of Dostoyevsky's Poetics* [Trans. C. Emerson]. Minneapolis: University of Minnesota Press.

Ball, S., Bowe, R. and Gewirtz, S. (1996). 'Social choice, social class and distinction: The realisation of social advantage in education'. *Journal of Education Policy*, 11 (1): 89–112.

Baranick, W. and Markham, P. (1986). 'Attitudes of elementary school principals toward foreign language instruction'. *Foreign Language Annals*, 19 (6): 481–489.

Bartram, B. (2010). *Attitudes to Modern Foreign Language Learning Insights from Comparative Education*. New York: Continuum International Pub. Group.

Beijaard, D. (2019). 'Teacher learning as identity learning: Models, practices, and topics'. *Teachers and Teaching*, 25 (1): 1–6.

Ben-Peretz, M., Mendelson, N. and Kron, F. (2003). 'How teachers in different educational contexts view their roles'. *Teaching and Teacher Education*, 19 (2): 277–290.

Bernstein, B. (2003). *The Structuring of Pedagogic Discourse, Volume IV: Class, Codes and Control*. London: Routledge.

Black, S., Wright, J. and Cruickshank, K. (2018). 'The struggle for legitimacy: Language provision in two "residual" comprehensive high schools in Australia'. *Critical Studies in Education*, 59 (3): 348–363.

Blackledge, A. and Creese, A. (2008). 'Contesting "language" as "heritage": Negotiation of identities in late modernity'. *Applied Linguistics*, 29 (4): 533–554.

Block, D. (2003). *The Social Turn in Second Language Acquisition*. Edinburgh: Edinburgh University Press.

Block, D. (2007). 'The rise of identity in SLA research, post Firth and Wagner (1997)'. *The Modern Language Journal*, 91 (S1): 863–876.

Block, D. (2014). *Social Class in Applied Linguistics*. London: Routledge.

Block, D. (2017). 'Political economy in applied linguistics research'. *Language Teaching*, 50 (1): 32–64.

Board, K. and Tinsley, T. (2014). *Language Trends 2013/14: The State of Language Learning in Primary and Secondary Schools in England*. Reading, UK: CfBT Education Trust.

Board, K. and Tinsley, T. (2015a). *Language Trends 2014/15: The State of Language Learning in Primary and Secondary Schools in England*. Reading, UK: CfBT Education Trust.

Board, K. and Tinsley, T. (2015b). *Modern Foreign Languages in Secondary Schools in Wales: Findings from the Language Trends Survey 2014/15*. Reading, UK: CfBT Education Trust/British Council Wales.

Board, K. and Tinsley, T. (2016). *Language Trends 2015/16: The State of Language Learning in Primary and Secondary Schools in England*. Reading, UK: CfBT Education Trust.

Board, K. and Tinsley, T. (2017). *Language Trends Wales 2016/17: The State of Language Learning in Secondary Schools in Wales*. Cardiff: CfBT Education Trust.

Board of Studies NSW (BOS). (2000). *Media Guide: Higher School Certificate and School Certificate*. Sydney: Board of Studies. Available online: https://www.boardofstudies.nsw.edu.au/bos_stats/media-guides.html (accessed 4 August 2019).

Board of Studies NSW (BOS). (2001). *Media Guide: New Higher School Certificate and School Certificate*. Sydney: Board of Studies. Available online: https://www.boardofstudies.nsw.edu.au/bos_stats/media-guides.html (accessed 4 August 2019).

Board of Studies NSW (BOS). (2013). *Learning through Languages: Review of Languages Education in NSW (Reference Paper)*. Sydney: Board of Studies. Available online: http://educationstandards.nsw.edu.au/wps/wcm/connect/e1df9b42-04e7-4ddd-b2d9-8bf9c2fde035/reference-paper.pdf?MOD=AJPERES&CVID= (accessed 25 June 2019).

Bonnor, C. (2019). *Separating Scholars: How Australia Abandons Its Struggling Schools. Discussion Paper*. Sydney: Centre for Policy Development.

Bourdieu, P. (1984). *A Social Critique of the Judgement of Taste* [Trans. R. Nice]. Cambridge and Massachusetts: Harvard University Press.

Bourdieu, P. (1991). *Language and Symbolic Power*. Cambridge: Polity Press.

Butler, R., Ho, C. and Vincent, E. (2017). '"Tutored within an inch of their life": Morality and "old" and "new" middle class identities in Australian schools'. *Journal of Ethnic and Migration Studies*, 43 (14): 2408–2422.

Caldwell, B. (2005). *School-Based Management*. Paris: The International Institute for Educational Planning/International Academy of Education.

Caldwell, B. (2008). 'Reconceptualizing the self-managing school'. *Educational Management & Leadership*, 36 (2): 235–252.

Campbell, C. (2005). 'Changing school loyalties and the middle class: A reflection on the developing fate of state comprehensive high schooling'. *The Australian Educational Researcher*, 32 (1): 3–24.

Campbell, C. and Proctor, H. (2014). *A History of Australian Schooling*. Crows Nest: Allen and Unwin.

Campbell, C. and Sherington, G. (2013). *The Comprehensive Public High School: Historical Perspectives*. New York: Palgrave Macmillan.

Campbell, C., Proctor, H. and Sherington, G. (2009). *School Choice: How Parents Negotiate the New School Market in Australia*. Sydney: Allen & Unwin.

Canning, J., Gallagher-Brett, A., Tartarini, F. and McGuinness, H. (2010). *Routes into Languages: Report on Teacher and Pupil Attitude Surveys*. Southampton: Languages Linguistics and Area Studies, Southampton University.

Cardak, B. and Ryan, C. (2006). 'Why are high ability individuals from poor backgrounds under- represented at university?' Available online: https://www.latrobe.edu.au/__data/assets/pdf_file/0010/130897/2006.04.pdf (accessed 6 August 2019).

Carlson, S., Gerhards, J. and Hans, S. (2017). 'Educating children in times of globalisation: Class-specific child-rearing practices and the acquisition of transnational cultural capital'. *Sociology*, 42 (6): 1089–1106.

Carr, M. J. and Pauwels, A. (2006). *Boys and Foreign Language Learning: Real Boys Don't Do Languages*. Basingstoke, UK: Palgrave Macmillan.

Center for Applied Second Language Studies (CASLS). (2007). 'Analysis of 2007 STAMP results: New Jersey Grade Eight proficiency assessment in world languages'. Available online: https://casls.uoregon.edu/wp-content/uploads/pdfs/NJElementsofSuccessLang.pdf (accessed 11 November 2018).

Centre for Educational Statistics and Evaluation (CESE). (2013). *NSW Trial of the Reliability and Validity of the EAL/D (English as an Additional Language/ Dialect) Learning Progression*. Sydney: NSW Department of Education. Available online: https://www.cese.nsw.gov.au/publications-filter/assessing-english-language-proficiency (accessed 4 August 2019).

Centre for Education Statistics and Evaluation (CESE). (2018). *Schools: Languages Diversity in NSW 2018*. Sydney: NSW Department of Education. Available online: https://www.cese.nsw.gov.au/publications-filter/schools-language-diversity-in-nsw-2018 (accessed 19 June 2019).

Chen, H. and Nordstrom, N. (2018). 'Teaching young second language learners in LOTE L2 contexts'. In R. Oliver and B. Nguyen (eds), *Teaching Young Second Language Learners: Practice in Different Classroom Contexts*, 109–126. London: Routledge.

Christian, D., Pufahl, I. and Rhodes, N. (2005). 'Language learning: A worldwide perspective'. *Educational Leadership*, 62 (4): 24–30.

Clyne, M. (2005). *Australia's Language Potential*. Kensington: University of New South Wales Press.

Clyne, M. (2008). 'The monolingual mindset as an impediment to the development of plurilingual potential in Australia'. *Sociolinguistic Studies*, 2 (3): 347–365.

Clyne, M. and Kipp, S. (2011). *Pluricentric Languages in an Immigrant Context: Spanish, Arabic and Chinese*. Berlin and Boston: De Gruyter Mouton.

Coffey, S. (2018). 'Choosing to study modern foreign languages: Discourse of value as forms of capital'. *Applied Linguistics*, 39 (4): 462–480.

Coghlan, P. and Holcz, P. (2014). *The State of Play: Languages Education in Western Australia*. Cannington, WA: School Curriculum and Standards Authority.

Coleman, J., Galaczi, A. and Astruc, L. (2007). 'Motivation of UK school pupils towards foreign languages: A large-scale survey at Key Stage 3'. *Language Learning Journal*, 35 (2): 245–281.

Colic-Peisker, V. (2011). 'A new era in Australian multiculturalism? From working-class "ethnics" to a "multicultural middle-class"'. *International Migration Review*, 45 (3): 562–587.

Connell, R. (2013). 'The neoliberal cascade and education: An essay on the market agenda and its consequences'. *Critical Studies in Education*, 54 (2): 99–112.

Connell, R., Ashendon, D., Kessler, S. and Dowsett, G. (1982). *Making the Difference: Schools, Families and Social Division*. Sydney: Allen & Unwin.

Considine, G. (2012). 'Neo-liberal reforms in NSW public secondary education: What has happened to teachers?' PhD thesis, University of Sydney.

Coyle, D., Hood, P. and Marsh, D. (2010). *CLIL: Content and Language Integrated Learning*. Cambridge: Cambridge University Press.

Cranston, N. (2001). 'Collaborative decision-making and school-based management: Challenges, rhetoric and reality'. *Journal of Educational Inquiry*, 2 (2): 1–24.

Cranston, N., Ehrich, L. and Billot, J. (2003). 'The secondary school principalship in Australia and New Zealand: An investigation of changing roles'. *Leadership and Policy in Schools*, 1 (3): 159–188.

Cross, R. (2010). 'Language teaching as sociocultural activity: Rethinking language teacher practice'. *Modern Language Journal*, 94 (3): 434–452.

Cross, R. (2012). 'Creative in finding creativity in the curriculum: The CLIL second language classroom'. *The Australian Educational Researcher*, 39 (4): 431–445.

Cross, R. and Gearon, M. (2013). 'Research and evaluation of the Content and Language Integrated Learning (CLIL) approach to teaching and learning in Victorian schools'. Available online: http://www.education.vic.gov.au/documents/school/teachers/teachingresources/discipline/languages/CLILtrialresearchrpt.pdf (accessed 7 December 2014).

Cruickshank, K. (2015). 'A framework for inclusion: Plurilingual teachers in day and community schools'. *Australian Review of Applied Linguistics*, 38 (3): 155–171.

Cruickshank, K. and Wright, J. (2016). 'A tale of two cities: What the dickens happened to languages in NSW?' *Australian Review of Applied Linguistics*, 39 (1): 72–94.

Culley, T. (2015). 'Second-generation migrant socioeconomic outcomes literature review'. Available online: https://migrationcouncil.org.au/wp-content/uploads/2016/06/2015_Culley.pdf (accessed 10 August 2019).

Curdt-Christiansen, X. (2009). 'Invisible and visible language planning: Ideological factors in the family language policy of Chinese immigrant families in Quebec'. *Language Policy*, 8 (4): 351–375.

Curnow, T., Liddicoat, A. and Scarino, A. (2007). *Situational Analysis for the Development of Nationally Co-Ordinated Promotion of the Benefits of Languages*

Learning in Schools. Adelaide: Research Centre for Languages and Cultures Education, University of South Australia.

De Costa, P. and Norton, B. (2017). 'Introduction: Identity, transdisciplinarity, and the good language teacher'. *The Modern Language Journal*, 101 (S1): 3–14.

de Kretser, A. and Spence-Brown, R. (2010). *The Current State of Japanese Language Education in Australian Schools*. Carlton South, VIC: Education Services Australia.

Department of Education and Early Childhood Development (DEECD). (2013). *Languages – Expanding Your World: Plan to Implement the Victorian Government's Vision for Languages Education 2013–2025*. Melbourne: Department of Education and Early Childhood Development.

Department of Education and Training (DET). (2017). *Languages Provision in Victorian Government Schools, 2017*. Melbourne: Department of Education and Training. Available online: https://www.education.vic.gov.au/Documents/school/teachers/teachingresources/discipline/languages/EduState_Languages_Provision_Report_2017.pdf (accessed 6 August 2019).

Department of Training and Education Coordination (DTEC). (1997). '*McGaw Report*'. *Shaping Their Future: Recommendations for Reform of the Higher School Certificate*. Sydney: DTEC.

de Silva, J. (2005). 'The language barrier'. *The Age*, 14 March, 6–7.

Donato, R. and Tucker, G. R. (2010). *A Tale of Two Schools: Developing Sustainable Early Foreign Language Programs*. Bristol, UK: Multilingual Matters.

Dörnyei, Z. (2009). 'The L2 motivational self system'. In Z. Dörnyei and E. Ushioda (eds), *Motivation, Language Identity and the L2 Self*, 9–42. Bristol, UK: Multilingual Matters.

Douglas Fir Group. (2016). 'A transdisciplinary framework for SLA in a multilingual world'. *The Modern Language Journal*, 100 (Supplement 2016): 19–47.

Duchêne, A. and Heller, M. (eds) (2012). *Language in Late Capitalism: Pride and Profit*. London: Routledge.

Duff, P. (2017). 'Commentary: Motivation for learning languages other than English in an English-dominated world'. *The Modern Language Journal*, 101 (3): 597–607.

Entzinger, H. (2003). 'The rise and fall of multiculturalism in the Netherlands'. In C. Joppke and E. Morawska (eds), *Toward Assimilation and Citizenship: Immigrants in Liberal Nation-States*, 9–86. London: Palgrave.

EREBUS Consulting Partners. (2002). 'Review of the Commonwealth Languages other than English Programme'. Available online: http://pandora.nla.gov.au/pan/39847/20040120-0000/www.dest.gov.au/schools/publications/2003/LOTE/reviewreport.pdf (accessed 24 June 2019).

Extra, G. and Yagmur, K. (2004). 'Methodological considerations'. In G. Extra and K. Yagmur (eds), *Urban Multilingualism in Europe: Immigrant Minority Languages at Home and School*, 109–138. Clevedon: Multilingual Matters.

Fielding, R. and Harbon, L. (2014). 'Implementing a content and language integrated learning program in New South Wales primary schools: Teachers' perceptions of the challenges and opportunities'. *Babel*, 49 (2): 16–27.

Foucault, M. (1982). 'The subject and power'. In L. D. Hubert and P. Rabinow (eds), *Michel Foucault: Beyond Structuralism and Hermeneutics*, 208–226. Chicago, IL: University of Chicago Press.

Francis, B., Archer, L. and Mau, A. (2009). 'Language as capital, or language as identity? Chinese complementary school pupils' perspectives on the purposes and benefits of complementary schools'. *British Educational Research Journal*, 35 (4): 519–538.

Francis, B., Archer, L. and Mau, A. (2010). 'Parents' and teachers' constructions of the purposes of Chinese complementary schooling: "culture," identity and power'. *Race Ethnicity and Education*, 13 (1): 101–117.

Fullarton, S. and Ainley, J. (2000). *Subject Choice by Students in Year 12 in Australian Secondary Schools. Longitudinal Surveys of Australian Youth Research Report*. Melbourne: Australian Council for Educational Research.

Gallagher-Brett, A. (2004). *Seven Hundred Reasons for Studying Languages*. Southampton: Languages Linguistics and Area Studies, Southampton University.

Gallagher-Brett, A. (2012). *Routes into Languages First-Year Undergraduate Survey in England and Wales: Students' Prior Engagement with Languages Outreach and Enrichment Activities*. Southampton: Languages Linguistics and Area Studies, Southampton University.

García, O., Zakharia, Z. and Otcu, B. (2012). *Bilingual Community Education and Multilingualism: Beyond Heritage Languages in a Global City*. Bristol: Multilingual Matters.

Gardner, R. C. (1985). *Social Psychology and Language Learning: The Role of Attitudes and Motivation*. London: Edward Arnold.

Garnaut, R. (1989). *Australia and the Northeast Asian Ascendancy: Report to the Prime Minister and the Minister for Foreign Affairs and Trade*. Canberra: Australian Government Public Service.

Gayton, A. (2010). 'Socioeconomic status and language – learning motivation: To what extent does the former influence the latter?' *Scottish Languages Review*, 22: 17–28.

Gayton, A. M. (2016). 'Perceptions about the dominance of English as a global language: Impact on foreign-language teachers' professional identity'. *Journal of Language, Identity & Education*, 15 (4): 230–244.

Gee, J. (1999). 'The future of the social turn: Social minds and the new capitalism'. *Research on Language and Social Interaction*, 32 (1 & 2): 61–68.

Gerhards, J., Hans, S. and Carlson, S. (2017). *Social Class and Transnational Human Capital: How Middle and Upper Class Parents Prepare Their Children for Globalisation*. Abington, Oxon: Routledge.

Gil, J. (2018). 'Why the NSW government is reviewing its Confucius Classrooms program'. *The Conversation*, 18 May. Available online: https://theconversation.com/why-the-nsw-government-is-reviewing-its-confucius-classrooms-program-96783 (accessed 6 August 2019).

Gobby, B. (2013). 'Principal self-government and subjectification: The exercise of principal autonomy in the Western Australian Independent Public Schools programme'. *Critical Studies in Education*, 54 (3): 273–285.

Hagger-Vaughan, A. (2016). 'Towards "languages for all" in England: The state of the debate'. *The Language Learning Journal*, 44 (3): 358–375.

Halse, C. (2015a). 'What makes Asia literacy a "wicked policy problem"'? In C. Halse (ed), *Asia Literate Schooling in the Asian Century*, 13–28. London: Routledge.

Halse, C. (ed) (2015b). *Asia Literate Schooling in the Asian Century*. London: Routledge.

Hansen, R. (2007). 'Diversity, integration and the turn from multiculturalism in the United Kingdom'. In K. Banting, T. Courchene and L. Seidle (eds), *Belonging?: Diversity, Recognition and Shared Citizenship in Canada*, 35–86. Montreal: Institute for Research on Public Policy.

Harbon, L. and Fielding, R. (2013). *Bilingual Education Programs in Four Primary Schools in New South Wales, 2009–2012: A Report to Continue the Conversation.* Sydney: University of Sydney.

Harbon, L. and Maloney, R. (2013). *Language Teachers' Narratives of Practice.* Cambridge: Cambridge Scholars Publishing.

Hardy, I. (2014). 'A logic of appropriation: Enacting national testing (NAPLAN) in Australia'. *Journal of Education Policy*, 29 (1): 1–18.

Hill, K., Iwashita, N., McNamara, T., Scarino, A. and Scrimgeour, A. (2004). *A Report on Assessing and Reporting Student Outcomes in Asian Languages (Japanese and Indonesian).* Canberra: Department of Education, Science and Training.

Ho, C. (2011). '"My School" and others: Segregation and white flight'. Sydney: *Australian Review of Public Affairs*. Available online: https://www.nswtf.org.au/files/my_school_and_others_-_christine_ho_may_2011.pdf (accessed 9 August 2019).

Ho, C. (2015). '"People like us": School choice, multiculturalism and segregation in Sydney'. Sydney: NSW Teachers' Federation. Available online: https://www.nswtf.org.au/files/people_like_us_-_school_choice_multiculturalism_segregation_in_sydney_-_christin_ho.pdf (accessed 19 June 2019).

Ho, C. (2017a). 'Selective schools increasingly cater to the most advantaged students'. *The Conversation*, 9 March. Available online: https://theconversation.com/selective-schools-increasinglycater-to-the-most-advantaged-students-74151 (accessed 30 January 2018).

Ho, C. (2017b). 'The new meritocracy or over-schooled robots? Public attitudes on Asian–Australian education cultures'. *Journal of Ethnic and Migration Studies*, 43 (14): 2346–2362.

Ho, C. (2017c). 'Angry Anglos and aspirational Asians: Everyday multiculturalism in the selective school system in Sydney'. *Discourse: Studies in the Cultural Politics of Education*, 40 (4): 514–529.

Ho, C. and Bonnor, C. (2018). *Institutionalised Separation: The Impact of Selective Schools.* Discussion paper. Sydney: Centre for Policy Development.

Hornberger, N. H. (2005). 'Opening and filling up implementational and ideological spaces in heritage language education'. *Modern Language Journal*, 89 (4): 605–612.

Hunt, M., Barnes, A., Powell, B. and Martin, C. (2008). 'Moving on: The challenges for foreign language learning on transition, from primary to secondary School'. *Teaching and Teacher Education*, 24 (2): 915–916.

Iannelli, C. (2013). 'The role of the school curriculum in social mobility'. *British Journal of Sociology of Education*, 34 (5–6): 907–928.

Jones, N., Ashton, K. and Walker, T. (2010). 'Asset languages: A case study of piloting the CEFR manual'. In W. Martyniuk (ed), *Aligning Tests with the CEFR: Reflections on Using the Council of Europe's Draft Manual (Studies in Language Testing) 33*, 227–248. Cambridge: Cambridge University Press.

Jones Díaz, C. (2014). 'Institutional, material and economic constraints in languages education: Unequal provision of linguistic resources in early childhood and primary settings in Australia'. *International Journal of Bilingual Education and Bilingualism*, 17 (3): 272–286.

Keddie, A. (2017). 'School autonomy reform and public education in Australia: Implications for social justice'. *Australian Educational Researcher*, 44 (4–5): 373–390.

Keddie, A., Gobby, B. and Wilkins, C. (2018). 'School autonomy reform in Queensland: Governance, freedom and the entrepreneurial leader'. *School Leadership & Management*, 38 (4): 378–394.

Keels, M., Burdick-Will, J. and Keene, S. (2013). 'The effects of gentrification on neighborhood public schools'. *City and Community*, 12 (3): 238–259.

Kenner, C. (2004). *Becoming Biliterate: Young Children Learning Different Writing Systems*. Stoke-on-Trent: Trentham Books.

Khoo, S.E., McDonald, P. and Giorgas, D. (2002). *Second Generation Australians: Report for the Department of Immigration and Multicultural and Indigenous Affairs*. Canberra: DIMIA.

Kleinhenz, E., Wilkinson, J., Gearon, M., Fernandez, S. and Ingvarson, L. (2007). *The Review of Teacher Education for Languages Teachers: Final Report*. Canberra: Department of Education, Employment, and Workplace Relations.

Kohler, M. (2017). *Review of Languages Education Policies in Australia*. Adelaide: Government of South Australia. The Multicultural Education and Languages Committee (MELC).

Kohler, M. and Mahnken, P. (2010). *The Current State of Indonesian Language Education in Australian Schools*. Melbourne: Education Services Australia Ltd.

Kohler, M. and Curnow, T., Australian Council for Educational Research, Spence-Brown, R. and Wardlaw, C. (2014). *Senior Secondary Languages Education Research Project: Final Report*. Melbourne: Asia Education Foundation.

Koopmans, R. (2006). *Trade-Offs between Equality and Difference: The Crisis of Dutch Multiculturalism in Cross-National Perspective*. Copenhagen: Danish Institute for International Affairs Brief.

Kramsch, C. (2002). 'Introduction. "How can we tell the dancer from the dance?"' In C. Kramsch (ed), *Language Acquisition and Language Socialization: Ecological Perspectives*, 1–30. London: Continuum.

Kramsch, C. and Uryu, M. (2012). 'Intercultural contact, hybridity and third space'. In J. Jackson (ed), *The Routledge Handbook of Language and Intercultural Communication*, 211–226. London: Routledge.

Lanvers, U. (2017). 'Contradictory *others* and the *habitus* of languages: Surveying the L2 motivation landscape in the United Kingdom'. *The Modern Language Journal*, 101 (3): 517–532.

Lao, C. (2004). 'Parents' attitudes toward Chinese-English bilingual education and Chinese- language use'. *Bilingual Research Journal*, 28 (1): 99–121.

Lave, J. and Wenger, E. (1991). *Situated Learning: Legitimate Peripheral Participation*. Cambridge: Cambridge University Press.

Li, W. and Zhu, H. (2011). 'Changing hierarchies in Chinese language education for British Chinese learners'. In L. Tsung and K. Cruikshank (eds), *Teaching and Learning Chinese in Global Contexts*, 1–28. New York: Continuum.

Liddicoat, A. and Curnow, T. (2014). 'Students' home languages and the struggle for space in the curriculum'. *International Journal of Multilingualism*, 11 (3): 273–288.

Liddicoat, A., Scarino, A., Curnow, T., Kohler, M., Scrimgeour, A. and Morgan, A. (2007). 'An Investigation of the State and Nature of Languages in Australian Schools'. Available online: http://pandora.nla.gov.au/pan/82870/20080401-1209/www. dest.gov.au/NR/rdonlyres/82B80761-70BD-47A6-A85A-17F250E11CBA/20743/ SNfinalreport.pdf (accessed 20 June 2019).

Lo Bianco, J. (1987). *National Policy on Languages*. Canberra: Australian Department of Education.

Lo Bianco, J. (2000). *After the Tsunami, Some Dilemmas: Japanese Language Studies in Multicultural Australia*. Melbourne: Language Australia, The National Languages and Literacy Institute of Australia.

Lo Bianco, J. (2003). 'A site for debate, negotiation and contest of national identity: Language policy in Australia. Guide for the development of language education policies in Europe: From linguistic diversity to plurilingual education'. Available online: https://rm.coe.int/a-site-for-debate-negotiation-and-contest-of-national-identity-languag/1680886e94 (accessed 12 June 2019).

Lo Bianco, J. (2009). *Second Languages and Australian Schooling*. Camberwell, VIC: Australian Council for Educational Research.

Lo Bianco, J. and Gvozdenko, I. (2006). *Collaboration and Innovation in the Provision of Languages Other than English in Australian Universities*. Melbourne: Faculty of Education, Melbourne University.

Lupton, R. and Hempel-Jorgensen, A. (2012). 'The importance of teaching: Pedagogical constraints and possibilities in working class schools'. *Journal of Education Policy*, 27 (5): 601–620.

Lytra, V. and Martin, P. (eds) (2010). *Sites of Multilingualism: Complementary Schools in Britain Today*. Stoke-on-Trent: Trentham.

Macqueen, S. (2013). 'Grouping for inequity'. *International Journal of Inclusive Education*, 17 (3): 295–309.

Marginson, S. (2006). 'Engaging democratic education in the neoliberal age'. *Educational Theory*, 56 (2): 205–219.

Marmion, D., Obata, K. and Troy, J. (2014). *Community, Identity, Wellbeing: The Report of the Second National Indigenous Languages Survey [NILS 2].* Canberra, ACT: Australian Institute of Aboriginal and Torres Strait Islander Studies.

Martin, N. and McPherson, R. (2015). 'The politics of the Local Schools Local Decisions Policy in a New South Wales public school: Implications for principals and the state'. *Leading and Managing,* 21 (1): 36–52.

Messinis, G. and Sheehan, P. (2015). *The Academic Performance of First Year Students at Victoria University by Entry Score and SES, 2009-2013.* Melbourne: Victoria Institute of Strategic Economic Studies, Melbourne.

Mills, M., Keddie, A., Renshaw, P. and Monk, S. (2016). *The Politics of Differentiation in Schools.* London: Routledge.

Mizoshiro, S. (2013). 'Teaching Japanese to gifted and talented girls'. In L. Harbon and R. Maloney (eds), *Language Teachers' Narratives of Practice,* 100–110. Cambridge: Cambridge Scholars Publishing.

Moloney, R. (2008). *Intercultural competence in young language learners: A case study.* PhD thesis, University of Sydney.

Mu, G. M. (2014). 'Learning Chinese as a heritage language in Australia and beyond: The role of capital'. *Language and Education,* 28 (5): 477–492.

Nicholas, H., Moore, H., Clyne, M. and Pauwels, A. (1993). *Languages at the Crossroads: Report of the National Enquiry into the Employment and Status of Teachers of Languages other than English.* Melbourne: NLLIA.

Niesche, R. (2019). 'School and principal autonomy: Resisting, not manufacturing, the neoliberal subject'. In J. Wilkinson, R. Niesche and S. Eacott (eds), *Challenges for Public Education: Reconceptualising Educational Leadership, Policy and Social Justice as Resources for Hope,* 31–43. Abington, Oxon: Routledge.

Nikolov, M. and Mihaljević Djigunović, J. (2011). 'All shades of every color: An overview of early teaching and learning of foreign languages'. *Annual Review of Applied Linguistics,* 31: 95–119.

Norris, L. (1999). *Pathways for Australian School Students to Achieve High Levels of Proficiency in Asian languages. A Report Prepared for the National Asian Languages and Studies in Australian Schools (NALSAS) Taskforce.* Perth: The Centre for Curriculum and Professional Development, Murdoch University.

Norton, B. (2001). 'Non-participation, imagined communities and the language classroom'. In M. Breen (ed), *Learner Contributions to Language Learning: New Directions in Research,* 159–171. Harlow: Pearson Education.

Norton, B. (2013). *Identity and Language Learning: Extending the Conversation.* Bristol, UK: Multilingual Matters.

Norton, B. (2016). 'Preface'. In S. Preece (ed), *The Routledge Handbook of Language and Identity,* xxii–xxiv. Abingdon, Oxon/New York: Routledge.

Norton, B. (2018). 'Identity and investment in multilingual classrooms'. In A. Bonnet and P. Siemund (eds), *Foreign Language Education in Multilingual Classrooms,* 237–253. Amsterdam: John Benjamins.

Norton, B. and De Costa, P. (2017). 'Research tasks on identity in language learning and teaching'. *Language Teaching*, 51 (1): 90–112.

Norton, B. and Toohey, K. (2011). 'Identity, language learning, and social change'. *Language Teaching*, 44 (4): 412–446.

Norton Peirce, B. (1995). 'Social identity, investment, and language learning'. *TESOL Quarterly*, 29 (1): 9–31.

NSW Department of Education. (2016). 'Community languages program K-6 guidelines'. Available online: https://www.languagesnsw.com/uploads/1/4/4/5/14456032/comlang-guidelines_final.pdf (accessed 12 June 2019).

NSW Education Standards Authority (NESA). (2019). 'Languages Stage 6'. Available online: https://educationstandards.nsw.edu.au/wps/portal/nesa/11-12/stage-6-learning-areas/stage-6-languages (accessed 6 August 2019).

OECD. (2011). 'Private schools: Who benefits?' *PISA in Focus 7*. Available online: https://www.oecd.org/pisa/pisaproducts/pisainfocus/48482894.pdf (accessed 5 July 2019).

OECD. (2012). 'Equity and quality in education: Supporting disadvantaged students and schools'. Available online: https://www.oecd.org/education/school/50293148.pdf (accessed 6 August 2019).

Opie, L. (2006). 'To be or not to be?: That is the question: LOTE education in the rural district of "Black Swan"'. *Teacher Learning Network*, 13 (1): 9–10.

Orton, J. (2008). *Chinese Language Education in Australian Schools*. Melbourne: University of Melbourne.

O'Rourke, P., Zhou, Q. and Rottman, I. (2017). 'Prioritisation of K-12 world language education in the United States: State requirements for high school graduation'. *Foreign Language Annals*, 49 (4): 789–800.

Ozolins, U. (1993). *The Politics of Language in Australia*. Cambridge: Cambridge University Press.

Pachler, N. (2007). 'Choices in language education: Principles and policies'. *Cambridge Journal of Education*, 37 (1): 1–15.

Paolino, A. (2012). *An Interdisciplinary Intervention: The Potential of the Orff-Schulwerk Approach as a Pedagogical Tool for the Effective Teaching of Italian to Upper Primary Students in Western Australia*. Joondalup, WA: Edith Cowan University.

Parrish, A. and Lanvers, U. (2019). 'Student motivation, school policy choices and modern language study in England'. *The Language Learning Journal*, 47 (3): 281–298.

Pennington, M. and Hoekje, B. (2010). 'Language program as ecology: A perspective for leadership'. *RELC Journal*, 41 (3): 213–228.

Pennycook, A. D. (2017). 'Language policy and local practices'. In O. García and N. Flores (eds), *The Oxford Handbook of Language and Society*, 125–140. Oxford: Oxford University Press.

Perry, L. and Lamb, S. (2016). 'Curricular differentiation and stratification in Australia'. *Orbis Scolae*, 10 (3): 24–47.

Perry, L., Ledger, S. and Dickson, A. (2018). *What Are the Benefits of the International Baccalaureate Middle Years Programme for Teaching and Learning? Perspectives from Stakeholders in Australia*. Perth: Murdoch University.

Perry, L. B. and Southwell, L. (2014). 'Access to academic curriculum in Australian secondary schools: A case study of a highly marketised education system'. *Journal of Education Policy*, 29 (4): 467–485.

Polesel, J., Leahy, M. and Gillis, S. (2018). 'Educational inequality and transitions to university in Australia: Aspirations, agency and constraints'. *British Journal of Sociology of Education*, 39 (6): 793–810.

Preece, S. (ed) (2016). *The Routledge Handbook of Language and Identity*. Abingdon, Oxon/New York: Routledge.

Prins, B. and Slijper, B. (2002). 'Multicultural society under attack'. *Journal of International Migration and Immigration*, 3 (3–4): 313–328.

Pufahl, I. and Rhodes, N. (2011). 'Foreign language instruction in U.S. schools: Results of a national survey of Elementary and Secondary schools'. *Foreign Language Annals*, 44 (2): 258–288.

Pufahl, I., Rhodes, N. and Christian, D. (2000). *Foreign Language Teaching: What the United States Can Learn from Other Countries*. Washington, DC: Center for Applied Lingustics.

Resnik, J. (2009). 'Multicultural education – Good for business but not for the state? The IB curriculum and global capitalism'. *British Journal of Educational Studies*, 57 (3): 217–244.

Rhodes, N. (2014). 'Elementary school foreign language teaching: Lessons learned over three decades'. *Foreign Language Annals*, 47 (1): 115–133.

Rhodes, N. and Pufahl, I. (2010). *Foreign Language Teaching in U.S. Schools: Results of a National Survey*. Washington, DC: Center for Applied Linguistics.

Rudd, K. (1994). *Asian Languages and Australia's Economic Future*. Brisbane: Queensland Government Printer.

Scarino, A., Scrimgeour, A. and Kohler, M. (2012). *Languages Teaching and Learning: Change in Context*. Adelaide: Independent Schools of South Australia.

Scarino, A., Scrimgeour, A., Elder, C. and Brown, A. (1998). *Development of Language-Specific Proficiency Descriptors: Chinese, Indonesian, and Korean*. Canberra: Department of Education, Training and Youth Affairs.

Scott, S. (2012). 'Pre-schoolers to learn second language under Tony Abbott and the Coalition'. News.com.au, 11 May. Available online: https://www.news.com.au/finance/economy/preschoolers-to-learn-second-language-under-tony-abbott-and-the-coalition/news-story/1b63e71289c7fb21b276a35375f37a35?sv=5f2e6aa8e28b8332e9bff2cab19ed184 (accessed 6 August 2019).

Singh, M. and Qi, J. (2013). *21st Century International Mindedness: An Exploratory Study of Its Conceptualisation and Assessment*. South Penrith: University of Western Sydney.

Singhal, P. (2018). 'The Aboriginal language taught more than Spanish in NSW schools'. *Sydney Morning Herald*, 8 October. Available online: https://www.smh.com.au/education/the-aboriginal-language-taught-more-than-spanish-in-nsw-schools-20180914-p503r3.html (accessed 16 June 2019).

Slaughter, Y. (2007). 'Asian languages: The study of Asian languages in two Asian states. Consideration for language-in-education policy and planning'. PhD thesis, University of Melbourne.

Slaughter, Y. (2009). 'Money and policy make languages go round: Language programs in Australia after NALSAS'. *Babel, Australian Federation of Modern Language Teachers Association*, 43 (2): 3–15.

Slaughter, Y. and Hajek, J. (2007). 'Community languages and LOTE provision in Victorian primary schools: mix or match?' *Australian Review of Applied Linguistics*, 30 (1): 07.1-07.22.

Smala, S., Paz, J. B. and Lingard, B. (2013). 'Languages, cultural capital and school choice: Distinction and second-language immersion programmes'. *British Journal of Sociology of Education*, 34 (3): 373–391.

Spina, N. (2018). '"Once upon a time": Examining ability grouping and differentiation practices in cultures of evidence-based decision-making'. *Cambridge Journal of Education*, online 6 November.

Spolsky, B. (2012). 'Family Language Policy – the critical domain'. *Journal of Multilingual and Multicultural Development*, 33 (1): 3–11.

Sriprakash, A., Proctor, H. and Hu, B. (2016). 'Visible pedagogic work: Parenting, private tutoring and educational advantage in Australia'. *Discourse: Studies in the Cultural Politics of Education*, 37 (3): 426–441.

Stein-Smith, K. (2019). 'Foreign language classes becoming more scarce'. *The Conversation*, 6 February 2019. Available online: http://theconversation.com/foreign-language-classes-becoming-more-scarce-102235 (accessed 6 July 2019).

Swain, M. and Lapkin, S. (2005). 'The evolving sociopolitical context of immersion education in Canada: Some implications for program development'. *International Journal of Applied Linguistics*, 15 (2): 169–186.

Swain, M. and Lapkin, S. (2013). 'A Vygotskian sociocultural perspective on immersion education: The L1/L2 debate'. *Journal of Immersion and Content-Based Language Education*, 1 (1): 101–129.

Tamis, A. and Gauntlett, S. (1993). *Unlocking Australia's Language Potential. Profiles of 9 Key Languages in Australia. Vol. 8 – Modern Greek*. Canberra: NLLIA.

Teese, R. (2007). 'Structural inequality in Australian education'. In R. Teese, S. Lamb and M. Duru-Bellat (eds), *International Studies in Educational Inequality, Theory and Policy (Volume 2)*, 39–62. Dordrecht: Springer.

Teese, R. (2013). *Academic Success and Social Power: Examinations and Inequality*. North Melbourne, VIC: Australian Scholarly Publishing Pty Ltd.

Teese, R. and Polesel, J. (2003). *Undemocratic Schooling: Equity and Quality in Mass Secondary Education in Australia*. Melbourne: Melbourne University Press.

Teese, R., Lamb, S. and Duru-Bellat, M. (eds) (2017). *International Studies in Educational Inequality, Theory and Policy*. Dordrecht: Springer.

Thomson, P. (2010). 'Headteacher autonomy: A sketch of a Bourdieuian field analysis of position and practice'. *Critical Studies in Education*, 51 (1): 5–20.

Thompson, G. and Harbaugh, A. (2013). 'A preliminary analysis of teacher perceptions of the effect of NAPLAN on pedagogy and curriculum'. *Australian Educational Researcher*, 40 (3): 290–314.

Thompson, G. and Mockler, N. (2016). 'Principals of audit: Testing, data and "implicated advocacy"'. *Journal of Educational Administration and History*, 48 (1): 1–18.

Tinsley, T. and Board, K. (2013). *Language Learning in Primary and Secondary Schools in England: Findings from the 2012 Language Trends Survey*. Reading, UK: CfBT Education Trust.

Tinsley, T. and Board, K. (2017). *Language Trends, 2016/7: Languages Teaching in Primary and Secondary Schools in England. A Survey Report*. Reading, UK: CfBT Education Trust.

Tinsley, T. and Dolezal, N. (2018). *Language Trends 2018: Language Teaching in Primary and Secondary Schools in England, A Survey Report*. Reading, UK: CfBT Education Trust.

Toohey, K. and Norton, B. (2002). 'Language learner identities and sociocultural worlds'. In R. Kaplan (ed), *The Oxford Handbook of Applied Linguistics*, 178–188. Oxford: Oxford University Press.

Tranter, D. (2012). 'Unequal schooling: How the school curriculum keeps students from low socio – economic backgrounds out of university'. *International Journal of Inclusive Education*, 16 (9): 901–916.

Universities Admissions Centre (UAC). (2007). *Report on the Scaling of the NSW 2006 Higher School Certificate*. Sydney: Technical Committee on Scaling.

Universities Admissions Centre (UAC). (2015). *Report on the Scaling of the NSW 2014 Higher School Certificate*. Sydney: Technical Committee on Scaling.

Universities Admissions Centre (UAC). (2017). *Report on the Scaling of the NSW 2016 Higher School Certificate*. Sydney: Technical Committee on Scaling.

Universities Admissions Centre (UAC). (2018). *Report on the Scaling of the NSW 2017 Higher School Certificate*. Sydney: Technical Committee on Scaling.

Ushioda, E. and Dörnyei, Z. (2017). 'Beyond global English: Motivation to learn languages in a multicultural world: Introduction to the Special Issue'. *The Modern Language Journal*, 101 (3): 451–454.

Vertovec, S. (2005). *Pre-, High-, Anti-and Post-Multiculturalism*. Oxford: ESRC Centre on Migration, Policy and Society, University of Oxford.

Vinson, T., Esson, K. and Johnston, K. (2002). 'Enquiry into the provision of public education in NSW'. Available online: https://www.nswtf.org.au/files/first_report.pdf (accessed 19 June 2019).

Watkins, M. (2017). '"We are all Asian here": multiculturalism, selective schooling and responses to Asian success'. *Journal of Ethnic and Migration Studies*, 43 (14): 2300–2315.

Watkins, M. and Noble, G. (2013). *Disposed to Learn: Schooling, Ethnicity and the Scholarly Habitus*. London: Bloomsbury Academic.

Watkins, M., Ho, C. and Butler, R. (2017). 'Asian migration and education cultures in the anglo- sphere'. *Journal of Ethnic and Migration Studies*, 43 (14): 2283–2299.

Watson, L. (2008). 'Private expectations and public schooling: The growth of private tutoring in Australia'. In P. Jeffrey (ed), *Australian Association for Research in Australia (AARE) National Conference Proceedings*, 1–15. Brisbane: Australian Association for Research in Education, 30 November–4 December.

Weedon, C. (1987). *Feminist Practice and Poststructuralist Theory*. Oxford: Basil Blackwell.

Windle, J. (2015). *Making Sense of School Choice: Politics, Policies, and Practice under Conditions of Cultural Diversity*. New York: Palgrave.

Wong, L., Garcea, J. and Kirova, A. (2005). *An Analysis of the Anti- and Post-Multiculturalism Discourses: The Fragmentation Position*. Alberta: Prairie Centre for Excellence in Research on Immigration and Integration.

Wright, J., Cruickshank, K. and Black, S. (2018). 'Languages discourses in Australian middle class schools: Parent and student perspectives'. *Discourse: Studies in the Cultural Politics of Education*, 39 (1): 98–112.

Zhang, J. (2009). 'Mandarin maintenance among immigrant children from the People's Republic of China: An examination of individual networks of linguistic contact'. *Language, Culture and Curriculum*, 22 (3): 195–213.

Zhou, M. and Kim, S. (2006). 'Community forces, social capital and educational achievement: The case of supplementary education in the Chinese and Korean communities'. *Harvard Educational Review*, 76 (1): 1–29.

Zhou, M. and Li, X. (2003). 'Ethnic language schools and the development of supplementary education in the immigrant Chinese community in the United States'. In C. Suarez–Orozco and I. L. G. Todorova (eds), *New Directions for Youth Development: Understanding the Social Worlds of Immigrant Youth*, 57–73. San Francisco: Jossey–Bass.

Index

Lightning Source UK Ltd.
Milton Keynes UK
UKHW020255040123
414799UK00007B/149